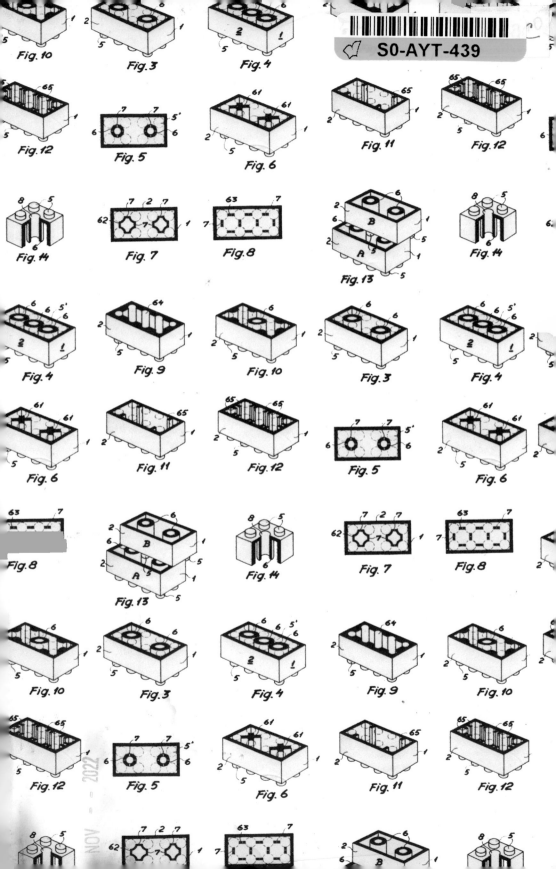

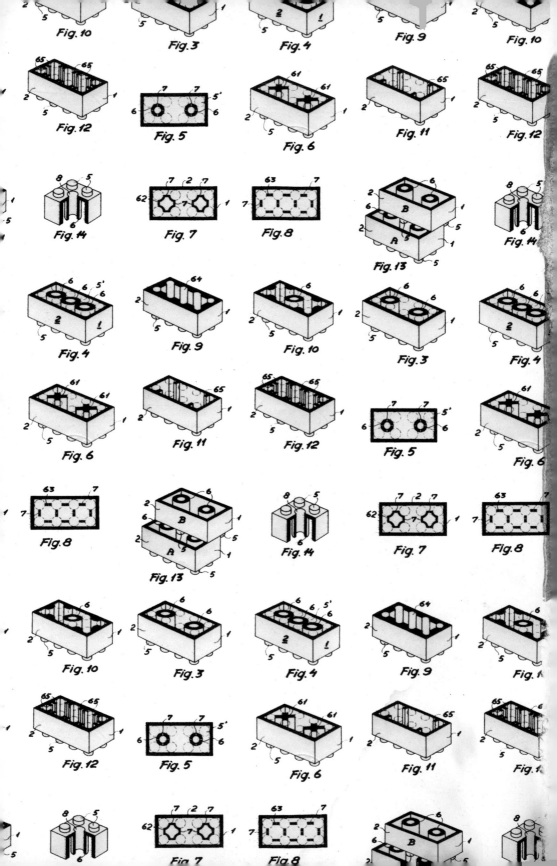

THE LEGO

STORY

How a Little Toy

Sparked the

World's Imagination

THE
LEGO
 STORY

JENS ANDERSEN

Translated by Caroline Waight

MARINER
BOOKS
New York   Boston

HarperCollins books may be purchased for educational, business,
or sales promotional use. For information, please email the Special Markets
Department at SPsales@harpercollins.com.

Originally published as *Et liv med LEGO* in Denmark in 2021
by Politikens Forlag.

FIRST U.S. EDITION

Designed by Leah Carlson-Stanisic

Library of Congress Cataloging-in-Publication Data has been applied for.

ISBN 978-0-06-325802-0

22 23 24 25 26   LSC   10 9 8 7 6 5 4 3 2 1

CONTENTS

FAMILY TREE

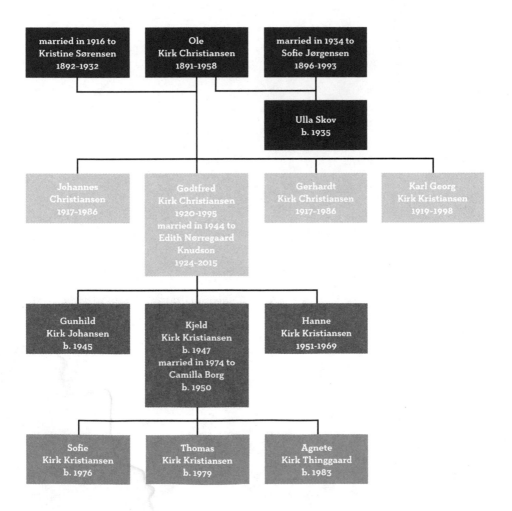

**married in 1916 to
Kristine Sørensen
1892–1932**

**Ole
Kirk Christiansen
1891–1958**

**married in 1934 to
Sofie Jørgensen
1896–1993**

**Ulla Skov
b. 1935**

**Johannes
Christiansen
1917–1986**

**Godtfred
Kirk Christiansen
1920–1995
married in 1944 to
Edith Nørregaard
Knudson
1924–2015**

**Gerhardt
Kirk Christiansen
1917–1986**

**Karl Georg
Kirk Kristiansen
1919–1998**

**Gunhild
Kirk Johansen
b. 1945**

**Kjeld
Kirk Kristiansen
b. 1947
married in 1974 to
Camilla Borg
b. 1950**

**Hanne
Kirk Kristiansen
1951–1969**

**Sofie
Kirk Kristiansen
b. 1976**

**Thomas
Kirk Kristiansen
b. 1979**

**Agnete
Kirk Thinggaard
b. 1983**

PREFACE

Dear reader,

It's estimated that each year between eighty and ninety million children around the globe are given a box of LEGO, while up to ten million adults buy sets for themselves. Yet LEGO is much more than a dizzying number of plastic bricks that can be put together and combined in countless ways. LEGO is also a vision of the significance of what play can mean for humanity.

This book tells the story of a global company and a Danish family who for ninety years have defended children's right to play—and who believe grown-ups, too, should make the time to nurture their inner child.

Since the early 1930s, LEGO has been creating toys and experiences for younger and older children alike, often crossing social and cultural lines, and always keeping pace with broader developments. This stretch of time has seen global crises and the emergence of the welfare state in Denmark and the other Nordic countries. There has been a shift from the patriarchal family—with the father firmly ensconced at the head of the table—to a world in which women entered the workforce and led their own households. Society has witnessed the advent of new gender roles and family structures and, with these changes, new ways of playing. Play used to be an exclusively physical activity; today, it's just as likely to be digital. LEGO has been there all along.

The idea behind *The LEGO Story* came to me in the autumn of 2019. This isn't a traditional business book, but rather a cultural history and biographical chronicle of three generations of the Kirk Kristiansen family, all of whom created and shaped LEGO into the company it is today, as the fourth generation is poised to take over: the world's largest producer of play materials and one of the most beloved brands in the world.

The book is built on my access to LEGO's own archives at Billund, as well as on monthly conversations that took place over eighteen months with Kjeld Kirk Kristiansen, former president and CEO of the LEGO Group and grandson of its founder, Ole Kirk Christiansen. Born literally in the thick of operations in 1947, Kjeld has helped shape the evolution of LEGO for nearly fifty years.

On the following pages, he is referred to as simply "Kjeld." That's what he wanted to be called in this book because that's what he's called at Billund, and that's how he's known to the 20,000 LEGO employees and to the official list of adult fans—more than five times that number—for whom LEGO is a passion and a lifestyle.

Speaking of names, the family's surname has caused some confusion from time to time over the years. There's no controversy about the middle bit—"Kirk"—but should the last part be "Kristiansen" or "Christiansen"?

According to old church records and certificates of baptism, it ought to be Kristiansen with a *K*, but for unknowable reasons, the founder, Ole Kirk, chose to spell his name "Christiansen" with a *Ch*, when he settled in Billund as a young carpenter in 1916. He continued spelling it that way, with the occasional exception, until his death, and this is how his name was chiseled onto his gravestone at Grene Parish Cemetery, just outside Billund.

Ole Kirk's son Godtfred also spelled his last name with a *Ch* instead of a *K*, and as a young, ambitious foreman in the 1940s he began to use the initials GKC. They stuck with him all his life, even becoming his nickname among the company's employees, as well as business associates, fellow townspeople, and good friends. GKC's son, Kjeld—the primary figure in this book—opted as a young man to stick to the church records and has always been known as Kjeld Kirk Kristiansen.

I have chosen to respect the wishes of each individual family member. So on the following pages, LEGO's founder is either "Ole Kirk" or "Christiansen," his son "Godtfred" or "GKC," and the third generation simply "Kjeld."

It may surprise some readers that I have written LEGO and other companies in the LEGO Group—KIRKBI, for example—in capital letters. I have found it more natural to follow the corporation's usual styling.

Readers who are employed by or connected to LEGO, however, will have to put up with my deviation from the company's internal orthographic guidelines on one point, where I have chosen to follow the conventions of standard English: I have largely avoided using the registered trademark symbol (®) after LEGO. This is purely for ease of reading.

Just as two classic eight-stud bricks can be put together in at least twenty-four different ways, there are many paths to take when telling the story of LEGO. I have opted for a broad, epic sweep, without references and notes. At the back of the book you'll find an extensive selection of literature as well as an index of names, and an acknowledgments section thanking everyone who made this book possible.

I should acknowledge upfront, however, that I would never have emerged from this project unscathed if not for the tireless help of Jette Orduna, director of LEGO Idea House, and archivist Tine Froberg Mortensen, the entire Kirk Kristiansen family, Niels B. Christiansen at LEGO A/S, Jørgen Vig Knudstorp, Ulla Lundhus and Søren Thorup Sørensen at KIRKBI A/S, as well as Kim Hundevadt and Ulla Mervild at Politikens Forlag. Thanks also go out to Caroline Waight for her deft translation into English and to Elizabeth DeNoma for her editorial insight and wordsmithing.

Lastly, especially heartfelt thanks are due to Kjeld, for offering me an insight into a fairy-tale episode in Danish history. The Danish words "*leg godt*"—meaning "play well"—are the origin of the name LEGO, so it seems only appropriate to adapt them here:

Read well!

Jens Andersen, July 2021

THE LEGO STORY

WOODWORK

THE 1920s

Ole Kirk's tools

A *long time ago in a galaxy far, far away . . .*
That's how a famous saga set in outer space begins, one that will come to play a role in the story you're about to hear. The story starts in Denmark, way out in the countryside in the autumn of 1915, when a young craftsman in Western Jutland heard about a woodworker's workshop for sale in the little provincial town of Billund.

Like his fiancée, the young man had grown up on the windswept heaths of rural Denmark, where money was tight and most people worked as day laborers. As a boy he looked after sheep and cows, learned to watch out for marl pits and adders, and when storms were brewing he could dig a cave better than anyone else in the area.

He'd become a journeyman carpenter, dreaming of a permanent roof over his head and talking of marriage and running his own business.

Several of his siblings had helped him borrow 10,000 kroner from the bank, and in February 1916 he took possession of a single-story white house with a workshop on the outskirts of Billund, a small village in the Jutland region of Denmark. With God's help—and that of the Varde Bank—everything would work out. On his twenty-fifth birthday in April, Ole Kirk Christiansen married Hansine Kristine Sørensen, and the following year she gave birth to the first of their four sons.

> **Kjeld:** *My granddad was born in 1891 in Blåhøj, which is roughly twelve miles north of Billund. He grew up in a family of six boys and six girls, each with a middle name my great-grandfather came up with himself. Well, the girls didn't get middle names, because of course they were supposed to change their names when they got married. One of the sons was called Randbæk, the second Kamp, the third Bonde. My granddad got his first and middle names—Ole Kirk—from a respectable West Jutland farmer and member of the Stænderforsamlingen, the Assembly of the Estates of the Realm, whom my great-grandfather had worked for and admired. By the age of six, my granddad was already looking after the animals, working on various farms, but he ended up as a carpenter's apprentice alongside one of his older brothers. Like other journeymen, he traveled around to work at first, but soon returned home to help his older brother build the post office in Grindsted. Then, in 1916, that was when he turned up in Billund.*

Toward the end of the First World War there were barely a hundred people in Billund, which was situated on the railway line between the much larger towns of Vejle and Grindsted. Apart from the station building, which also functioned as the post office, in 1916 Billund consisted of four or five large farms, several houses reserved for elderly people who could no longer work the land, a school, a cooperative dairy, a food shop, an evangelical meeting house called the Mission House, and the pub, which was soon to lose its license to sell spirits and reopen as a temperance hotel. There were roughly thirty buildings in all, lining a gravel country road with deep ditches along both sides. If you wanted to get out onto the road itself, you needed to balance on a couple of boards across the ditch to reach it.

Ole Kirk and Kristine's house, with the workshop around the back, was at the very end of the road leading out of Billund. Beyond that there were a few cultivated fields, and then nothing but the heath, as far as the eye could see. Mile after mile of brownish heather trying to take root along a sandy rural road leading west.

They said that a rich man from Kolding once traveled through the parish of Grene and called Billund a "godforsaken place." It's true that Billund in the 1910s was only a small dot on the arc traced through town by the country road, but there were plenty of signs of life there in the years after the First World War—especially where God and the Holy Spirit were concerned.

On Ole Kirk's twenty-fifth birthday, April 7, 1916, he and Kristine married. In Billund, Karen and Peter Urmager, who were on the board of the Inner Mission, took particular care of the young newcomers. A warm friendship developed, and years later, when Karen fell ill as an elderly widow, Ole Kirk brought her to their home, where she convalesced in his bed until she recovered.

The young couple settled down in Billund during a period in Danish history when religious movements were spreading rapidly across the country. Except for the growing trade union movement in the major cities, the Inner Mission, an evangelical revivalist group, was the country's largest popular organization. Mission Houses sprang up among God-fearing, thrifty farmers all across Denmark, and by around 1920, more than three hundred thousand people, mainly from the ordinary agricultural and working classes, had formed small, local communities based around the principles of the Inner Mission. Not a sect, it was a religious network with many branches, each living its own piously Christian life within the overall framework of the Danish National Church, although many priests in the National Church at that time denied members of the Mission access to the houses of God.

Several waves of revival had already washed over the parish of Grene since the 1880s. Many different religious voices had rung out over the decades, from Catholic and Lutheran priests, pietists, and Moravian Brethren to devoted modern-day worshippers and the so-called Grundt-vigians, adherents of the psalmist Nikolai Frederik Severin Grundtvig and his ideas about Christianity, culture, church, and the fatherland.

Fundamentally, the members of the Inner Mission believed that human beings are sinful by nature. Only through understanding God and accepting his help can we be redeemed and live acceptable lives. The town's new carpenter and his wife cleaved to these same beliefs, although the Christiansen household was often rather merrier than many others in the region.

Kjeld: *In those days, people in Billund fell into one of two camps. Those with the Inner Mission were thought of as the stern saints who spent all their time at the Mission House, and then there were the Grundtvigians, who were supposed to be more down-to-earth in their relationship with God. They liked to meet in the town hall. Like my grandparents, most of the townspeople were involved in the Mission, but both groups felt that it was better not to mingle with "the others" more than strictly necessary. It was like that all the way up until the 1950s, in fact, when I was growing* *up. My two sisters and I knew who was with the Mission and who was Grundtvigian. Both my granddad and grandma were very religious people, but from stories about my grandfather, it's clear he was also a happy man, "simple" in the best sense of the word. He was very open and honest about his faith and loved putting "God willing" and things like that in his letters about the running of the company. I don't think he ever really taught people directly about God and Jesus, but his own faith was unshakable, and until his dying day my granddad was convinced he would never have come up with the toy and founded LEGO without God's help.*

At the top of invoices from the new tradesman were the words *Billund Woodworking & Carpentry*. Although most people in town only had positive things to say about Ole Kirk's professional skills, good intentions, and strong faith, the business wasn't as profitable as he and Kristine had hoped it would be, even after a few years, despite its promising start.

Farmers in Billund and other districts benefited from Denmark's neutrality during the First World War, by selling grain and meat to the warring nations and earning some extra hard cash by producing peat. In other words, they had the money to repair, rebuild, and expand their businesses, so between 1916 and 1918 there was plenty of work for a diligent young joiner and master carpenter to sink his teeth into. Once the war ended, however, the international financial crisis hit Denmark, too, and suddenly local farmers realized that money wasn't as readily available. In Billund and the surrounding areas, they had meager, sandy soil to contend with, too.

Still, there was always demand for a good carpenter, and Ole Kirk was confident. He employed both a journeyman and an apprentice, and for bigger building projects he took on local workmen. He was known as a kind and approachable boss who required careful and conscientious work from his men.

The boss had a low tolerance for idleness, and if you were of a lazy disposition, you wouldn't keep your job at Christiansen's for very long. If, however, you were willing to make a sustained effort, to really put your back into the work, then you'd be in good, thoughtful hands. Ole

Kirk only rarely spoke harshly to his men if they made a mistake. "It's just something to learn from," he'd say.

One of the workmen who grew close to Ole Kirk and his family over the years was Viggo Jørgensen, called "Joiner's Viggo." In 1917 he landed an apprenticeship at Billund Woodworking & Carpentry, where he would remain for the next eight years. It had a profound impact on the young man's approach, not just to his craft and his high ethical standards, but to other people and life in general.

Like Ole Kirk's four sons, Viggo, who had grown up at an Inner Mission orphanage near Vejle, learned that life wasn't merely a gift, but also a duty. As human beings, we had an obligation to make the most of what had been entrusted to us. Viggo never forgot this, and he emphasized it time and time again in the handwritten memoir he'd later write about his years with the Christiansen family, a memoir that he'd eventually share with his boss's sons.

Fourteen-year-old Viggo arrived in Billund on the train from Vejle on a spring day in 1917, carrying nearly everything he owned in his little suitcase. His pocket contained his entire fortune—one kroner and eighty-two øre, or about twenty-five cents. Ole Kirk picked the lad up at the station and walked him back to the house and the workshop, walking his bike beside him. They lived across from the co-op, where far too many people bought goods on credit from the manager and his wife and where the accounts were a total mess. Ole Kirk put the bike down in the little courtyard behind the house and showed the shy boy the place he'd be living, in a cool gable above the workshop.

"This is your room, Viggo. I bet you're scared of sleeping alone up here in the attic?"

"No," answered Viggo bravely, although having his own room with a bed, table, and chair was a new and overwhelming experience for this boy from the orphanage. Downstairs in the front room he met the boss's wife, who scrutinized him thoroughly.

"He looks a bit weedy to me, Ole."

"Yes, but that can be remedied," replied the boss.

Viggo soon felt at home. No longer was he just one of fifty or sixty

lilsen fra Billund

Postcard from the 1910s. Billund seen from the west, with the heather creeping across the gravel road. The white buildings to the left are the house and workshop Ole Kirk bought in 1916. *Local History Archive, Grene Parish.*

parentless boys at the Bredballe Orphanage. Now he had his own place in a family where every single mealtime began and ended with a prayer and sincere thanks to God. When guests came round they sang hymns, and Viggo was allowed to join them at the table and be part of the community. On ordinary days he had his own permanent seat among the other workers—at times there were six or seven of them—who gathered around the dining table with the boss at one end. Often, Christiansen read aloud from the Moravian Brethren's Devotional Calendar, finishing with a verse or two from the hymnal, which he particularly liked.

As was customary in early-twentieth-century Denmark, Viggo wasn't paid a wage during the four years he apprenticed there, although his room and board were covered. Instead, Ole Kirk allowed him to collect the tiny shavings of wood from the workshop, which he sold as kindling for 10 øre a bag. Sometimes, too, local parents would need childcare when they went to the Mission House in the evening, or for coffee at one another's homes, and this was another opportunity for Viggo to earn some money. Once he'd gotten familiar with the tools, Ole Kirk allowed him to use the shop after work hours, and he practiced his handiwork by making stools, hat racks, small bookshelves, dollhouse furniture and other small toys, and selling them in town.

"Just remember to keep track of the materials, Viggo!" said Christiansen. "And make sure you're paid for what you sell." That last bit could be a bit of a challenge in Grene Parish, where there was rarely much cash in circulation, and bartering was commonplace. Even when it came to small jobs like repairing a window or replacing parts of an old door, the farmers asked Ole Kirk if they could pay him in kind or be given a reduced price.

The same thing happened during the construction of Skjoldbjerg Church, which took place over the years between 1919 and 1921. Billund's by then much-sought-after master carpenter was commissioned to make Grene Parish Church's new gallery, with space for a big organ and even more seats. But Skjoldbjerg Church, south of Billund on the road to Vorbasse, was Ole Kirk's biggest assignment to date. He was in charge of all the important carpentry: the huge main door with its wrought-iron fittings, the pews, the pulpit, and the altarpiece. A wood-carver from out of town was tasked with crafting the twelve apostles, which Viggo installed in the small niches in the altarpiece, while the gilder, waiting to cover Jesus's disciples in gold leaf, looked on.

Ole Kirk was never to be paid the balance of what he was owed after the completion of Skjoldbjerg Church, but contented himself with knowing that, as he later put it, "It went to a good cause." If it got him into God's good books, it was probably a wise investment.

The fact that the authorities in Skjoldbjerg got away with underpaying for their new church made it clear, however, that Ole Kirk wasn't quite as punctilious with his accounting as he was with his craft. Several times in the first half of the 1920s, Viggo discovered that Christiansen was in dire financial straits. Whenever the business was truly under threat, and God, despite the boss's prayers, didn't leap into action, Viggo would be sent off on the bike to the bank in Grindsted.

The journey was eighteen miles there and back, down gravel tracks and

Billund Station

Billund Station was completed in 1914 and became one of the busiest stations on the line between Vejle and Grindsted, due to the trade in peat, marl, and manure. Viggo Jørgensen (left), who got off the train one day in 1917, wrote in his memoirs, "I still remember two people, Christiansen and his wife, who took care of a homeless boy and gave him good professional training and taught him the etiquette of life." *Local History Archive, Grene Parish.*

against the west wind on the outward journey. In the apprentice's pocket was an envelope of money intended to keep the creditors from the door.

"We'd better hope you don't get a flat, Viggo, because if you don't make it to the bank by three, they'll take the workshop and the house from us," Christiansen admonished him earnestly, but soon a mischievous smile spread across his face.

As Viggo later recalled, "It took much more than that to put the boss in a bad mood."

Ole Kirk was the kind of believer that Vilhelm Beck, the founder of the Inner Mission, described as "men with a brighter outlook on, and a more liberated approach to, their faith." At the core of Ole Kirk's personality was his unswerving conviction that human beings are the children of God and that they'd been forgiven their sins through baptism, yet he was also playful and given to banter. At times his sense of humor could be rather unconventional; for example, on New Year's Eve, he liked to throw firecrackers between people's legs, and as an elderly man he once made his grandchild pretend to be a dog and get into the trunk of the car.

> **Kjeld:** *I remember him as a happy, smiley, and very gentle man who couldn't help joking around with people in town and at the factory. One time he locked me into the trunk of his Opel Kaptajn because he thought I ought to see what it was like in there for the dog, which he and Grandma used to shut in there when they were driving. It wasn't much fun, actually, because suddenly someone came over to speak to him, and he forgot to let me out. I was in there for quite a while before someone heard me banging and managed to get me out.*

Throughout his life, humor and practical jokes were as defining an aspect of Ole Kirk's character as his unstinting religious faith. Perhaps it was this lightheartedness combined with deep faith that explained his nonchalance in the face of debts, overdue loans, and even bankruptcy petitions. Often, even as the darkest clouds loomed over Ole Kirk's business, he ended up on a cheerful, friendly footing with the debt collectors and lawyers his numerous creditors unleashed on him. Even the bailiff himself left Billund with his business unfinished but with an armful of beautiful wooden items for his family.

In November 1921, Viggo finished his apprenticeship, but there wasn't much full-time work to be had in this part of Jutland. "What will you do now, Viggo? Do you have anywhere to go?" asked Christiansen. Viggo didn't.

"All right, then I've got a suggestion for you, and you can take it or leave it. We'll be good friends regardless."

The boss offered Viggo room, board, and ten kroner a week if he stayed on to help with the bigger jobs that, God willing, would soon be coming through the door. "And don't think I'm just after cheap labor, because I'm almost as strapped for cash as you. I just want you to get something good out of your apprenticeship. You've got the skills, Viggo, it's only the work that's lacking."

Of course Viggo said yes. He'd been working with Christiansen in Billund for four years at that point and he knew what the life of a workman was like. When there weren't any big jobs, you got on with the smaller tasks back home at the workshop. In one room there were the machines: the band saw, drill, planer, and router, all of which were connected by long drive belts to the big axle under the roof. In the other room, overflowing with shavings and sawdust, were the benches and the stove they used to heat the glue. This is where they'd collect the individually worked pieces of wood, ready to be turned into doors, window frames, kitchen furniture and fittings, coffins, boxes for carts, as well as wardrobes and chests of drawers for young men and women going into domestic service.

Viggo concentrated on the joinery in the workshop, but within only a few weeks there was a bigger undertaking at a nearby farm. Christiansen made sure from the outset that Viggo got the full pay owed to him as a journeyman—one krone and eighteen øre per hour.

Kjeld: *What really motivated my granddad all those years, as a master carpenter and as a manufacturer, wasn't just perfection and quality, but* *also decency, which meant having a good relationship with his staff. It was a sense of social responsibility, which was all part of the respect he had for a job well done. Everything had to be of the best quality.*

You couldn't cut corners; my dad got told off for that at a young age. One day in the 1930s, after they'd started making toys, Dad sent out a consignment of wooden ducks much faster than normal. He thought he'd be praised when my granddad heard what he'd discovered—that the ducks only needed two coats of varnish instead of the usual three. He'd saved the company time and money, right? My grandfather looked at my dad and asked him to fetch the whole consignment back from the station so that the ducks could get another good, thorough coat of varnish. The quality of the product—and thus the satisfaction of the consumer— meant everything to him.

It wasn't long before there were more mouths to feed at Ole and Kristine's. After Johannes in 1917, Karl Georg came along in 1919, then Godtfred (Kjeld's father) in 1920, and finally Gerhardt in 1926. So, in 1923 Ole Kirk decided to add another level on top of the workshop, build an apartment in the attic and rent out a room on the ground floor. Any and all forms of income were welcome.

One Sunday toward the end of April 1924, during their midday nap, there was suddenly yelling from outside. "It's on fire!" The workshop was in flames, and the fire quickly spread to the main house. In a few hours, the whole property had burned to the ground.

Afterward it turned out that five-year-old Karl Georg and four-year-old Godtfred, the boy who'd eventually become LEGO's dynamic managing director, had sneaked into the workshop to play and make some dollhouse furniture for the neighbor's daughters. But the brothers were freezing cold, so they found some matchsticks on a workbench and tried to light the oven. An ember escaped, setting some wood shavings alight. The two boys tried to beat out the fire with sticks, but it only made the flames leap higher. Soon there was a real blaze, and an apprentice sleeping upstairs noticed the smoke. He rushed downstairs and broke through the door of the workshop, which the boys had locked.

In 1923, things were going so well for Billund Woodworking & Carpentry Shop that Ole Kirk built an attic over the machinery workshop. Behind the window in the wing on the right was another workshop, with planing benches, tool cabinets, and a glue heater, as well as the journeyman's room upstairs.

Nobody had been hurt. Some furniture and tools were able to be rescued from the fire, but the machines couldn't be salvaged. Viggo, who had few possessions, was hit hard. A keen reader and writer, he lost not just his clothes and clogs, but also his collection of books, including several that Christiansen had helped him bind.

Seeing his life's work suddenly in ruins was a shock for Ole Kirk, but the local community came through. The family was rapidly rehomed in the attic above the co-op, just across from the site of the fire, so at least they'd have a roof over their heads and Ole Kirk could keep working. He and numerous other tradesmen were busy erecting Billund's new co-operative dairy in the middle of the town, where LEGO House is today.

The dairy was a vital building, not just for the town of Billund but for the whole area, and Ole Kirk persevered, trying to keep his mind off his personal misfortunes and on his prospective house that would replace the one that had burned down. In the course of working on the dairy, he'd had several conversations with the architect, a man from nearby

Kristine and Ole Kirk in 1924, with Godtfred (left), Karl Georg, and Johannes. Gerhardt wasn't born until 1926.

Fredericia, a town east of Billund, who, like many of his colleagues in the 1920s, was a devotee of the "Better Building Practice" movement, a style of construction that focused on simple materials and good, healthy craftsmanship, often incorporating picturesque details.

Ole Kirk convinced the architect, Jesper Jespersen, to design him a new house with an adjoining workshop. The result was a large, beautiful building, but also a significant amount of debt, which in Christiansen's own words "pursued me for many years to come." Many parishioners looked askance at the master carpenter's new home. Even on quite sizable farms, you'd usually start with the cowshed when expanding on the property. Then would come the grain barn, and then finally, if there was money left over, the farmhouse. Christiansen worked it the opposite way. He thought big. The design was forward-looking, visionary, with the living rooms, bedrooms, kitchen, and workshops—all the living and work spaces, essentially—combined into a single, functional unit.

During the summer of 1924, the house took shape. In a letter to the architect in August, clarifying a few points about the windows and doors in the main house and workshop, Ole Kirk inquired whether Jespersen might ask the management of the dairy to pay his outstanding fee as an advance on the work he was doing: "Money is a bit tight for us." The architect forwarded his request, along with a note asking them to kindly send two thousand kroner to Ole Kirk Christiansen as soon as possible.

And, just like that, Billund's perennially insolvent master carpenter managed to end up with the most elegant and modern villa in Grene

In the garden one Sunday in summer, early 1920s, showing two delighted parents with their children. To the left is Ole Kirk with Karl Georg on his back, in the middle is the housemaid with Johannes, and to the right are Kristine and Godtfred.

Parish, with a workshop and courtyard around the back. "It was an entire mansion, and as usual Dad bit off more than he could chew," one of his sons later recalled.

At one end of the stately brick home was a huge window overlooking the street, with a kind of shop set up behind it where Ole Kirk could display his wares in a similar fashion to that of other respectable master tradesmen. To emphasize the craftsmanship of the house—which "would in itself attract new customers," Ole Kirk declared—they poured a stretch of cement pavement, the only one in all of Billund, and positioned two watchful, majestic cement lions on either side of the front door. Hardly were they in place and the building in use before people started calling it "the Lion House."

Kjeld: *In a way it was Granddad himself who designed the house. The architect simply followed his instructions. He knew exactly how it was supposed to be, but of course it turned out way, way, too big, even for two adults, four kids, and an ever-changing number of workmen lodging with*

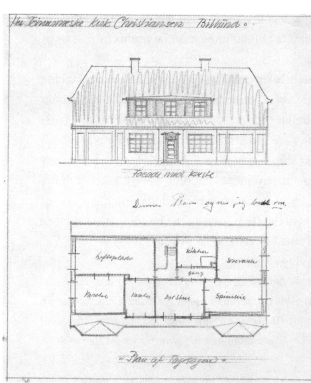

Architect Jesper Jespersen designed Ole Kirk's new house in 1924, and he followed the ideals of Better Building Practice: use of masonry and simple, beautiful execution with high-quality, solid materials. Good proportions were matched with practical and modern décor, with a focus on the entrance area, which was a visitor's first impression. And what could be more stately and decorative than two vigilant cement lions? *Drawing: Fredericia Local History Archive.*

them. But Granddad's construction projects were always like that, all through his life. Everything always had to be big, and later on he and my father had several heated discussions about it. Since the building, including the main house, was much too big right from the start, they rented out the first floor. Downstairs, the ground floor housed an office, in addition to the display area with the window facing the street, and in the other half of the house there was a sitting room, a bedroom, and the kitchen. The place is slap-bang in the middle of Billund to this very day, diagonally opposite LEGO House, and it's a memorial not only to Ole Kirk Christiansen and what he accomplished, but also to contemporary Danish building practices.

The first decades of LEGO's history were plagued by accidents. One day in August, only a year after the family first moved into the Lion House, lightning struck the new workshop and it burst into flames. Machines, furniture, and fittings as well as a huge number of half-finished commissions went up in smoke. The fire damage was estimated at forty-five thousand kroner, and once again Ole Kirk had to rebuild his business from scratch.

The following year, in November 1927, misfortune hit again. This time, it had to be said, the accident was self-inflicted, although the insurance company was never informed of this. Chatting merrily with various other workers and tradesmen on a local farm where a major construction project was in progress, Ole Kirk declared in one of his waggish, jaunty moods that he could easily stop the farmer's new petrol generator with a specific part of his body. Naturally, everyone around him insisted on visual confirmation.

Afterward, no one could say for sure what made the machine tip at the very moment Christiansen put his backside against the drive belt. At any rate, he got the worst of this encounter, hitting the ground hard and fracturing his skull. A few days later, the newspaper reported that "Doctor Lange drove in a screeching hurry to the site of the accident with a white flag on his car, followed by the ambulance. The injured man was treated in hospital soon afterward. His condition is serious and cause for concern."

The "injured man" recovered relatively quickly, however, and his condition improved still further when he was awarded 4,500 kroner by the insurance company. This large and unexpected sum enabled the technology-mad Ole Kirk to buy a crystal radio receiver; but no sooner did he have that device than he was dreaming of a "modern automobile," of which there was only one in Billund. In the autumn of 1928, Ole Kirk was thinking big once again, ignoring all his debts, and investing in a used Ford Model T.

Kjeld: *Granddad always had to have the latest gadgets. Not to show off, but because he was so incredibly curious and playful when it came to new technology. He was also the first person in Billund to get a TV in the 1950s. It was a huge deal, I remember, for the kids and grown-ups alike. We sat, goodness knows how many people, in Granddad and Grandma's old living room in front of this enormous box of a TV. That was very characteristic of him: he was never afraid to try things out if he could see—or if he just had a hunch—that there was a sensible idea behind it.*

But certain circles in Billund were beginning to wonder if Ole Kirk was showing a lack of respect for God. First he built a house that was beyond his means, then he bought a radio, and finally even a car. On the other hand, the carpenter wasn't the only one who suddenly had money to splurge on things. "When farmers are rich, everybody's rich," as the Danish saying goes, and 1928–1929 was an extraordinarily good year for harvests. In the period that followed, there was a boom in masonry, carpentry, and painting in Billund and the surrounding district.

Kristine felt Ole Kirk was taking his enthusiasm a step too far, however, when he suddenly started devoting all his time—and, crucially, his finest wood—to a large, beautiful sleigh for Pastor Frøkjær Jensen. "Did you even get anything for it, Ole?" she asked.

Ole didn't expect remuneration, saying, "If you can make your priest happy, then surely that's got to count for something with the Lord."

And wouldn't you know it, he started getting even more commissions for homes and barns, which meant he was busier than ever, al-

A young man leans up against Ole Kirk's "HGF," a contemporary nickname for a Høj Gammel Ford ("Tall Old Ford") with pedal gears. It was bought in installments in the autumn of 1929, becoming only the second car in Billund. The first was a German Brennabor with carbide headlamps and a canvas roof, belonging to Jensen, the painter.

though at this point he could race off to meet with clients in his Model T, which had three pedals instead of gears. Costing him 1,400 kroner, it was purchased in installments.

For a while, the future looked promisingly bright, but shock waves from the Wall Street Crash in October 1929 that wiped out billions of dollars in wealth quickly spread to Europe. Germany and England, Denmark's biggest trading partners, were badly affected, and the price of grain, butter, and pork crashed. The widespread agricultural crisis affected not only farmers but also tradesmen, leading to a rapid slump in construction, and resulting in massive unemployment, strikes, and riots and an explosive rise in the number of bankruptcies in rural areas. Many farm owners and master craftsmen were forced to put down their tools, and before long the net tightened around Billund Woodworking & Carpentry, too.

FAITH

THE 1930s

Duck, 1937

One morning in the autumn of 1931, a man headed out of town in his Ford Model T with a heavy heart. He had a long day ahead of him. Master carpenter Ole Kirk was going to try to claim some of the money owed to him around the district. At the very least he'd try to get some of his debtors to sign promissory notes, which was a common way of helping one another out in the countryside when money was scarce.

Debt collecting had never been Ole Kirk's strong suit. He usually sent ten-year-old Godtfred with the bills when they were due to be renewed because, unlike his father, his son rarely came home empty-handed. But on this day Ole Kirk—now threatened with bankruptcy—needed to step up and protect the Lion House and the workshop from the law.

The last person he visited that day was Jens Riis Jensen, who owned a farm on the Grindsted road. Ages ago he'd had a hay barn built, and he still owed thirty-five kroner on it. When the tall Ford Model T swung into the yard, Jens Riis came out to greet the driver. Ole Kirk opened the door but remained sitting inside.

"Don't suppose you have the thirty-five kroner you owe me, Jens Riis? I've been to fifteen different places today where I'm owed money, but nobody's got two coins to rub together, and they don't dare write promissory notes anymore."

The farmer shook his head despairingly. "Sorry, Christiansen. Last time I took full-grown pigs to the slaughterhouse I got less than I paid for them when they were tiny little piglets. Now I don't have so much as a krone to my name, but you can take some cheese home, if you like."

"I thought that might be the case, but will you sign a promissory note so I can get through tomorrow?"

"Well, the thing is, I'm not sure when I can pay you for the rest of the barn . . ."

"When the time comes, you can call me, Jens Riis, and I might have a bit of money you can borrow."

The farmer smiled, fetched a pen and signed the note.

Ole Kirk thanked him. "Your signature is the first and only one I've gotten after all this driving round today, but now I know that we'll manage at least one more day."

Neither Jens Riis nor any of the other Danish farmers were being paid enough for their goods, and in the early 1930s nobody could afford to repair anything much or to replace their doors and windows. Then one day Ole Kirk discovered that he could no longer buy wood on credit. When a nearby farm burned down and he was asked to rebuild the barn and house, he ordered the wood, as usual, from Johannes Grønborg's Lumberyard in Kolding. Because so many tradesmen were going bust, Grønborg was apprehensive about approving credit even for small orders, and he asked the bank for advice: Is Christiansen in Billund credit-worthy?

The answer was promptly returned. "We advise against that, even for the amount that is insured, since the carpenter you mention is in such unfortunate circumstances that he could go under at any moment."

In the 1930s, the co-op in Billund acquired an electric coffee grinder, as well as a petrol pump by the roadside. Hans Nielsen was the manager, and he had a close relationship with the Christiansen family on the other side of the street. He would gladly take unsecured checks from Ole Kirk's employees, which he would send to the bank only once he knew there was money back in Ole Kirk's account. People helped one another as best they could in this small town. *Local History Archive, Grene Parish.*

Ole Kirk was in a precarious position, indeed. Still, at the beginning of 1932 he was optimistic, perhaps due to his faith that God would help him in all aspects of his life. Little Knud, an apprentice who'd been with Ole Kirk since 1928 and lived, as Viggo once did, in the attic above the workshop, the one where the washbasin froze over in winter, worked on Christiansen's last home-building project in Billund in 1931, along with another journeyman. Now these two were helping the workshop produce various wooden items that the family hoped to sell during the Christmas season: stepladders, stools, ironing boards, Christmas tree bases, and a few toy cars, about which the boss surveyed his four boys for ideas.

Making these small toys was a source of tremendous enjoyment for Ole Kirk. It came to him quite easily, and although they weren't exactly selling like hotcakes, it did him good to make things for children with as much care and attention as he devoted to his products for adults. Throughout his sons' childhood in the 1920s, he'd occasionally pick up lumps of wood from the floor and whittle them with a knife or saw into horses, cows, or houses—or into one of the miracles of the speed-loving modern era: cars, trains, or planes.

> **Kjeld:** *My granddad was a good, considerate father who also had certain ideas and principles when it came to bringing up boys. He played with them when he had time, which was basically only on Sundays, which he always considered a holiday and an opportunity to spend time with his family. He carved and built little toys for them, and I know he would have given them the chance to put their own stamp on them too. When he started producing toys for real in 1932, it was his two youngest—my dad and Gerhardt—who put them to the test. Is this any good? Is what you're supposed to do with it good enough? In a way, my dad did exactly the same thing with me in the 1950s, when he'd suddenly appear in the basement playroom to see what I had made this time, and what a child might do with the new plastic bricks LEGO had started focusing on.*

One day in the early spring of 1932, there was a knock at the door of the Lion House. Outside was Jens V. Olesen, also known as "Wood Olesen," a lumber merchant from Fredericia. He'd brought a colleague, and the two men asked whether they could come in and see what Christiansen was doing in his workshop, since the building trade was so quiet those days and one carpentry business after another was having to close its doors. The two men praised Ole Kirk for the level of quality that distinguished his ladders, stools, and ironing boards. They were especially enthusiastic when shown all his beautiful toy cars, several of which were painted in gorgeous, shiny colors. Olesen ordered a large consignment of Ole Kirk's merchandise on the spot, for delivery in August. He could easily find a market for them among the shopkeepers and co-op managers across the countryside, all of whom needed to stock potential Christmas presents for the whole family. These may have been trying times, but children shouldn't be the ones to pay the price, Wood Olesen opined.

The two men were invited for coffee, and at some point, Olesen started talking about "Dansk Arbejde" ("Danish Work"), an organization that encouraged Danes to buy Danish-made products and helped master craftsmen set up a new type of production. Wooden items—especially toys—would be particularly sought-after in the coming years, predicted Olesen. He also said that Dansk Arbejde was offering new manufacturers free booths at Købestævnet, the annual trade fair in Fredericia where businessmen could display their products. As well as making new contacts with vendors and wholesalers, they might also get a lot of orders.

Ole Kirk had never heard anything like it, but as he later observed, he and Kristine were "receptive to the propaganda." After the two lumber merchants had gone, he said, "This might be the way to go, eh? We can always dip our toe into the water with a couple of ironing boards, stepladders, wooden cars, and some other toys."

It proved to be a turning point in Ole Kirk Christiansen's working life. He decided to revamp his production and pour all his efforts into practical wooden items and toys, and in order to afford help in the workshop and get a price list together, he borrowed money from some of his siblings. It was money he wouldn't be able to pay back for a decade.

Not everyone in the family understood his decision—far from it. The same went for many of Billund's other residents, who didn't put much stock in Ole Kirk's jumble of wares. Toys were simply ridiculous in the hands of a grown man! They'd always respected his hard work and skill, but now they shook their heads; some even came out and told him point-blank, "I think you're much too good for that, Christiansen—why don't you find something more useful to do!"

Kjeld: *In those first years, Granddad felt that it wasn't just people in town and the local parish who looked down on the fact that he was making wooden toys, but also some of his older siblings. They thought it was total nonsense, and the business didn't take off immediately. Sometimes, in the interviews he gave as an older man, he called himself the black sheep of the family, but I think we need to see that in the context of the fact that he wasn't able to keep his carpentry business afloat, and had to resort to making smaller items for women's household use and children's games. They didn't understand that in those days.*

Meanwhile, Ole Kirk worked hard to fulfill Olesen's order. The selection of wooden toys gradually took up as much space as the various other objects in the newly named O. Kirk Christiansen's Woodwork & Toy Factory, which was immortalized one summer's day in 1932 in a photograph taken in the family garden behind the workshop. Wooden cars, trams, planes, and numerous other toys were displayed on ironing boards and ladders. Behind them, Ole Kirk's group of assistants—including his son Johannes, Harald Bundgaard, Little Knud, Niels Christensen (known as Niels the Bricklayer), and thirteen-year-old Karen Marie Jessen, who was employed to paint the toys—stood in a line. The photographer might have been Ole Kirk himself, but it could also have been Kristine, who was pregnant with the couple's fifth child.

What wasn't visible in this historic photograph was the period's most sought-after and internationally best-selling toy, the yoyo. For Ole Kirk, the arrival of the yoyo had been a sign from above. As he later explained, "God gave me faith in the toys. It was those yoyos."

The worldwide yoyo craze appealed to both children and adults, serving as a brief distraction from a crisis that was becoming ever worse. The yoyo reached Denmark in late 1931, and could be seen and tried out for the first time at the Danish Christmas Gifts exhibition at the Technological Institute in Copenhagen. Through that winter and the spring of 1932, the obsession with yoyos spread to the rest of the country, and woodworkers like Ole Kirk enjoyed a brief halcyon period. Danish newspapers fueled the new popular phenomenon, which was said to have originated with the Ancient Greeks: "Yoyo fever is raging; people are playing with yoyos on the tram, on bikes, at work, in public offices; and if the assistant at the post office doesn't have time to serve us, it's because he's practicing with his yoyo under the counter."

In 1932, early summer. Kristine was expecting her fifth child, and the pregnancy took such a toll on her that she had to use a walking stick. Photographed here with Ole Kirk and their youngest son, Gerhardt, along with journeyman Harald Bundgaard.

For Ole Kirk, the demand for yoyos emerged so suddenly that it wasn't even on his initial price list in 1932, but he leapt at the unexpected chance and began to churn them out. For the men at the workshop, the small toy was quick and easy to make, and afterward the women in this small, industrious community of townspeople and family members painted and varnished them behind the Lion House. The cotton strings were added, then the yoyos were packed into crates and dispatched from Billund Station to wholesalers and distributors across the nation.

Thanks to the yoyo craze of 1932, there was work to be had at Christiansen's factory for a few lucky individuals like Niels the Bricklayer. Ole Kirk paid one øre per yoyo, and on his best days Niels could do a thousand of them. That added up to a daily wage of ten kroner, which was more than he earned as a bricklayer. Still, Ole Kirk tried to get most of his help from his wife and sons.

As he later explained, "We worked like dogs, my wife, my children, and I, and gradually things began to pick up. Many days we were working from morning till midnight, and I bought a cart with rubber wheels so the neighbors wouldn't be disturbed when I took the packages to the station late at night."

All seemed peaceful and idyllic in the old photograph taken in the summer of 1932, where the proud, loyal team were surrounded by the various beautiful wooden objects they'd made. Somehow it was especially reminiscent of the first lines of one of Ole Kirk's favorite hymns: "None are safer when in danger / than the children of the Lord."

Yet there was more hardship in store for the now forty-one-year-old master craftsman and prospective manufacturer. In August, production of the yoyos was at its height, and it seemed for the first time as though they might actually be able to earn decent money from making wooden toys, when the heavily pregnant Kristine fell seriously ill and was admitted to hospital in Grindsted, where it became clear that her fetus had died. She appeared to recover from the miscarriage, but abruptly came down with phlebitis, and on September 6 she, too, died, at the age of only forty.

The whole thing happened shockingly fast, and in the period that followed, a deeply grief-stricken Ole Kirk struggled to master his thoughts and emotions. The boys, especially twelve-year-old Godtfred, never forgot the sight of their father in mourning.

"I remember him coming into the front room, where I was playing around on the organ, and he told us what had happened. That was the first time I saw my father cry. We prayed to God before we went to fetch two of my brothers, who were out working."

Ole Kirk was so shaken that his faith in God wavered. He withdrew from the board of the Mission House, remaining an ordinary member for the next ten years. Not until 1944 does Ole Kirk Christiansen's signature appear on the records of the board meetings. Much later, looking back on the hardest and unhappiest period in his life, he wrote, "I tried to say, 'Thy will be done, Lord Jesus,' and to truly live it, but remained sickened by grief."

In the summer of 1932, the proud employees assembled behind the first assortment of wooden products. From the left: Karen Marie Jessen, Little Knud, Jens T. Mathiesen, Niels Christensen, "Mejse," Harald Bundgaard, and Johannes, the eldest of Ole Kirk's sons.

Kjeld: *It was typical of my grandfather that he refused to give up even when things looked darkest and most impossible. He must have had quite remarkable drive. No matter what, he was able to convince himself that things would be all right. To simply give up just like that—that wasn't in his nature. I recognized that same trait in my father, too, and I have it, as well. It's a kind of stubbornness that's been handed down, and it's connected to faith. Not necessarily in a religious sense; it's more about a broader and more general faith—faith in the future and in everything you're responsible for. And out of that grows the thought and the feeling that "This, this I can cope with!"*

Later in life, when Ole Kirk was an elderly man and director of LEGO, he was asked to explain how he coped during the financial crisis and throughout the personal problems that beset him between 1931 and 1933. His response, in summary, was, "You've got to pray a lot, pray you get the orders in, pray you get the goods made, and pray you get the money."

He expounded upon his vision about the concept that God had carried him, his family, and his business through the crisis—and about a revelation:

I was sitting there one night brooding on all the setbacks I'd been through. My creditors had sent lawyers after me, and my family and friends reproached me for "not doing anything useful." What should I do? It felt as though help was so far away that it could never reach me in time. And then something wonderful happened, something I will never forget. As though in a vision, I saw a large factory where busy people were bustling in and out, where raw materials were brought in and finished goods dispatched. The image was so clear that I never again doubted I would one day reach my goal: it was the factory that today is a reality. It's funny how you can gain faith and confidence in the middle of something so hopeless. I'm certain that it's God who gives us visions like that. The God I learned to believe in as a child.

Suddenly, having just restructured his business, Ole Kirk found himself with the sole responsibility for managing the household and raising four sons between the ages of six and fifteen, all of whom mourned their mother deeply. Six-year-old Gerhardt was still too young to be of much real help to his father, and thirteen-year-old Karl Georg would soon begin his carpentry apprenticeship. Back at the Lion House was twelve-year-old Godtfred, who was so weak as a little boy that Ole Kirk and Kristine once thought they might lose him. Now, the bright, intelligent lad helped out in the workshop with his brother Johannes when they weren't at school. Godtfred was good with his hands and a whizz with numbers, while the ever-smiling Johannes had been marked for life by the epilepsy he suffered from as a child.

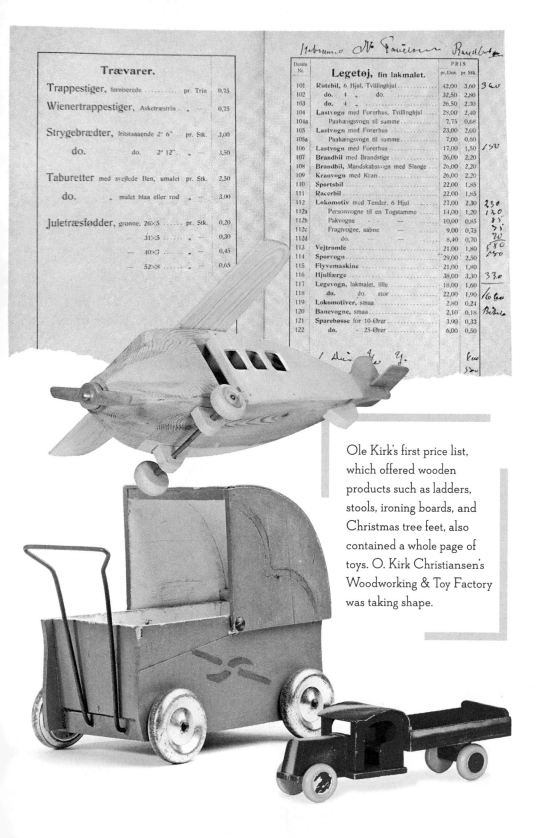

Ole Kirk's first price list, which offered wooden products such as ladders, stools, ironing boards, and Christmas tree feet, also contained a whole page of toys. O. Kirk Christiansen's Woodworking & Toy Factory was taking shape.

On top of all this grief and sadness, Olesen's huge toy order was caus-ing additional problems. It was supposed to have been picked up in Au-gust, but was still gathering dust on the shelves. Ole Kirk had assumed it was a sure thing, but it transpired that Olesen had gone bankrupt. As always when he needed a little help from the next world, Ole Kirk got down on his knees and laid his troubles before God, who showed him a way out. The next day he rose early, packed the old Ford Model T with Olesen's unclaimed order, asked the boys to look after one another, and set out to try to sell his wares, going from shop to shop and co-op to co-op.

It wasn't a great success. He did manage to get most of the items off his hands, but Ole Kirk had to admit that he wasn't a natural salesman. He found it hard to just show up and sing the praises of his own prod-ucts, because in his mind their quality spoke for itself. He was disabused of this notion, however, when he reached the town of Esbjerg: "The lady in the shop absolutely savaged my products, and I didn't dare make a proper retort. After this hatchet job she said she did want to buy some if she could get an additional 30 percent discount. I was so pleased when I left the shop."

Elsewhere, Ole Kirk had to settle for bartering, and he returned home to Billund with raisins, tapioca, and twenty kilograms of almonds in their shells, which meant that the little family in the Lion House—which had by this time acquired a housekeeper—could have a slightly better Christmas than other families in the area. Many of them couldn't afford meat or desserts, having to content themselves with potatoes, cabbage, and a modest financial contribution from the parish council's relief fund.

Nearly as soon as it had begun, the yoyo craze was over, and in the autumn of 1933 it had become increasingly difficult to make ends meet, despite a small increase in the annual turnover. Ole Kirk was stuck with a large stockpile of yoyos he couldn't get rid of. As he put in an advertise-ment printed in the Jyllands-Posten on November 4: "Offers requested for toy wheels or painted yoyos. For immediate delivery. Cheapest price per 1,000 pcs. Billund Toy Factory, O. Kirk Christiansen. Billund."

Ole Kirk took such a big bet on the yoyo craze that he was left with a large supply of them in 1933.

These financial troubles piled up just as Ole Kirk was struggling with the loss of Kristine, the lynchpin of their home for fifteen years, who'd taken care of all the household work and the raising of their four sons. Meanwhile he was being pursued by old debts, in particular by a contract of guarantee that he signed in good faith in the late 1920s to keep a local construction project going.

> It was something we tradesmen often did without risking anything, and my guarantee was almost a formality. But circumstances were such that the other guarantors were struggling, so they tried to pin the whole thing on me. There were distresses levied on my property, which I didn't really notice, but when the people who had lured me out onto thin ice and assured me in the friendliest terms that I was risking nothing now started confiscating my stock, then I thought everything was going to collapse.

Ole Kirk was on the verge of giving up and declaring bankruptcy when, one day in the late summer of 1933, Flemming Friis-Jespersen arrived on his doorstep. Friis-Jespersen was a lawyer from Vejle who, while on an errand in the neighborhood, decided to drop in on the local carpenter who hadn't been responding to his reminder letters or writs and had therefore been issued a sentence for failure to appear in court. Perhaps a solution could be found to satisfy both the creditors and the debtor, Friis-Jespersen thought. Many years later, in a letter addressed to Godtfred Kirk Christiansen, Friis-Jespersen recalled his first meeting with a deeply unhappy and disillusioned Ole Kirk:

> *In a virtually empty workshop behind what was really quite a large house, all things considered, I met a man who from the very first struck me as sympathetic.*
>
> *"To be honest, I've given up," he explained immediately. "Last year I built two houses, one for a client, the other for sale, but the client couldn't pay and nobody wanted to buy the house. Now I've been forced to sell them both at auction, and my own house will probably be going the same way soon enough. I owe debts everywhere, my wife is dead, and I'm left with four children who depend on me. What am I supposed to do? I might as well pack it in right now."*

Friis-Jespersen told him that to do nothing was the stupidest thing of all, because then every tiny claim increased exponentially with compound interest, and before you knew where you were, the debt had doubled. He advised the insolvent carpenter to draw up a list of his creditors and their demands immediately. Friis-Jespersen would then use this to file a letter of indemnity on the Lion House, which would not only give the creditors some assurance but also—for a while—give Ole Kirk some breathing room to consolidate his little business and to find a new housekeeper.

Nina, the competent and hardworking woman who had been looking after the family in the year since Kristine's death, resigned from her post abruptly on October 1, 1933. In his reference for the pious young woman, Ole Kirk wrote that she was "eager to do the work of God's Kingdom" and explained that not only had she been cooking and cleaning for twelve people every single day, but could also play the organ and sing. Where on Earth was he going to find a new Nina?

Few people realize that the first owner of LEGO was a woman. This would never have been the case had it not been for the newspaper lying on a chair in the kitchen one October day in 1933, when Sofie Jørgensen came to visit a friend in the South Zealand town of Haslev. Thirty-seven-year-old Sofie had just returned to her hometown from the larger town of Aarhus in the hopes of getting a job as manager of the local "Tatol," a chain of businesses that sold soaps, perfumes, and other articles of personal hygiene.

For the past few years, Sofie had been working at a home for troubled boys in Aarhus, sedulously saving up for the day she could realize her dream of running her own shop. Unfortunately, she had not been offered the job in Haslev that day, and a disappointed Sofie cycled over to her friend's house to take her mind off the episode. As the coffee brewed and they set the table, Sofie flipped through the *Kristeligt Dagblad*, which was lying on a chair. When she reached the employment page, her eye quickly fell on an entry entitled "Housekeeper":

> *A genuinely devout girl who is thrifty and capable of all the cooking, and who can take on all the duties of a housewife in a home, is sought for 1 November in favorable environment. Good community. I have two boys aged twelve and seven, so someone who can help bring them up with love and can make the place homely for them is preferred. Additional information from O. Kirk Christiansen, Billund Woodworking. Please send references from prev. employment as well as proposed salary.*

After Hougesen, the manager of the dairy, had helped him read and evaluate the various replies to the advertisement, Ole Kirk selected Sofie Jørgensen, who had good references, was a committed Christian, and came from Haslev, the Inner Mission's key stronghold in Denmark. Godtfred picked up the new housekeeper at Billund Station and brought her home to the Lion House, where Ole Kirk opened the front door and spontaneously exclaimed, "If I'd known you had such short hair, Sofie Jørgensen, I'd never have taken you on!"

And perhaps Sofie wouldn't have applied if she'd known that the big house with the beautiful pavement and grand lions was such a mess inside. And if she'd known that the family included four brothers, rather than two, as the job listing had said. Still, Karl Georg and Johannes returned from their respective apprenticeships only for an occasional visit. Godtfred, thirteen, went to school and helped his father in the workshop, he told Sofie, while seven-year-old Gerhardt climbed up onto the strange woman's lap and said, "Did you know my mother? She was so nice!"

Despite her short hair, the new housekeeper turned out to be a godsend. As the four brothers said in a television interview fifty years later, all talking at once: "Sofie became a really great mother to us. She was competent, she was loving, and she brought order back to the household."

Thirty-seven-year-old Sofie Jørgensen, who answered the ad in the *Kristeligt Dagblad*, found herself at a crossroads. After having worked for ten years at a boys' home and an Inner Mission "rescue home" for young female prostitutes, she wanted to try her luck as a housekeeper.

From the beginning, there was also strong, genuine rapport between Sofie and Ole Kirk, and seven months after she arrived, their wedding took place at her family home in Haslev. It occurred a bit too quickly, if you were to have asked his late wife's Jutland family. For the celebration on May 10, 1934, Sofie wrote a song for Ole Kirk, to be sung to the melody of "På Tave Bondes Ager" by B. S. Ingemann. In the song, she described the love that blossomed so quickly on Ole's fields in Billund:

> *No dreams she had of an equal life*
> *till Ole asked her to be his wife.*
> *And as he stood there in his yard,*
> *naught this sunlit moment marred.*
> *What words the two exchanged that day*
> *no one present now can say.*
> *The path to understanding there*
> *is a secret only those two share.*

For the rest of his life, Ole Kirk often repeated that if Sofie hadn't come to Billund in 1933, and if she hadn't allowed him to use her savings, LEGO would never have existed.

It was that simple. With the thousand kroner Sofie brought to their marriage—equivalent to thirty-seven thousand kroner in today's currency—she saved her husband from yet another bankruptcy in March 1934. And along with several smaller loans from some of Ole Kirk's siblings, Sofie's "dowry" formed the financial basis of the company that was to come. In his words: "In 1934 I married my housekeeper. She had a thousand kroner, and with some of this money I settled the most pressing of my debts. My family also helped me as best they could, so I got off relatively lightly."

The following year, O. Kirk Christiansen's Woodwork & Toy Factory was rechristened. Friis-Jespersen, who had previously saved Ole Kirk from imminent bankruptcy, suggested he find a name for his toy factory that customers would remember. Ole Kirk had been to the big trade fair at Fredericia for the second year in a row in 1935, and he realized that all the major firms at the fair were called something original, so he gathered his eight employees and announced that he was offering two bottles of cider as a prize to the person who could come up with a really good name.

Maybe it was the disincentive of the boss's sour home brew, but the two best suggestions—LEGIO and LEGO—came from the manufacturer himself. The first suggestion had something to do with "legions of toys," as Godtfred later explained. "Dad thought that if this toy-manufacturing business was ever to get off the ground, it would have to be through mass production." The other suggestion—LEGO—is a contraction of the Danish words *leg godt,* meaning "play well," and it was much more in keeping with the zeitgeist than Ole Kirk realized. The latter suggestion won out, since it sounded good and could be pronounced by grown-ups and children. Not until years later, when the toy company from Billund started exporting plastic bricks to the whole world, did they discover that LEGO in Latin means "I gather."

Kjeld: *There's another story in the company name, too, about how it wasn't just necessity and poverty that drove my grandfather to make toys. He originally started making useful household items, after work in the construction industry dried up, but soon moved on to making wooden toys. First and foremost it was because he was a playful person himself, who always enjoyed the company of children and thought, "Kids should have fun, and I can make children happy by giving them good toys." That idea played a major role for him, I think, particularly in the difficult phase when they were starting up, and that's why the name LEGO came to him so easily. But he liked to put it this way: "What I'm doing now is at least as important as ordinary joinery and carpentry."*

Throughout the 1930s and the early 1940s, the marriage between Ole Kirk and Sofie and the strong family bond formed the cornerstone of the "LEGO Factory," as their company was described on its elegant new letterhead. In the spring of 1935, Ole and Sofia had their first and only child, their daughter Ulla. She grew up in a small town where everybody knew everybody else, people helped one another out, and where ever more of the local population earned a living in the dusty, noisy workshops behind the Lion House, which smelled of wood and varnish. By the year's end, their turnover had nearly doubled compared to the previous year, now reaching 17,200 kroner. In 1936, turnover doubled again, and the workshops looked increasingly like the large-scale facility that God once showed Ole Kirk in a vision.

The little company was still dogged by liquidity problems, however, because of its founder's old debts and his tireless urge to invest in new technology. The year 1937 found Ole Kirk at a trade fair in Germany, where he couldn't take his eyes off a state-of-the-art router from ELZE & HESS, a device that could make elaborate cutouts in wood and would add exactly the right soft, rounded corners to LEGO's popular wooden animals on wheels. Unfortunately, the machine cost a fortune: four thousand kroner. Two months later, he ordered one through a supplier in Copenhagen. At that point it was all or nothing.

He took the same approach a few years later, when their accountant, Johansen, sat in the LEGO office writing out paychecks. He'd nearly finished when the telephone rang. It was Vejle Bank.

"Johansen, this can't go on any longer," the banker said. "No more writing checks that the company can't afford!"

The accountant had heard this before, so he brushed it off, arguing that the bank had plenty of money while LEGO had almost none, and so on. When the chilly voice on the other end of the line replied that this decision had come from the top, Johansen decided that Ole Kirk ought to be informed.

When he found the boss kneeling in his garden, planting flowers, the latter's only response was that Johansen ought to simply keep writing the checks as needed. "I've had bigger problems!"

Ole Kirk's financial recklessness and all the old debts he was still saddled with were the reason why the company was in Sofie Kirk Christiansen's name between the years of 1935 and 1944. If he were to have been declared personally bankrupt, they couldn't have seized her property. This arrangement also meant that, legally speaking, all LEGO's income and assets up until 1944—when it became a limited company—belonged to Sofie.

Slowly but surely, the little toy factory in Billund made progress. The first time the new name and logo were presented to the world was at the trade fair in Fredericia in the summer of 1936, when the fair outdid itself, and 82,000 people—including King Christian X of Denmark—visited the exhibition space, a magnificent complex within encircling ramparts.

Ole Kirk's booth was on the third floor of the main building, alongside big, prestigious firms and smaller contractors and entrepreneurs from across the country, all of whom were displaying a wide array of items, from pianos, corsets, and fruit wine to washing powder, meat extracts, and cigar-drying boxes. In previous years, passersby had already noted the excellent quality of Ole Kirk's toys and admired the detail on the various types of cars. They were called Billund Auto, and their wheels were made of old yoyos. All the spools that Ole Kirk didn't sell in 1933 had been sawed up and repurposed as car wheels. They had an uncannily realistic finish, for which thirteen-year-old Karen Marie Jessen had been responsible. As she recalled:

> Each wheel went through my hands three times. First, they had to be primed and dried. Then painted gray, then dried again, and then finally they had to have a fine red color in the middle, following the edge very precisely. I got one øre for every three wheels, and I could paint nine hundred a week, which gave me three kroner, and I still remember how pleased my mother was when I gave her the money every Saturday night.

A majority of LEGO employees in the 1930s were young men who'd not been apprenticed in any particular trade, as well as girls, housewives, and widows from Billund and the local area whose stories Ole Kirk knew well. Most came from families that had been hard hit by the agricultural crisis and needed to supplement their household income by taking on a few jobs at home during the Christmas rush, when it was always extra busy at LEGO.

The major challenge faced by Danish companies in the second half of the 1930s was working capital, needed both for wages and to pay for raw materials and invest in machinery. In the lumber industry, liquidity was still an issue at the end of the decade, and suppliers were reluctant to offer credit. Even so, LEGO was on its way to becoming a reputable company, even outside of Jutland, and it approached an annual turnover of 40,000 kroner. In 1939, when Ole Kirk put in a large order with Davinde Sawmill on Funen and was asked to prove his company's creditworthiness, Vejle Bank sent the following assessment to the mill:

> *The owner of LEGO is Mrs. Kirk Christiansen, while her husband is the actual head of the organization. It is our impression that they are respectable and energetic people who live frugally, and we believe it is possible they can build up a profitable business. Mr. Christiansen has shown us the balance sheet for 1938, which shows a small working profit, and therefore it is our assessment that there is unlikely to be excessive risk involved in giving the company credit for reasonable quantities.*

The LEGO Factory was charging full steam ahead, and in 1939 they hit 50,000 kroner in turnover, thanks to a range of toys designed for

The year 1936 was the last time Ole Kirk participated in the trade fair in Fredericia, which for many years had been very important to his small business. The toy factory in Billund presented its new name, LEGO, in the catalog, and the telegram address was of course "Leg." *Fredericia Local History Archive.*

boys and girls, including even more of their popular pull-along animals, led by a half-mechanical duck that could peck with its bill, a red high-speed train, doll carriages, games to be played at the beach, and various makes of car.

Ole Kirk had started traveling abroad. Several times he had gone to the Leipzig Fair, looking for inspiration and ideas to take home, which he would then duplicate and put into production. In the toy industry, copying was rife and patent law was a foreign concept. He also flirted with the idea of exporting products, and in January 1938 he wrote to the Foreign Ministry to explore "the possibility of selling wooden toys in the Scandinavian countries and Great Britain." The reply from the ministry contained a number of addresses of importers, information about duties and tariffs in the respective countries, as well as a questionnaire, asking the owner of LEGO to describe his company and its products in more detail.

For decades, the European toy market had been dominated by Germany, Denmark's much larger neighbor. They produced wooden and mechanical toys, which the quality-conscious Ole Kirk made a point of calling "Nuremberg tin trash." He was unimpressed by Germany's toy industry and believed that LEGO could compete on craftsmanship.

Unlike many of his colleagues in the industry, Ole Kirk didn't use cheap raw materials such as wood with "blue stain," that is, wood that had been discolored by fungus, which could be hidden if the wood pieces were dipped thoroughly in paint. LEGO's wooden toys were always completely knot-free, and at all stages of the production the team prioritized rigorous, skilled work, rounding each piece off with additional finish and a quality-control check.

The raw material, beechwood, had to be of the very best quality. It wasn't cut until it reached Billund, where it was seasoned and air-dried before being steamed and oven-dried. From the earliest days in 1932, LEGO's core offering had been good, solid, long-lasting wooden toys. Quality sells itself, Ole Kirk believed. As the slogan of a German teddy bear company he saw at the fair put it, "For children, only the best is good enough."

Richard Christiansen operated the expensive router Ole Kirk bought in 1937 for a small fortune. It turned out to be a wise investment, given that pull-along animals were becoming more and more popular—not just the classic gray duck, but also cats and chickens, which were attached to wheels, and a string, allowing little hands to pull them along.

In the 1920s and 1930s, increasingly progressive ideas about children and play swept across Europe, ideas that were, in many ways, a continuation of Friedrich Fröbel's much older theories. Fröbel was a German educator who created the first kindergarten in 1840, and who also designed toys for children and published a journal with the motto: "Come, let us live for our children!"

Published in 1900 and translated into seventeen languages, Swedish writer Ellen Key's book *The Century of the Child* dealt with similar themes. In a way not previously seen in child-rearing literature, she discussed the ideal upbringing, pleaded for love between parents and children, and argued that humanity's most important raw material would always be the children we bring into the world.

Childhood was also a topic of debate in Sigmund Freud's later essay on the function of play, "Beyond the Pleasure Principle," in which the psychoanalyst claimed that children play primarily because games are associated with pleasure. Also in the 1920s, the Swiss psychologist Jean Piaget described in various scientific articles how children explore the world through play, arguing that it helps them understand cause and effect.

Many other interwar psychologists, educators, authors, and philosophers researched childhood and the universal significance of play, including Maria Montessori, Margaret Mead, A. S. Neill, Bertrand Russell, and Johan Huizinga, the Dutch historian who in 1938 published the book *Homo Ludens* (*Man at Play*), building on the thesis that all human culture arises and develops through play.

In Scandinavia, the 1930s and subsequent decades witnessed the development of a distinctive perspective on childhood and children, one that expressed itself concretely in toys and literature. In 1932, as Ole Kirk revamped his carpentry business, the artist and craftsman Kay Bojesen garnered international attention with his gorgeously designed wooden toys at a major exhibition in Copenhagen. The year before that, a Swedish toy company owned by the Ivarsson brothers located in Osby began emblazoning their company name, BRIO, onto their colorful wooden toys. They'd been working on their products for twenty years, mindful of the importance of play and hoping to give children the best possible experience.

In the 1940s and early 1950s, several landmark children's books were written in Scandinavia. For the first time in world literature, adult writers dared to make children and childlike characters the first-person narrators of children's books, giving children natural-sounding voices. These groundbreaking changes are evident in the work of the Swedish writer Astrid Lindgren, Danish Egon Mathiesen, Norwegian Thorbjørn Egner, and Finnish Tove Jansson. Like the toys made by the Ivarsson brothers, Kay Bojesen, and Ole Kirk, their works of art—created by adults for children—helped expand parents' understanding of the world of the child and the nature of play.

Amid this boom in Scandinavian youth culture and the associated focus on children, games, and toys, LEGO continued to expand production. Ole Kirk, meanwhile, evolved as a toy manufacturer. At first he was scarcely aware of this sea change, although his toys comprised a key component of it. Words and concepts like "functionalism" and "progressive education" would have been unfamiliar to Ole Kirk, but repeated trips to exhibitions and trade fairs abroad during the latter half of the 1930s gave him new knowledge and insight. It was no accident that he kept a lengthy newspaper article published around this time in a Danish newspaper, about the increasing interest in children's games and toys, particularly among scientists:

The educator speculates on its value for upbringing, the doctor on the harm or good it may do for the child's health, the chemist on the composition of the pigments to be used, which must be entirely nontoxic, the inventor creates new models, the engineers transform the ideas into reality, and the businessman speculates on the most advantageous sales tactics. While in olden days one might have been content to give one's child a carved horse, a few colorful paper cutouts, or a rag doll to play with, children have become more demanding, and toys have become such a significant factor that they have an impact on Denmark's balance of trade.

Kjeld: *There's no doubt my grandfather realized instinctively that quality toys were the foundation of good play, but I don't think he was thinking so much about the educational aspect or the connection between games and learning, which is so important to LEGO these days. Nor was my father. For him, it was more about the system of the products, although he did use expressions like "the child's creative urge." The concept of learning through playing with LEGO was something I brought to the company in the 1980s.*

Later in life, Ole Kirk's four sons remembered their father as "a good pal" in the years after their mother's death. They all described him as such in a lengthy TV interview from the 1980s, in which Godtfred added, "Dad never lost his sense of humor. It was at his request that I stayed home to help him, although for a while there were plenty of other things I wanted to do more."

The Kirk Christiansen family in the mid 1930s, when Ulla was born. Back, from left: Karl Georg, Johannes, and Godtfred. Front: Sofie, Gerhardt, Ulla, and Ole Kirk.

Godtfred, even more than his three brothers, had sawdust in his veins, and on top of that he was good with numbers and good with people. Even as a child he assisted in the workshop, helping his father with the accounts and bicycling around with the bills that had to be paid and the promissory notes that had to be signed. As a reward, he was allowed to drive his father's Model T when he reached adolescence—occasionally at the risk of other people's life and limb, according to his cousin Dagny Holm, who in the 1960s became famous as the model-builder and artist behind the various towns and fairy-tale characters in LEGOLAND.

In the early 1930s, Dagny was living in Skjern, where her father had a bike shop. When the family from Billund came to visit on Sundays, Godtfred drove occasionally.

"One time he drove into a pole in the middle of Skjern. The electricity company called us afterward and said, 'Next time you get a visit from those scamps from Billund, call us in advance so people can get home in time.' The whole town had been plunged into darkness, you see, because of the crash," explained Dagny.

She also remembered that the four brothers were remarkably like their father, especially when it came to pranks and teasing. For a while, when she was eighteen, just before leaving for Zealand to work at a home for troubled boys, Dagny lived in Billund. The brothers decided to help see her off properly, so late one night they tried to coax a live pig into their cousin's room. Although she just managed to close the half-open window in time, her cousins returned the following night, and this time they succeeded in playing a prank on her. When Dagny got up the next morning and drew back her curtains, she was in for a shock. Outside her window was a dangling figure of a man, who turned out to be a scarecrow with a noose around his neck.

It wasn't just Dagny—and later Godtfred's brothers—who left Billund, each in turn, to find work or learn a trade. So did most of Godtfred's schoolmates. At fifteen, Godtfred looked forward to starting a promised apprenticeship at Sørensen's Auto. But this dream would never be realized. One night, Ole Kirk sat down on the edge of his son's bed and explained that he couldn't do without Godtfred's brains and technical ingenuity at the workshop.

> **Kjeld:** *The factory became my father's destiny. He never had any real education beyond his schooling here in Billund, which was every other day and ended after seventh grade. After that he worked with his father in the workshop, helped out with the development and production of the toys, and kept an eye on the books and went to the bank. Money was never my grandfather's strength, and that responsibility fell on my father's shoulders early on. He learned a lot from that.*

As far as higher education went, Godtfred had to settle for attending the Technical School in Grindsted a couple of nights a week. During the day he assisted in the workshops, where by now they were producing more than fifty different kinds of toys. In addition to the various makes of car, there were animals on wheels, prams, ironing boards and irons, gliders, fire engines with ladders, and something they called "Kirk's Sand Game." This consisted of long wooden pieces that could be assembled into a track, which traveled down a pile of sand in a sandpit or on the beach.

The 1930s were also a period in which Danes became increasingly fond of the outdoors, flocking to the forests and the beaches on Sundays with their families. In Billund, LEGO played into that trend by, for example developing the Sand Game. It was sold in a box printed with the following perfectly targeted rhyme: "Sun, beach, and woods, wherever you wend, Kirk's Sand Game is a child's best friend." In addition to the wooden pieces, the box also contained a flag with the Danish colors, printed with the words "Kirk's Ball Track," which could be placed on top of the child's heap of sand. And for Mom and Dad, there was the following relevant bonus information: "Excellent for developing your child's aptitude."

In the years 1936–1940, Ole Kirk and Godtfred's relationship developed into a creative and enterprising partnership that was the basis for

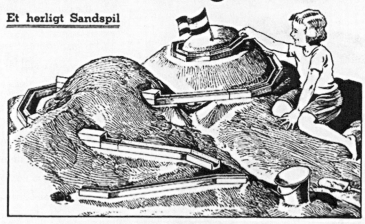

Kirk's Kuglebane

Et herligt Sandspil

Hvert Barn sit Sandspil.

Kirk's Ball Track, from the mid 1930s. This toy contained educational instructions for playing the game, but in the sand pit behind the dairy, Ulla used her own imagination, playing with her friend Kurt, the son of the dairy manager, Hougesen. *Private collection.*

During this decade, the car was becoming the preferred form of transportation, although they were still far from common, unless you were content with a quality sealed car from LEGO. These were initially very simple and angular, but softer, more streamlined shapes were developed toward the end of the decade, when Godtfred was designing new models at the technical school in Haslev and sending them home to his father at the factory.

LEGO's growing sales and success throughout the 1940s. The collaboration between father and son was virtually frictionless; Ole Kirk focused on the quality of the product and the well-being of their staff, while Godtfred was the inventive designer, simultaneously realistic and intuitive, with the ability to think strategically.

In his mind, Ole Kirk had already chosen Godtfred as the son who'd take over the running of the company when the day came that he, himself, no longer had the energy. A stay at the well-regarded Inner Mission trade school in Haslev would be an investment that wouldn't just stimulate his son, but also eventually prove useful for LEGO. But the venture wasn't a success. Godtfred was out of his element. He missed home and drew endless models of upcoming, streamlined LEGO wooden cars, all of which were immediately mailed back to his father in Billund:

Dear everybody! Dear Dad!

I enclose a few drawings! You'll have to see if they are usable. I can draw more cars if you want. I like the system with the mudguards, and they're also cheaper than the lathed ones, but it would be best if we could use the same size for several different cars.

Godtfred felt disliked and excluded from his peers at trade school because he wasn't going to be a "real" tradesman like the others but simply someone who cobbled together toys for children. As he later remarked, "It wasn't considered a real subject. I probably experienced a little of the same disdain as my father did when he first started producing toys."

To pass the time at the trade school, Godtfred worked on his own car designs. He sat at the back of the class, giving the old, slightly clunky and awkward wooden cars softer shapes inspired by Ford and Chevrolet, while the future joiners, bricklayers, carpenters, and smiths around him practiced their technical drawing, keeping their attention focused on the teacher at the blackboard.

Ole Kirk, meanwhile, had bigger and better plans for Godtfred's further education. He was busy arranging a year's traineeship at a lumber company in Germany, to begin as soon as his son finished in Haslev. But when Germany occupied Denmark on April 9, 1940, his plans were brought to an abrupt halt. Godtfred had to stay home in Billund and help out at the factory with a new job title: foreman.

On the eve of a new decade, the world was on the verge of a long and immensely destructive war, a war that paradoxically ended up offering companies like LEGO some new and unexpected opportunities.

WAR

THE 1940s

Peace Pistol, 1945

Bernhard Bonde Christiansen, a young journeyman carpenter from West Jutland, arrived for his first day at LEGO in December 1941. His job was to look after the expensive router Ole Kirk had invested in. It carved the various animals on wheels, which the children of that period loved to pull along in their wake. His starting salary was thirty-five kroner per week, plus room and board. Bernhard got his meals at the Lion House, while his bed and a small amount of storage space was in the room above the woodworking shop, which he shared with three other employees.

In the beginning he was astonished by the motley assortment of older boys and old women working at LEGO. There were eighteen of them in total, and Bernhard Bonde, as far as he can tell, was the only one to have completed an apprenticeship. But the atmosphere was good with a strong sense of team spirit. Every day, Christiansen walked round in his khaki overalls, chatting with "the lads," as he called the young men, and joking with the girls who did the painting and packing.

The workweek was forty-nine hours, but the world was at war and Denmark under occupation, so during certain periods the staff were let go earlier in the day and asked to come to work at daybreak instead to save electricity, which was being rationed. A normal working day at LEGO started at seven. Bernhard had a half-hour break in the morning, an hour for lunch, when a hot meal was served at the Lion House, and then a half hour in the afternoon for coffee. They worked right up until half past five and spent no more than five minutes or so preparing for the end of the day. That said, all employees were obliged to clean up after themselves, which happened after closing time.

The highlights of Bernhard Bonde's day were the hot lunch and particularly the afternoon coffee, both of which he took at Lion House. For a brief while, he felt like a part of one big family. At the end of the table heaped with food, made by Sofie and the girl who helped with the housework, sat Christiansen in his shabby work clothes. He was the one who said grace: "Dear Heavenly Father, we thank you for all your gifts to us. Amen!" Around the table, in addition to the host and hostess, were their daughter, Ulla, and their sons, Godtfred, Johannes, and perhaps Gerhardt or Karl Georg, if they were home visiting, and the other people from the factory who, like Bernhard Bonde, got room and board.

Once in a while, Christiansen kept them waiting if he was on a phone call or had fallen into a reverie in his beloved garden. As time dragged on and the hungry crowd waited to start, it was tradition for everyone around the table to sing, at steadily increasing volume, a verse written by the family's high-spirited sons:

We're waiting for the boss
WE'RE WAITING FOR THE BOSS . . .
AND WE'RE STARVING TO DEATH!

On one icy night in March 1942, Bernhard Bonde was woken by one of the other men in the room, who shook him awake and told him he could hear strange noises coming from below. Sitting up, Bernhard immediately smelled smoke. He dashed downstairs and flung open the door to the workshop, where the flames had taken hold of the dry wood. Bernhard rushed across the yard, where snow had gathered in heavy drifts, hammered on the back door, and knocked on the windows of the Lion House, shouting, "The workshop's on fire! The workshop's on fire!"

Soon, voices and shouting could be heard from inside, where nobody could see anything because the power had gone out.

After that, everything seemed to run on instinct, as Ole Kirk later explained. Over the course of the night, the snowstorm had torn down most of the telephone and power lines in Billund. Only one remained intact, and Sine, Karl Georg's girlfriend and later wife, at the telephone exchange managed to alert the fire service in Grindsted. The message had already gone around to the local men and older boys, who rapidly gathered outside the Lion House with buckets and other firefighting equipment. Ole Kirk tried to burst his way into the workshop with a fire extinguisher, but was forced to retreat because it was so blisteringly hot that even the machinery was melting. Sofie wrapped Ulla in blankets and carried her to the dairy, where she and the dairy manager's daughter sat in the window and watched the smoke and flickering glow against the night sky. It was a sight she would never forget.

Thanks to the direction of the wind and the help of the fire brigade, only the workshop building burned to the ground—not the Lion House or the several other nearby homes. Aided by the firemen and the volunteers from the town and the workshop, Ole Kirk and three of his sons saved what could be saved, including Godtfred's generator, which always went *hwirw, hwirw, hwirw* when you cranked it, as Bernhard Bonde recalled.

Karl Georg was in Filskov with an uncle whom he was helping to build a house, but Sine called him immediately. It was impossible to drive or get a lift, so Karl Georg decided to make the six-mile walk through the snow on foot. He borrowed a pair of thick socks to pull over his shoes so he could progress across the slippery ground. Then Karl Georg half walked, half jogged home to Billund over the heath and the marshes, where reasonably solid footing could be found in the hard, frosty weather.

He was too late to see anything but the smoking ruin: sooty and dilapidated walls, charred stumps of workbenches, and melted remnants of machines and tools. Their losses totaled seventy or eighty thousand kroner, not including a correspondingly large sum in orders they were either working on or about to ship. They were insured for only sixty thousand kroner, and the next day Ole Kirk was seized with a sense of fear and dejection he hadn't experienced since Kristine's death. For the first time since Sofie had come into his life, Ole doubted the plan that God had laid before him.

> *As everyone knows, adversity is there to be overcome. It's through it that we humans are being refined. This was the third time I had to see my company burn to ashes. And this time it really was a big shock. I had to go to my bedroom to pray in my despair. Then I experienced something remarkable: the prayer became a thanks and a blessing for me. I was given invisible help. It was as though my difficulties were taken from me.*

As he had done so many times before, LEGO's founder sought help and renewed strength from his Heavenly Father, and a few days after the disaster he once again saw his life and occupation in an optimistic light. Ole Kirk was at a crossroads: was this the moment he was meant to leave Billund and put down roots elsewhere in Denmark?

A couple of days after the fire, a composed, resolute Ole Kirk sent several important letters. One was to LEGO's sales rep in Copenhagen, Axel Barfod, advising him of the unfortunate situation and letting him know that they couldn't take new orders for the time being. The letter concluded with the words:

> *Our future plans are not yet laid, but we intend, assuming we find the right place, to take over another factory, potentially one not currently*

in use, in a central location near a town, but not in the town itself. If
you get wind of anything that might suit us, we would be very interested
to hear from you.

Another more concise and formal letter was dispatched to the
Jyllands-Posten and the *Berlingske Tidende*. It contained an adver-
tisement, which ran in both newspapers seven days after the fire, on
March 28, 1942:

FACTORY PREMISES. Ideally with woodworking machinery, approx.
seven thousand square feet of floor space as well as offices and accom-
modation near national railway. Centrally located. Required for im-
mediate purchase or rent. Must be six apartments on site as well as a
number of rooms. LEGO Factory, Billund.

More than thirty replies came in from owners and landlords in various towns, primarily in Jutland. Ole Kirk, Sofie, and Godtfred looked
at several options. A couple of offers in Copenhagen and Aarhus were
discarded right away because one of Ole Kirk's core beliefs, which he
passed on to his son and grandson, was that industry should be spread
across Denmark, instead of being concentrated in and around the major
cities. The family looked at several interesting locations, not only in Jutland. They also made a trip to Funen, crossing what was then the new
Little Belt Bridge, where the cars drove right next to the Danish State
Railway's high-speed red train, the Litra MS, which in the 1940s was one
of the biggest hits in the LEGO catalog.

After traveling far and wide through western Denmark, Ole Kirk was
sure of what he wanted and what felt right: "The more we looked, the
fonder we were of Billund."

Kjeld: *My dad was definitely involved in Granddad's proposal to move*
the production and the family, and later he considered doing the same
thing himself. At one point, Hedensted was suggested as a new home for
the LEGO Group because it was more central and closer to the main

The day after the fire, only the charred remnants of walls, machinery, and furniture remained. At this fateful moment, Ole Kirk gathered his employees and their families for a group photograph in front of the ruins. He sits in the front row, with Ulla in front of him. Standing on the far left are Godtfred and his fiancée, Edith.

All the undamaged toys were gathered up and sold, allowing Ole Kirk to repay his old debts to his siblings and friends from the Inner Mission.

roads, Dad thought. But, like my grandfather in 1942, he came to the con-
clusion that Billund was where our roots were—and where they should
stay. It was here we had employees who would go through fire and flood
for LEGO, here we had all our family connections. I think it was tre-
mendously significant for LEGO that back then they decided to stay in
Billund and rebuild the factory from the ground up. I have always felt the
same strong sense of veneration for the town and the area, which is why
Billund remains our headquarters.

Taking out new loans, Ole Kirk designed, by the standards of the age
and given his situation, a very large and modern factory. Work began in
the late summer of 1942 and finished before the New Year. At the helm
was a local master mason, Søren Christensen, with whom Ole Kirk had
worked since the 1920s and had also known from meetings and activities at the Mission House. The new LEGO factory was a long redbrick
building with two stories, plus an attic and basement. Architecturally,
it was reminiscent of the Lion House, and was built surrounding Ole
Kirk's garden, which were intended both for the family and the factory
workers to use during their breaks.

After the fire, while the new factory was still under construction, a
makeshift production line was set up in Billund School of Handicrafts,
which Ole Kirk had helped to found a few years earlier. Godtfred got
permission to use master carpenter Tage Jensen's workshop at night to
make the models so that they'd be ready for mass production when the
new building was finished and ready for use.

Some of this hefty expenditure was financed by the "Total Clearance
Sale" that Ole Kirk announced shortly after the fire, which included the
undamaged stock that had been in the Lion House on that fateful night.
The sale brought in so much money that Ole Kirk was able to do something he'd been dreaming of for many years. He repaid the money he
owed to his siblings and a couple of close friends from the Inner Mission, who had helped him through the worst of his crises in the 1930s
and acted as guarantors for the overdraft that had made it possible to
invest in machinery.

The long factory building behind the Lion House (left) was ready by the end of 1942, and soon housed a more efficient mode of production, although most of it was still done by hand. There were now thirty-five to forty employees, and in the group photo outside the main entrance, Ole Kirk and Sofie can be seen sitting on the far left. Godtfred stands just behind his father.

Including interest, these debts had now reached 9,000 kroner, equivalent to 200,000 kroner or $35,000 today. Being able to repay the loans gave Ole Kirk renewed faith in what he was trying to build. With a few months distance from what had looked like financial chaos and potential liquidation, or having to relocate his business, he sat down at his typewriter one day in the summer of 1942. Ole Kirk needed to explain himself to his God, the one who'd given him faith in toys:

We are now laying the foundation stone of our new warehouse and workshop building, knowing full well that we will not be able to accomplish it on our own. Yet we also know that God said, "For which of you, intending to build a tower, sitteth not down first, and counteth the cost" (Luke 14:28). We believe, in accordance with this, that we have thought through our plans and made our calculations, but we have come to the result that without Him we can do nothing. We are living with the horrors of war. Denmark is occupied by a rapacious people. Food is in increasingly short supply. It is a struggle to obtain the necessary commodities. The war may be why we have had such a large turnover, yet that does not mean we wish the war to continue. We wish for peace across the whole world, and pray, "Lord, take this into your hands!" Our aim is to produce such genuinely good, solid, and decent work that people must always acknowledge that LEGO makes quality products. My prayer to the Lord for LEGO is that he will help us run a business that is honest in every way, in our life and dealings, so that our actions and our lives are lived in his honor and with his blessing. God preserve our king and country.

Billund, June 19, 1942

The war was now being keenly felt in Billund. During the summer of 1943, all employees at LEGO, led by Christiansen and his sons, headed out onto the heath to cut peat in the marsh, ensuring they'd be able to heat the new factory premises, as well as the rebuilt Lion House, during the winter months. Blacking out the windows and rationing daily provisions had become part of everyday life in the small town, and in the co-op on the other side of the road, the selection of products was becoming increasingly minimal.

Cars, now a more significant presence in Billund, had been forbidden for personal use and kept off the roads, although the doctor and a few haulers were allowed to mount a gas generator, known as a "stove, which must be fed with wood waste on their vehicles." Electricity was rationed too, and each family was allotted a daily share of power. Coffee had become a rare, exotic drink, like the tobacco Ole Kirk enjoyed most in cigar form and had begun to grow himself in his fertile, well-tended garden. He dried the tobacco plants in the attic, then chopped them up, rolled them into cigars and sprinkled them with a few drops of prune extract before finally sealing them with egg white.

The only thing that, for once, seemed to be plentiful for everyone was cash, but there wasn't much to buy in the nation's shops. Wooden toys, as always in times of crisis and shortages, were much in demand.

During the war, fuel was scarce, so in order to keep warm at the factory, the employees had to head out into the bog with Ole Kirk (far left) and Godtfred (far right) to cut peat.

Many Danish parents were keen to protect their children from hardship, and during the five years of occupation, LEGO brought in more than a million kroner. The year of the fire, 1942, notwithstanding, their annual turnover was trending in only one direction: rapidly upward, rising from 74,000 kroner in 1940 to 357,000 kroner in 1945.

Yet production wasn't without its challenges. This was due partly to a scarcity of high-quality wood and decent paint, glue, and varnish, but also to the growing number of German soldiers in the town. They'd been posted there in connection with the proposed airfield at Vandel, "*Fliegerhorst Vejle,*" and were now moving into Billund, demanding accommodation and commandeering some of the town's larger buildings.

One day in 1943, a German officer marched into LEGO's offices and explained that the Wehrmacht wished to use the new factory as a barracks and depot. Godtfred didn't speak any language except Danish, though he quickly grasped what was happening but acted as though he didn't understand, as he later explained in an interview:

The Germans needed space for their equipment, and of course they had total power to act as they pleased. It's probably the only time not speaking German proved to be an advantage for me. The officer barked a few sentence fragments, and we stared coldly at each other. Then he abruptly turned around and left the office, and I never saw him again.

Additional German soldiers were stationed in the local area in 1943 and 1944, and the town hall, the scouts' hut and Billund School's new gymnasium were filled with the rank and file in their hobnailed boots which, to the indignation of the entire town, caused a lot of wear and tear on the varnished floor of the gymnasium. The more senior soldiers were given private quarters, and in the Lion House, Sofie's aging mother had to share the first floor with two German officers. She had moved from Haslev to live with her daughter and son-in-law in Billund, and she didn't speak a word of German, either. She did, however, know how to play chess with the two foreigners.

Ole Kirk kept communication with the uninvited guests to a minimum, always ensuring he maintained a polite, appropriate façade. He had good reason, too, although neither his sons nor his family friends knew anything about the reason why. He was involved in the illegal resistance, and in the confidential papers circulating in the movement in 1944–1945, "Manufacturer Christiansen" appeared as a Town and Group Leader in the Danish underground army, which included some fifty thousand men and women across the country. He was also listed as the head of Billund town's Watchmen, which kept law and order in the local area after the Danish police were dissolved by the occupying German forces in September of 1944. This position gave Ole Kirk access to several BSA rifles, which were put to use during the liberation in May 1945, when he and the rest of the Watchmen in Billund were tasked with guarding the many German refugees. More than three hundred thousand German refugees, civilians from Eastern Europe, had fled in advance of the Red Army to Denmark in crowded ships across the Baltic. In the last months of the war many thousands of women, children, and elderly people arrived in West Jutland on special trains from Copenhagen.

The founder of LEGO never participated directly in sabotaging the railways, a frequent act of resistance among the very active groups in Grindsted and Brande. But he did often help in the extremely important task of transporting and storing weapons, ammunition, and explosives that were dropped in containers from British planes. In the movement's confidential papers, he was also mentioned as the leader of a "Response Group in Grindsted District," composed of seventeen men in Billund, including a railway worker, an agricultural laborer, a mechanic, a gardener, a tailor, a furniture manufacturer, a bookkeeper, a town council chairman, and a toy manufacturer.

The group's mission was to fetch the weapons airdropped in the area and to get rid of the parachutes and containers before the Germans arrived. As it happened, Billund was never used as a drop site during the war, so instead, Ole Kirk acted as an intermediary in the crucial transport of weapons and ammunition. He did so by sending out innocuous-looking horse-drawn carts packed with boxes marked

"LEGO," apparently full of wooden toys going to distributors in West Jutland. Many years after his father's death, Godtfred told the story:

> *I only found out about it after the war. Dad would transport hand gre-*
> *nades, among other things, in the empty wooden boxes they would usu-*
> *ally use for wooden toys. We had German officers staying with us, like so*
> *many other people in the area, but that didn't bother my dad. He didn't*
> *let it affect him, anyway. The boxes were stored in our warehouse with the*
> *beechwood, and that's how the resistance movement was passed supplies.*

Christiansen, armed, also headed out to patrol the streets during the frantic and chaotic days after the liberation in May 1945, when the Danish police weren't yet back in operation and the mob was out for blood, rounding up traitors across the country. Starting on May 4, Ole Kirk went on evening patrols with LEGO's bookkeeper, Axel Svarre, and Christian Horsted, chairman of the town council, each with a rifle slung over his shoulder. They were sending a message that no one would be punished in Billund without a trial, and were also protecting the German refugees who'd been housed in the town hall, where they slept on piles of straw brought in from the farms.

Despite the fire in 1942 and the shortage of raw goods and materials, the war proved extremely lucrative for LEGO. The sale of toys rose 30 to 40 percent year after year, while the number of employees quadrupled between 1939 and 1946. LEGO was now one of the biggest and most highly regarded toy manufacturers in Denmark, next to Dansk Legetøjsfabrik (Danish Toy Factory), which had been producing wooden toys through the prison system since the First World War.

If you asked a Danish girl immediately after the war what kind of toy she most wanted to play with, it would have been an iron and ironing board from LEGO, while most boys preferred LEGO cars or trains. Many parents of young children invested in a painted red box of educational "LEGO Blocks," polished wooden blocks with letters and numbers in primary colors on their varnished sides. These small, handcrafted items

Four members of the illegal resistance group in Billund fall into conversation outside their leader's house one day in 1943. From the left: Frandsen, tailor; Alfred Christiansen, hauler; Thorvald Christensen, LEGO employee; and Gunnar Sand, sales assistant. Below is Ole Kirk's identification card as leader of the town Watchmen. *Local History Archive, Grene Parish.*

reflected Ole Kirk's uncompromising insistence on quality and his defi-
nition of success in the toy industry: "The right toy is the one parents
are happy to buy and that children want to play with more than just on
their birthday or at Christmas."

The enormous progress the factory at Billund had made during the
war continued throughout the rest of the decade, when Danish toy makers still benefited from a ban on imports. Another reason for LEGO's
growth was Ole Kirk's decision to make LEGO a limited company. In
1944, "The LEGO Toy Factory, Billund A/S" was registered, with a share
capital of fifty thousand kroner. The goal was to eventually become self-
financing, so they didn't have to borrow money every time they wanted
to buy extra machinery or expand the factory.

The decision brought Sofie Kirk Christiansen's nearly ten years of
company ownership to an end. Her husband's old debts had now been
repaid, and Ole Kirk could call himself the rightful owner, managing
director, and chairman of a family-run board and group of shareholders,
which included his four sons, in addition to himself and Sofie. Because
of LEGO's continued growth trajectory, a decision was made in 1946
to divide up the company and set up a subsidiary, "A/S O. Kirk Kristiansen," which would be solely responsible for production, while the
parent company remained in charge of everything to do with sales and
marketing. Kristiansen, here, was spelled with a K, since it's officially
recorded as such on Ole Kirk's birth certificate.

Restructuring the company wasn't Ole Kirk's idea. It was suggested
by an enterprising accountant with an understanding of tax legislation
and how to safeguard a family company. Ole Kirk later explained all
this in an interview, in which he also emphasized the patriarchal line of
succession that underpinned LEGO. Sofie was on the board, and in time
their daughter, Ulla, would be allotted her quota of the LEGO shares as
well, but there could be no doubt that it was the men in the family who
ran the company:

"My sons and I have arranged things so that we have registered two
limited companies. One is called LEGO and deals solely with selling

our products, while the other company is called O. Kirk Kristiansen and deals with the manufacturing."

Another major change took place in the Christiansen family during the final year of the war, when Godtfred proposed to twenty-year-old Edith Nørregaard Knudsen, the daughter of the Billund's grocer. She had a clear sense of her future with the energetic, ambitious Godtfred, picturing their future child as "a little craftsman at home in his father's workshop." It didn't quite work out that way over the following decades, but at the time in 1945, Edith's cozy idea of a small family company and a husband who worked partly from home wasn't too off-base. LEGO was still small enough that Ole Kirk's daughter-in-law helped clean the offices and pack wooden toys during the peak season.

Kjeld: *When my father and mother got married, they needed a car. It was all part of starting a family, they thought. But Dad couldn't afford one on his own, so he agreed to go in together with Hougesen, the manager of the dairy, to buy a 1931 Chevrolet. Hougesen would have it one week and my father the next. Many years later, Dad found the exact same car at a secondhand dealership. It was in terrible shape, but he had it all fixed up nicely, painted it its original black, and added the same number plate as it had had back then—Z8300. Today it sits gleaming in my car collection.*

Godtfred and Edith got married in October 1944. The wedding was celebrated with real coffee beans from Knudsen the grocer's private storage room, as well as extra rations of butter from the dairy co-op board. These were trying times in Denmark, and the couple's wedding presents included bedding and tea towels sewn from sacks of flour and sugar. The bridegroom managed to build a house for the family he and Edith were about to start. Situated along a stretch of road off the main street, Hovedgaden, which ran past the rear courtyard and the factory, this road would later be named Systemvej, and in the 1950s and early 1960s it became the central thoroughfare in the ever-growing part of Billund that included LEGO's factory and office buildings.

On October 29, 1944, twenty-four-year-old Godtfred and twenty-year-old
Edith Nørregaard Knudsen were married in Grene Parish Church. She was
the daughter of Knud N. Knudsen, a grocer, and his wife, Theodora (left).
The bridesmaids were Edith's younger sister, Birgit (front left) and Godtfred's
younger sister, Ulla. *Private collection.*

From their redbrick home, Godtfred and Edith had a view over the
factory and Ole Kirk's garden, which still opened onto the flat, endless
expanses north of Billund, where in the not-so-distant future a major airport and a family park and hotel would be built. While building his house
in 1943–1944, Godtfred had to get creative about fetching materials from
the brickworks in Sønder Omme to Billund. As he would later explain:

*The hauler whose truck I borrowed worked for the Germans during the
day at the airfield in Vandel. That meant I could only borrow his vehicle at night to pick up the bricks. We were building a house with a 600
square foot footprint, with a whole basement and a first floor where the
bedrooms were, and there were two toilets each with a washing sink, one
upstairs and one downstairs. I remember lots of people in Billund thinking it was very grand building a house with two indoor toilets!"*

Godtfred and Edith's house with a view over the Lion House and the long factory building. On the far right is the timber barn where all the wood was stored, and Ole Kirk's kitchen garden with his beehives and greenhouse. *Aerial photo: The Royal Library.*

Shortly after the liberation and the end of the Second World War in May 1945, Godtfred realized his vision for a product he'd been tinkering with for a year: a semi-automatic toy pistol made of wood. Design-wise, it was a far cry from traditional boys' weapons such as wooden swords, bows, and cowboys' guns. In 1945, selling toy and replica pistols was still prohibited in Denmark, but that didn't stop LEGO's inventive foreman from applying for a patent. The little wooden gun was a stroke of technical genius. Combining wood and steel and incorporating various spring mechanisms, it could be loaded automatically with wooden bullets from the chamber above the grip. The pistol wasn't overly noisy when it was fired, but it made a nice *bang* that boys appreciated when they played.

Godtfred had no intention of inciting anyone to violence, so he decided to call his invention the "Peace Pistol," and on the back of the packaging, LEGO made sure to educate the toy's new owner: "All healthy boys want a Peace Pistol. Will you, as the owner, remember the law of the gun—never aim at a playmate in jest or in earnest!"

Once the prohibition on selling toy or replica guns was lifted in the autumn of 1945, the pistol became a huge success. LEGO simply couldn't keep up with demand. Just after the start of the new year, Axel Barfod, the sales rep in the capital, impatiently chased after them for "another 1,000 pistols and 1,000 packets of ammunition," although he knew there was a major shortage of wood in Billund. They were also

The Peace Pistol with its "ammunition," red wooden projectiles. Seen here in a 1945 wooden version and on the right, the later plastic version, which Ole Kirk had dreams of mass-producing and exporting in 1946.

running out of the varnish mix that gave the black gun its authentic sheen.

The shortage of wood prompted Ole Kirk to look for other materials. Bakelite had long been known in the toy industry and was an obvious option for the next run of Peace Pistols. So was plastic, which many people believed to be the wonder material of the future, although nobody in the Danish toy industry had tested it yet.

Laboratories across the world had been experimenting for decades with synthetic materials such as celluloid, Bakelite, PVC, polystyrene, and melamine, but during the Second World War plastic began to be developed in earnest, creating new industrial opportunities in various industries after 1945. Unfortunately, it was very difficult to get production up and running in Europe, since so much of the machinery had been either destroyed or worn out during the war, and prospective plastics manufacturers in Denmark also would have had to hack through a bureaucratic jungle of rules and regulations if they wanted to buy equipment or raw materials.

Nevertheless, raincoats, shoes, nylon stockings, and other items made of plastic started appearing in post-war Danish shops in 1946 and 1947. Within the toy industry, it was widely believed that plastics would breathe new life into a market that had been stagnant for ten years. Parents and children were sick of the wooden toys on the shelves every wartime Christmas, and experts had no doubt that the age of plastic was just around the corner. As a Danish newspaper observed in 1947, "The toys of the future will be made of colorful plastic. The material is ideal for the purpose, because it is wonderful to the touch, hygienic and harmless, and practically indestructible. Improving plastic toys is also very easy, since the models are molded."

It was at this point that the fifty-five-year-old Ole Kirk revealed his true entrepreneurial spirit. He thought originally and unconventionally and was willing to run huge risks to turn his ideas into reality. Unlike his son, he had confidence in the new materials, especially plastic, which would be ideal if they decided to mass-produce the Peace Pistol for export.

Along with his brother-in-law, Martin Jørgensen, a mechanic and blacksmith, Ole Kirk decided in January 1946 to do a special run of toys in a material other than wood. The plan was to mold 11,500 Peace Pistols in Bakelite or plastic, working out of Martin's basement on Bjørn-

Martin Jørgensen, Sofie's younger brother, lived in Copenhagen. After the war, he helped Ole Kirk get the plastics production up and running. The two brothers-in-law exchanged long, intense letters between 1945 and 1946 about all the challenges facing entrepreneurs at the time, as well as about details of their personal lives. *Private collection.*

sonsvej in Copenhagen. The toy guns would initially be meant for the domestic market, but if the plan succeeded they'd soon be looking further afield. As Ole Kirk wrote in a letter to Jørgensen: "We can easily sell this batch at home, and it's not enough to start exporting yet."

The pair had only an empty basement in which to house a molding machine, molds, smaller machines for adjustments and polishing, various tools, plus five tons of Bakelite or plastic powder. Simply obtaining all of it was quite a feat in 1946. They soon agreed that plastics manufacturing was the more attractive option, because a plastics molding machine injected 160 pistol halves in an hour, while the Bakelite machine could only do 15, which then also needed to harden. On the other hand, the plastics molding machine costs six times as much as the Bakelite equivalent. But surely it was worth the investment? As Martin Jørgensen wrote to Ole Kirk, there was a rumor going round that Tekno, another toy company, had ordered a machine from England that could mold plastic cars. Shouldn't LEGO try to be first out of the gate with that technology?

They agreed that they absolutely should, so while Martin focused on ordering plastic powder, inviting offers for molding machines and molds, and coming up with a logo for the Peace Pistol that could be printed on the grip, Ole Kirk decided to set aside a large portion of LEGO's profits for new machinery and tools. He wrote to his business partner in Copenhagen, "By doing so we will store up a fortune in tools, which doesn't have to be included in the stock, and that can make a big difference if we go through difficult times."

Ole Kirk didn't initially involve his foreman in the decision to buy a molding machine, knowing that Godtfred wouldn't approve of an idea that pushed the firm's available funds to their limits. When it came to risk, father and son had very different perspectives.

Kjeld: *The financial stuff was incredibly important to my father at that time. He felt that he was the one who had to keep things reined in. He had to stay at the office and make sure, not just that the accounts added up, but also that their hard-earned money wasn't being frittered away.*

*There's no doubt that when my granddad rushed out and bought an ex-
pensive plastics molding machine—in fact, at one point he was even on
the verge of buying two—my father was distinctly unenthusiastic. After
all, they'd only just got their finances back on an even keel after the fire in
1942 and forming the limited company.*

When Martin Jørgensen wrote in May 1946 that a company called
Hoffmann & Co. had a Windsor SH triple-injection molding machine
at the port in Copenhagen and that they were offering demonstrations,
Ole Kirk couldn't get to the capital soon enough. He closed the deal
on the spot, and at the end of July, Martin confirmed that "So far, the
injection molding machine has been purchased and an order has been
placed for molds."

The English machine cost thirty thousand kroner, more than half of
LEGO's most recent working profit, and on top of the other expenses—
molds, powder, polishing machines, springs, and screws—the company
needed to invest a total of fifty thousand kroner before they could start
producing plastic Peace Pistols. That's equivalent to one million kroner
or one hundred sixty thousand dollars today, and in the uncertain, un-
predictable post-war period, this financial outlay might well have ended
in bankruptcy. Still, Ole Kirk was undaunted. He'd been through worse,
and he liked to describe those intensely difficult years in the early 1930s
with the words "Yes, we went bankrupt every once in a while. Well, I say
bankrupt; there was nothing to bankrupt."

After the summer holiday, the problems started to mount. Hoffmann
& Co. informed them that the molding machine wouldn't be delivered
until November, and the molds would also be delayed. Martin's ongoing hunt for plastic powder was hampered by the restrictions issued by
the Directorate for the Supply of Goods. They could have been lucky
and gotten half a ton of plastic powder from a Danish importer, Martin
wrote, but only if it had a license to import the powder and they had
stock available. Alternatively, they could have tried obtaining an "import authorization," but they'd have had to ask the Danish central bank
to approve the application to buy foreign currency.

The red tape seemed endless, and time was running out for the pair's ambitious plan to have 11,500 plastic Peace Pistols ready in time for Christmas. Still, they hadn't given up, and to keep the longer-term dream of exporting the pistols alive, they started looking at an American injection molding machine, one that was even more expensive than the one from England. It was worth the added cost, though: the American machine was much quicker, more efficient, and could be used for more complicated molding processes.

In August 1946, Ole Kirk and Martin Jørgensen headed to Stockholm to witness a demonstration of the American machine, which turned out to be just as impressive as advertised. LEGO's owner ordered a second molding machine, this time at the dizzying price of fifty-three thousand

Godtfred was full of ideas but believed more in wood than plastic. In 1945, he patented a "collapsible doll carriage," which was a combination of toy car, doll carriage, and high chair. Using his daughter Gunhild as a model, he tried to sell his idea to BRIO in Sweden but received a final rejection from the Ivarsson brothers in Osby in 1947. It was a great idea but never made it to production.

kroner. Their subsequent application to authorize a foreign-currency transaction of eleven thousand dollars, which Martin had immediately started writing on LEGO's behalf, noted that: "The molding machine will be used for exports, which assumes large-scale, low-cost production of our patented articles."

One of the few advantages of the post-war bureaucracy around imports and exports was that a person rarely had to put down any money when placing an order. This meant that in the winter of 1946–1947, Ole Kirk was the future owner of two whole plastics molding machines without having paid a single krone for them. There were, however, numerous other items that did need to be paid for, all of which were currently piling up in Martin Jørgensen's basement on Bjørnsonsvej in Copenhagen: a polishing machine, eccentric press, cardboard packaging, tools, screws and nails, as well as a typewriter with a tabulator.

Seeing all these objects gathering dust, as well as the unbearable wait for the two machines, made Ole Kirk take a more realistic view of the makeshift assembly line in his brother-in-law's basement. Could they really pull this off? And would the Danish Working Environment Authority even approve the premises for that use? After further consideration, Ole Kirk decided that the only sensible move was to transfer production from Copenhagen to Billund. Before discussing the situation with his business partner, he bought old German barracks from a farmer in Vandel, which were dismantled and later rebuilt close to the factory in Billund.

It was high time the two men sat down and made a decision. In November 1946, Ole wrote to Martin, "I know Rome wasn't built in a day, and perhaps it's for the best that this is taking awhile, because at the same time, of course, it will allow things to fall into place." "Falling into place," in Ole Kirk's eyes, would mean moving not only the production of plastic goods but also Martin and his family to Billund, even though he knew his brother-in-law would prefer to remain independent. In a long, beautiful letter dated November 19, 1946, Martin made up his mind. He turned down the offer and wished his brother-in-law the best of luck with what he prophetically describes as "realizing your grand plans of creating a town of toys in Billund—Denmark's Nuremberg."

In the spring of 1947, Ole Kirk was still waiting for the English Windsor SH. Godtfred was now involved in his father's plans to bring plastics production to Billund, and to his relief, his father had canceled the American molding machine. Deep down, Godtfred hoped that his father would give up on the Windsor machine, too, and on the idea of manufacturing toys from plastic altogether, which the young foreman viewed with profound skepticism. He sent a confidential letter to Martin Jørgensen in Copenhagen:

> To date, the history of plastic has resulted in nothing but disappointments and expense; the future doesn't look especially promising, since they have now banned the production of plastic toys, knick-knacks and trinkets, office or household items. And exporting is difficult, since so many countries are closed.

In the early summer of 1947, however, something utterly decisive in the history of LEGO occurred. A Mr. Printz, the managing director of Hoffmann & Co., and the person who sold Ole Kirk the Windsor machine, came to visit Billund. He'd just returned from England, bringing with him a box filled with small, bricklike plastic blocks in various colors, which he'd seen at the British Industries Fair in London. Perhaps, he suggested, LEGO could make something similar once the Windsor molding machine arrived in Denmark and was set up in Billund.

Ole Kirk was spellbound by the English bricks, which were hollow and featured studs on the top. With a handful of pieces like these, any child would be able to copy real-life tradesmen and become their own masons. He also immediately noticed the superiority of the material. Plastic was even more durable than wood, not to mention more hygienic, as well as being quick and easy to produce. Unlike wood, plastic didn't have to be seasoned, steamed, oven-dried, milled, polished, painted, varnished, and finally assembled with screws, nails, and labels. And while a piece of wood had to pass through many different human hands and undergo numerous processes, plastic seemed designed for simple, rapid mass production by a machine operated by a single person.

At the factory, several employees noticed that the director was rattling something in his coat pocket on his daily strolls around the workshops. Orla Jørgensen in accounts and Bernhard Bonde in the woodworking shop recalled Christiansen stopping and showing them some small, colorful plastic bricks. Would these be suitable for Danish children?

Not if you asked Godtfred at the time, although eight years later he'd be the primary strategist behind the system of LEGO bricks, which was to conquer the European market in record time. As late as 1951, Godt-

Kiddicraft's first box of Self-Locking Building Bricks in 1947 made it clear that the bricks were patented. They were hollow on the underside, with slits on the sides for doors and windows, and there was a small extra raised piece on top of the studs. The colors were red, yellow, blue, and green. *www.hilarypagetoys .com*

fred was still skeptical about plastic toys, telling a Danish newspaper, "Plastic will never supersede good, solid wooden toys."

Godtfred found support for his skepticism in Jørgensen, the book-keeper, and Lorentzen, the auditor, both of whom were concerned about the costly experiment with plastics. A glance at the company's finances on any arbitrarily chosen day in the late 1940s spoke for itself: 100 kroner in the cash box, 2,400 kroner in a giro account, and 3,364 kroner in an account with Vejle Bank, to which LEGO owed 150,000 kroner. Later, Godtfred would recall frequent arguments with his father about the financial management of LEGO:

> Dad often said to me, "If you just make sure we sell some products and earn some money, I'll deal with the construction and buying the machines." We had a lot of heated discussions about the financial issues. And I simply hated it when we were low on funds, and I had to plod off yet again to see Gunnar Holm, the managing director at Vejle Bank, and borrow more money or get the repayment of a loan deferred for another month or two.

According to Lorentzen, these disagreements arose most often when Ole Kirk was in an innovative mood: "Time after time, he emptied Godtfred's available funds, which were reserved for strictly necessary settlements of our credit obligations, which at that time were significant."

In a video clip from the 1980s, Godtfred's three brothers recalled that one day he persuaded them to march down with him to their father's office, to "get Dad to stop all this plastics nonsense, which ran the risk of our destroying ourselves." Karl Georg also remembers Godtfred speaking loudly to their father shortly after the Windsor machine first arrived, while they were still experimenting with it: "We should never have got that bloody plastics machine, it's bankrupting us!"

By the time the Windsor machine arrived in Billund in November 1947, Ole Kirk had prepared the wooden barracks that would house the plastics department, and they were also waiting for the molds for various plastic toys. They spent Christmas and the first few months of the new year assembling and getting accustomed to the machinery. All of this took place in Godtfred and Edith's basement, during the same time period as they were expecting another child. On December 27, 1947, Edith gave birth to a boy they named Kjeld.

Summer, 1948. Little Kjeld safe in his grandfather's arms. *Private collection.*

Kjeld: *It was a home birth, the same as with my big sister Gunhild and little sister Hanne. Each time they sent for the midwife in Jelling, who was married to my father's cousin. I've been told that when I was born, the new molding machine was in the basement, and at various points during the day the whole house was echoing with the racket, which obviously made my mother very unhappy during the first weeks and months after I was born, when she was at home with me all day long. But that's just how it was. The molding machine took priority, and at first it was in the basement, which later would become my playroom, where I built houses, bridges, and ships out of LEGO bricks on two big tables.*

It usually takes a while to switch from one material to another, but before the molding machine could be thoroughly tested at Billund, Ole Kirk had produced smaller plastic items "out of house," including pieces for the LEGO board game Monypoli, which was a traffic-themed game for children. In the summer of 1948, the very first LEGO-produced plastic toys went on sale. They were small colorful balls, designed for babies, sold at eighty-three øre each, and the following year a small range of plastic toys appeared on LEGO's price list: a fish, a sailor, some miniature animals, baby rattles, and a plastic pistol (no longer called the Peace Pistol). A few small, colorful plastic bricks became available for purchase in Danish toy shops in the autumn of 1949.

What to call the bricks was a contested question until the very last minute. As usual, Ole Kirk wasn't afraid to turn to other people for advice, and in the spring of 1949, his sales rep Axel Barfod in Copenhagen was tasked with asking his friends and acquaintances if they could come up with a good name.

Barfod replied, "Several people are busy finding the right name. And I hope in the course of a few days to be able to share the result with you." In the end there was no need, because it was decided that the plastic blocks would be called Automatic Binding Bricks.

The origin of LEGO's very first plastic bricks isn't in dispute. Godtfred explained on several occasions that they were inspired by the English firm Kiddicraft, founded by Hilary Fisher Page in the 1930s. Page was a pioneering figure in the world of educational plastic toys for small children, which in England were sold under the name "Sensible Toys," but the Second World War, a divorce, and an extended stay in America called a temporary halt to production of Page's innovative toy.

In 1942, when Page returned home to England and resumed his work on developing plastic toys for various age groups, he immediately applied for a patent for a system of plastic building bricks for older children, Self-Locking Building Bricks. The patent was granted in 1947, not just in England but also in France and Switzerland, and on the front of the box that Printz brought home to Ole Kirk were the words "British and foreign patents."

After nearly eighteen months' wait, the Windsor plastic molding machine arrived in Billund in December 1947, and was initially assembled in Godtfred and Edith's basement. Later that month, Kjeld was born.

This information didn't go unnoticed by Godtfred, who'd learned something about Danish patent law through several of his own inventions, including the Peace Pistol. And in January 1949, before LEGO began production of its bricks, Godtfred applied to the Nordic Patent Bureau. He wanted to know whether Kiddicraft had a patent on their plastic bricks in Denmark, which turned out not to have been the case.

Ole Kirk wasn't as knowledgeable about plagiarism and copyright law as his son. He was a self-taught toymaker who practically stumbled into the industry in the 1930s, when people didn't worry so much about protecting original ideas. Even after the war, many toy manufacturers continued to imitate and copy one another's products. "That's just how it is in the toy industry," he told his lawyer, Flemming Friis-Jespersen, who recounted the incident in a letter to Godtfred many years later, describing how Ole Kirk showed him some small, hollow plastic bricks from England one day in the late 1940s and asked for his advice. Friis-

Jespersen replied that it was a splendid idea, but that the English might have a patent. Was it somehow protected? To that, Ole Kirk replied:

That's not something we take very seriously in our industry. If we agree that there's a future in it, I'll just go ahead. Denmark is a small country, anyway, and it might be years before the English discover what we're up to, if they ever do. Toys are usually a rather short-lived affair.

Godtfred, however, who had been given more responsibility for the production and sale of LEGO's products, realized that the toy industry was undergoing a transformation, including the prevailing attitudes toward copyright and patent law. Unlike his father, he was sure that clearer limits were coming regarding the extent you could be inspired by, or imitate, a patented toy.

Decades later, during a lengthy court case in Hong Kong in 1986, in which the American toy company Tyco challenged LEGO's patents in the American market by making their version of the LEGO bricks, Godtfred found himself on the witness stand. In court, the Americans used the argument that LEGO had originally copied their bricks from an English invention. Godtfred, now sixty-six, was asked to explain how the very first LEGO bricks were created in 1949.

"We had decided to produce some components that strongly resembled Kiddicraft, but before we started production, we wanted to make sure that there was no protection in Denmark that made that impossible for us."

Godtfred also explained that they asked Bodnia, a tool company in Copenhagen, to make molds for small plastic bricks with four studs and eight studs, so that, as the court records show, they would:

. . . look like the samples we had from Kiddicraft, but there were three differences. We wanted sharp corners, flat studs and an eight millimeter [0.315 inches] module. You understand, the difference is that in Europe— apart from England—we use the metric system, while in England they use the imperial system.

Kjeld: *There were lots of people making different types of plastic bricks back then. Even in the 1930s, before Kiddicraft made its bricks, people around the world were experimenting with bricks that had buttons on the top, and they were made of wood, rubber, clay, and plastic. So we can't say—and we have never said—that we were the ones who invented the brick. It was my grandfather who immediately saw the possibilities in the bricks from England, and it was my father who developed it in the 1950s into a bigger building system, then in 1958 invented the interior tubes. That meant they could interlock, which they hadn't done before. In the 1940s there was virtually no legal protection of the shape, appearance and design of a product. It was "open source," we'd say today, meaning freely accessible. Over the years, Dad was never comfortable having to explain where the idea originally came from. I think he couldn't help feeling that we had once done what other people were now doing to us.*

The very first LEGO-produced plastic bricks went on sale in 1949, under the name Automatic Binding Bricks. They had slits on the sides for doors and windows and were hollow underneath. In 1950, LEGO launched the somewhat larger and taller plastic building bricks, which were also inspired by a Kiddicraft product. Two-year-old Kjeld was featured on the box, his debut as a model. *Private collection.*

The Kiddicraft bricks didn't sell especially well in England in the late 1940s. On Danish soil, meanwhile, LEGO couldn't drum up much interest in its Automatic Binding Bricks either. Maybe it was the name. Maybe it was the dated packaging, featuring a colorful drawing of two children that made the product look like a box of old-fashioned wooden blocks. Toy sellers had no faith in the small plastic bricks, and only agreed to put the boxes on their shelves if they could return anything that went unsold.

The extremely modest sales were a source of frustration for Godtfred, compounding his aversion to plastic toys. Again he turned to his brothers, hoping that together they could persuade their father to concentrate on what LEGO was known for and can sell—toys made of wood!

Ole Kirk sat in his office behind his big, dark desk by the window, which overlooked Hovedgaden. He listened to Godtfred speak.

When he finally fell silent, his father looked all four sons in the eye and said slowly, "Don't you have enough faith, boys? *I* have prayed to God, and *I* believe in these bricks!"

Many years later, Gerhardt and Karl Georg would point to this as a decisive moment in LEGO's history. It was decided that they would keep manufacturing plastic bricks and give the product one more chance. "We just had to leave it in God's hands, and he would make sure everything worked out! Those were Dad's words. Then we just slunk quietly out of the office, and that was the end of the discussion."

SYSTEM

THE 1950s

It looks almost like colorful gravel or pebbles, and it comes in all sorts of colors. Before it's used, it's dried to reach a specific degree of humidity, then it's placed into a trough on top of the machine and gradually trickles down into the machine itself, where it's heated to 200 degrees, so it becomes a fluid. Then it's injected into the mold at a pressure of about 100 atmospheres, and a moment later the molded piece, in pure pastel colors, is removed from the machine, which can produce a hundred pieces per hour . . .

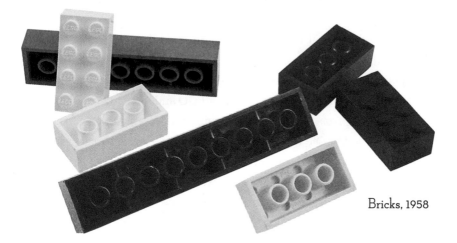

Bricks, 1958

LEGO's Junior Managing Director was showing a journalist and photographer around the factory in Billund. The year was 1951, and sales of the once-popular Peace Pistol, now available in transparent plastic, had been overtaken by the small, realistic Ferguson tractors, symbolizing peace and Marshall Plan aid. "They are also available as a kit, and LEGO can produce more than thirty of those per hour," said Godtfred, adding that all the waste material could be reused.

The journalist wanted to hear about the small, hollow plastic bricks with the funny name, but accidentally wrote "America" in his notepad instead of "England" when Godtfred explained where the idea for the colorful bricks came from. What was also mentioned in the paper, and here the journalist hadn't misheard, was the young managing director's surprisingly negative take on the future of plastics in the toy industry. In response to the journalist's question, "Will plastic toys ever supplant wooden toys?" Godtfred answered:

> That will never happen! If people took the trouble to investigate the plastics market, they would discover that most of the time it breaks after the children have been playing with it for a day. It's not so much the fault of plastic, it's the construction. That's why plastic is losing its allure. In America, for example, it's rapidly going out of fashion. What's happened is simply that the use of plastics has spun out of control. You can produce useful and handy things out of plastic, but wood is just more solid.

There were several reasons why Godtfred, and not his father, was the one talking to the press. Godtfred may have lost the power struggle over plastics, but on his thirtieth birthday in the summer of 1950, he was named Junior Managing Director of A/S LEGO and A/S Kirk Kristiansen.

He got the promotion itself in a joyful and ceremonious birthday telegram signed by Ole Kirk, Sofie, Johannes, Karl Georg, and Gerhardt, which concluded with some familiar words from Numbers, "The Lord bless thee and keep thee: / The Lord make his face shine upon thee, and be gracious unto thee: / The Lord lift up his countenance upon thee, and give thee peace!" Recalling that special moment in his life, Godtfred later commented:

> I don't think I ever asked my father why he chose to reference that passage in the Bible in the congratulatory telegram. That he wished in his own way to give me a blessing—that's obvious. But at the same time, it was important for my father to emphasize the responsibility I was now taking on.

In the autumn of 1951, Ole Kirk had a stroke. It wasn't life-threatening, but he was weakened, and in the years that followed he went on several lengthy visits to health resorts abroad. More and more of the daily grind during the first half of the 1950s fell to Godtfred, assisted by his brothers, all three of whom were now involved with the company. Karl Georg and Gerhardt functioned as heads of operation in the plastics division and wood division, respectively, while Johannes took care of driving and

Son Johannes (right) and daughter Ulla, along with happy employees, welcome Ole Kirk home after his stay in the hospital after a cerebral hemorrhage in 1951. *Private collection.*

odd jobs, and was given the title of Manager. As far as his strength allowed, however, Ole Kirk remained in charge of purchasing wood. As bookkeeper Jørgensen later explained:

He really knew everything about wood, and he'd drive the family car, a gorgeous blue Opel Super Six, out to the forest at Boller, near Horsens, to buy a carload of quality beechwood, whole trunks of it. It would be

chopped up later at Billund Sawmill. When the payment was due, the
forest supervisor would call to remind him and demanded, always a little
acerbically, to speak to the boss in person. Several times I had to go out
into the garden to fetch him.

Even after settling their differences over the issue of manufacturing
with plastics, father and son often disagreed, vociferously, about how
to manage and invest their money. They had a major argument shortly
after celebrating Ole Kirk's sixtieth birthday in the spring of 1951, when
Barfod and Breckling, the two traveling sales reps, announced that they
didn't think it was worthwhile going to see all their regular customers
before the summer break. Most retailers, after all, didn't place their final Christmas orders until August.

Based on that, the senior managing director decided that LEGO
would cease production and close the factory for a couple of weeks in
July, a decision Godtfred didn't entirely agree with. He thought they
ought to keep the wheels turning—constantly. The stream of orders
shouldn't be allowed to dry up, and if the mountain won't come to Mohammed, then Mohammed must go to the mountain, he reasoned.

Godtfred already had a reputation in Billund and the local area for
being resolute, dynamic, stubborn, and occasionally a bit of a know-it-
all. He filled the black Chevrolet, which he still shared with Hougesen,
the dairy manager, with samples of LEGO's products. He also asked
Edith to pack a suitcase and large lunch, because the two of them were
about to set off on a road trip. The plan was to visit as many Jutish
customers as humanly possible so that they could get some orders on
the books and give management an idea of what position LEGO was in
before entering the crucial autumn months, when the factory always
transformed into Santa's busy workshop.

Edith brought her knitting but spent most of her time writing. The
orders started pouring in and were immediately dispatched to Billund.
Godtfred managed to bring in a whole sixty thousand kroner, or about
ten thousand dollars (what would be almost one hundred sixty thou-

AMLESÆT TIL *Ferguson* MODEL TRAKTOR

FREMSTILLET AF LEGO · DANMARK

LEGO's first truly successful plastic toy was the Ferguson Model Tractor, which sold seventy-five thousand units in 1952. A rolling symbol of modern, industrialized agriculture in Europe, LEGO's version had rubber tires. The front wheels were connected to the steering, which could be turned, and as Ole Kirk demonstrates, it could also pull various farming implements.

sand dollars today), during the couple's trip, keeping production going and ensuring employment for the nearly one hundred employees.

Driving all those miles and meeting all those customers was also something of an education for the Junior Managing Director, opening his eyes to the importance of direct contact with distributors. Unlike his father, he had no problem whatsoever praising LEGO's products to the skies. Godtfred—or GKC, as he was also known at the factory—was a born salesman.

The scent of wood, shavings, and sawdust from the workshops behind the Lion House, which Billund's five hundred residents had grown accustomed to over the years, now mingled with the somewhat sweet aroma of heated plastic. The old, familiar whine and howl of the woodworking tools and machines had been joined by a monotonous, jerky banging sound coming from the barracks at the bottom of Ole Kirk's garden, where the plastic toys were molded. The new material accounted for half their turnover, and LEGO's annual price lists contained more than 250 different items.

> **Kjeld:** *I loved the odor of wood as a child, and at the age of ten or twelve I often used to creep into the Craftyard, as we called it. There were these little workshops for smiths, painters, joiners, and electricians, and it really was a glorious world to run around and play in. I learned a little about the various tools—what they were used for, and how to hold them properly. And they'd also let you make things.*

At the South Jutland Exhibition in the summer of 1951, LEGO's list ran the whole gamut of toys, from baby rattles, beach balls, hobbyhorses, pull-along animals, and classic wooden cars, to the small plastic building bricks and the latest bestsellers from the Billund factory, like a "Ferguson Model Tractor with original plastic tools" and a "Diesella," a wooden motor that could be mounted on the back wheel of a bicycle and made boys' push-bikes sound like mopeds. The trade magazine *Legetøjs-Tidende* was at the fair and reported enthusiastically on the Diesella:

In addition to being able to reproduce the familiar bangs in a lively way, LEGO's bicycle motor can be primed and filled with "petrol." Furthermore, since a driving license for the happy "moped driver" is included, we can say with confidence that this whole original toy will soon be much in demand.

There were tremendously exciting toys for boys and girls at LEGO's stand, almost too many. The range of products was huge and extremely varied. The company had even started producing plastic photo frames for slides and was also considering selling steam engines imported from England—all to increase turnover, of course, which crossed the one million mark for the first time in 1951.

At toy shows, LEGO showed off its wide range, from baby rattles to "engines" that could make a bike sound like a moped.

Godtfred realized that they needed to focus and prioritize more sharply, ensuring the longevity of LEGO's range and making the company less dependent on short-lived hits like the yoyo, the Peace Pistol, and the Ferguson tractor. From 1952 onward, "concentration" became a key word for Godtfred, synonymous with the product and marketing philosophy of the entire company, meaning having a specialized focus. Many years later, Kjeld defined this approach in a presentation at a marketing conference:

> *In the toy industry, which is filled with one-hit wonders that come and go, the "concentration philosophy" we have pursued so far and intend to build on has been very unique. We wish to nurture and cultivate this underlying idea, which is quite simply the foundation of the company, and it's an underlying idea that continues to offer ample opportunity for growth.*

One thing that sharpened Godtfred's feelings on this issue was Ole Kirk's latest idea that came in 1952. Whether it was exacerbated by his father's illness Godtfred couldn't tell, but he knew that there was neither the need nor the money to expand the factory to the extent and at the cost (350,000 kroner) his father wanted. Godtfred still firmly believed that investments shouldn't come at the cost of the company's healthy financial development.

This disagreement over Ole Kirk's desire to keep building flared up one summer's day in 1952, and Godtfred ended up resigning. He marched across the street back to his house and asked Edith if she wanted to go on a road trip to Sweden. Before leaving Billund, he tried to offer Ole Kirk a compromise.

"Let's start with a third of your plan, Dad!"

Ole Kirk was having none of it. "I'm the one who decides what we build here, and your job is to find the money!"

Godtfred saw that his father had tears in his eyes, but he didn't want to give in. So he turned on his heel and headed off to Sweden, disappointed and furious.

After a week of thinking, Godtfred and Edith come home to Billund. He still didn't agree with his father, but said to him, "We're relying on your faith now, not mine."

This decision proved momentous for LEGO's development over the coming years, as Godtfred later recalled. "The expansion of the factory in 1952 was a landmark moment in our history. It forced me to start thinking beyond the borders of our country, initially in Norway in 1953. I remember I came home from Norway with a major contract just as the new building was being constructed."

The following year, Godtfred traveled to Germany and England to test the waters of the toy industry there and made contacts with distributors and colleagues. At the trade fair in Nuremberg in 1953, there was a gathering of Danish industry professionals one evening, and Godtfred heard several of the buyers say that once the Danish import restrictions were lifted, which they soon would be, toy factories in Denmark might as well pack up. Godtfred was frustrated. For more than ten years, he and his father, as well as other manufacturers, had invested money and elbow grease into developing the best possible toys, which many people believed were on par with the best-quality German brands.

Indignant, and goaded by what he saw as this utterly unfair assessment, Godtfred had a crazy idea: if a company like LEGO could find exactly the right toy, something unique that could be sold everywhere and that had staying power, would it be so completely inconceivable that they could turn defense into offense and conquer the German market, a primary route into Europe's other countries and markets? As Godtfred explained to LEGO's management some years later, after they'd started exporting to Norway and Sweden:

> If we combine the population of fifteen million we have here in the Nordic countries with Germany's forty-five million, and we are capable of dominating a market like that, then not only will we be able to fully compete with the Germans, but also, assuming we can effectively build up sales opportunities, we will be one step ahead, and we will also have the same export opportunities as the Germans.

These fearless, expansion-oriented ideas were still on the thirty-three-year-old Godtfred's mind in February 1954, when he set off across the North Sea to the British Toy and Hobby Fair in Brighton. Joining him on the trip was his personal secretary, Bent N. Knudsen, Edith's brother, who helped Godtfred with English, which he understood somewhat but couldn't speak.

After a busy and inspiring week in the seaside town of Brighton, where Godtfred discovered that Hilary F. Page's Self-Locking Building Bricks still existed but hadn't apparently become a big commercial success in Great Britain or any other country, he relaxed over a whiskey and cigar in the bar on the DFDS ferry from Harwich.

Also on board were other Danes in the industry who had been at the fair, and Godtfred got to chatting with Troels Petersen, a young head buyer for the toy department at Magasin du Nord. Petersen was far from impressed by the state of the toy industry, expressing exasperation at the fact that there was no system to it. Godtfred pricked up his ears. Petersen had put his finger on a problem he, himself, had been ruminating over for a couple of years. It wasn't simply about the diversity of LEGO's products, but also about approaching production and sales more purposefully and systematically.

This conversation on the ferry was eye-opening for Godtfred. Suddenly, his task became utterly clear: LEGO needed to concentrate on a single idea. They had to coalesce around *one* product that was unique and lasting, that could be developed into a wider range of toys that were easy to play with, easy to produce, and easy to sell.

But what should that product be? Once again Godtfred put LEGO's product offering under a magnifying glass, and this time it was obvious that only one of their 265 different wood and plastic products fit the bill: the colorful plastic bricks that had entranced Ole Kirk. They were still being produced at Billund, and in 1952–1953 were relaunched under the name "LEGO Bricks."

Unlike his father, Godtfred had never before had much faith in the small hollow bricks, and the sales figures during those initial years had seemed to prove him right. In 1953–1954 they performed a little better,

Edith and Godtfred's three children enjoyed playing together. They biked, played games, built round LEGO towers, and pretended to be on the bus, on the lawn at the cottage in Hvidbjerg. Kjeld was driving, while his mother Edith came along for the ride. *Private collection.*

but the numbers still weren't exactly overwhelming. The question was whether LEGO Bricks were the product that could become something bigger and more enduring.

Ole Kirk, of course, never doubted it. Nor did his grandchildren when they played with the bricks. Six-year-old Kjeld, in particular, was a whizz at constructing all sorts of different buildings.

Kjeld: *When I was little, I built towers around me. Only two studs overlapped, so I could turn the bricks and make rounded walls. The towers were often so big I could walk into them and hide. Later, I constructed whole cities out of LEGO bricks in our playroom in the basement, where the first molding machine had been. I never followed any instructions; I just used my imagination. I don't think there's any question that Dad was inspired by me and my sisters playing with the bricks and saw the potential to create a system. He was often interested in what we were building, but he never sat down and played himself, not even when we were a bit older. It's always astonished me that he didn't think it was fun to sit down and tinker around with LEGO bricks. On the other hand, he did love coming down to the basement to see what I'd come up with now, and he often showed them off to business associates who came to visit us.*

The "LEGO System" Godtfred had begun to visualize wasn't just about putting together five, six, or more bricks into a building, but also about collecting LEGO bricks and expanding the possibilities they offered by asking for LEGO gift sets and supplementary boxes every Christmas and for each birthday. Soon, the formula behind Godtfred's business idea became apparent: the more bricks a child had, the more playing they did. The more playing they did, the more sets and boxes they asked for. The more sets and boxes, the bigger the turnover.

It's hard to quantify exactly how much impact Edith and Godtfred's children had on their father's invention of the "LEGO System in Play," mainly because Godtfred never discussed it. The only thing we know for sure is that he was so proud of Gunhild, Kjeld, and Hanne and their games that in 1953 he decided to use them to advertise a new series of LEGO Brick sets in the run-up to Christmas.

In the original image photographed by Hans Lund from Grindsted, six-year-old Gunhild, five-year-old Kjeld, and little Hanne, aged two, were building with the bricks on the tile-topped table in their living room. Hanne didn't end up in the final photograph printed on the front of LEGO boxes in 1953–1954, because Godtfred had decided that the primary target audience would be boys and girls around the age of Gunhild and Kjeld.

Godtfred's idea of a "LEGO System in Play" was born at a point in the post-war era when the upbringing and education of children was becoming a hot topic in Denmark and elsewhere. There was a lot of discussion about "healthy play" and the need for good toys. Experts in the field also argued that parents should think of caring for their children as something joyful, rather than a duty.

As much as he could, LEGO's hardworking Junior Managing Director kept up with the pedagogical debate raging in the country's major daily papers and on the radio. Godtfred clipped out articles and interviews with leading Danish child psychologists and education experts like Jens Sigsgaard, Thea Bank Jensen, and Sten Hegeler, keeping them in LEGO's big scrapbook, where they lay side by side with the very first mentions of the little Billund toy factory and its big ideas.

Many adults in post-war Denmark still viewed play as something to be grown out of. In the Kirk Christiansen family, this has never been the case. When Godtfred and his siblings were children, Ole Kirk and Kristine—and later Sofie—never saw it as a waste of time. Godtfred and his brothers found the bits of wood in various colors, shapes, and sizes that were always lying around their father's workshop very engaging. Now and again the blocks would be carved into an animal or a car, or were simply stacked one on top of another like blocks, and when Ulla was growing up in the 1930s, Ole Kirk built her and her friend a playhouse in one of the trees in the back garden.

The women in the town who'd earned money by working from home in the 1930s, painting wheels and ducks that Ole Kirk would deliver in a

Two-year-old Hanne plays at the tiled table, but only Gunhild and Kjeld were featured on the box of LEGO Bricks, because they were in the target group.

basket, recalled that he would sometimes also knock on their front door on a Sunday afternoon with the following message: "Don't sit indoors; come outside and play with the children!" The whole of Billund became a playground.

Even during Ole Kirk's own truncated childhood in the 1890s, he and his numerous siblings would play and sing at home in Blåhøj. As a young farmhand, his most beloved toy, he later explained in an interview, was a "hwolkow" (meaning "hollow cow")—a stone with a hole through it and a string threaded through the hole, which children could drag around after them and tether to a post like a real cow. But times had changed. As Ole Kirk remarked, "We are undeniably living in the age of the child. Every year, attentive parents in Denmark spend an estimated fifty to one hundred million kroner on toys for their children. When I think that boys my age only had a rusty nail and a stone with a hole to play with, it's easy to sigh and feel that you were born too soon."

Like his father and contemporary experts on childhood, Godtfred agreed that good play demanded good playthings, and as a toy manufacturer he believed it was important to "be able to adjust to the child's level and make sure the toy affords enough options." Other similar statements reflected how attuned Godtfred was to the pedagogical debates of the time. At the same time, he sought inspiration for the wording LEGO would use once the System in Play was eventually launched. Looking at an advertisement for LEGO Bricks in 1953, it's obvious how close he was to his goal. The ad bears the tagline "Do you want to LEGO with me?" and is accompanied by the following thorough sales pitch:

Children who "play well" become enterprising and active adults. The importance of giving children developmental toys that can stimulate their imagination and creativity is therefore obvious. LEGO Bricks are just such a toy, loved by boys and girls alike—and grown-ups, for that matter. They are recommended by countless nurseries, recreation centers, and kindergartens.

"Do you want to LEGO with me?" Advertisement for LEGO Bricks from 1953, which presents the bricks not just as toys for children, but for use by architects when building models.

Due to his ailing health and lengthy stays at various resorts and spas, Ole Kirk was only partially involved in Godtfred's grand plan to gather and consolidate the production of plastic toys around the LEGO Bricks. From the early spring of 1955, the word "system" was ever-present in the management offices and on the factory floor in Billund, although the term "LEGO System in Play" wasn't known to anyone but Godtfred himself until the very last moment.

The first management meeting of the year included Ole Kirk, his sons Karl Georg and Gerhardt, the three traveling sales reps, and the bookkeeper Orla Jørgensen. They were welcomed by Godtfred, who rose to his feet in honor of the occasion, giving a solemn speech, hailing not just a new year but also a new beginning:

Our Senior Managing Director has worked with God's blessing, and I wish to congratulate us on being employed at a company that, first, gives

us the opportunity to do what any person with a healthy mind feels the
urge to do, namely to help create something—responsibly—and second,
offers us the opportunity to live a good life. In this new year, let us con-
tinue to work from this fundamental perspective on life and pray for
God's blessing going forward—everything rests on that.

One month later, Godtfred unveiled the details of the company's major new investment. It took the form of a town plan printed on a plastic
mat that could be placed on a table or the floor. The slogan was, "Build
a LEGO town out of LEGO Bricks!" On marked areas on the town plan,
children could build houses out of LEGO Bricks, plant trees and bushes,
and drive small, richly detailed LEGO cars on the gray roads with white
markings and pedestrian crossings.

The new LEGO system promoted free-form, individual play, Godtfred explained. The idea was that children learn something, because
in increasingly traffic-heavy Denmark, children ought to know something about traffic rules and safety. As well as getting his system rubber-
stamped by the Council for Greater Road Safety, Godtfred hired a real
police officer for the advertisements to give advice to the children and
recommend that parents buy the new toy, which combined play and
learning. This was still twenty-five or thirty years before Godtfred's son
was to introduce the concept of "play and learning" and make it a key
principle of the LEGO Group.

At a meeting in June, Godtfred (or GKC, as he was referred to in the
minutes) presented the thinking behind that autumn's big sales push.
The plan was for a small leaflet, *LEGO News,* to be sent around to the
distributors and shop staff, and then followed up by a visit from one
of LEGO'S three sales reps. Their task was to present the philosophy
behind the new toy system, explain the promotional initiatives, and,
crucially, to bring in as many orders for the LEGO System in Play as
conceivably possible.

The last item on the agenda was arguably the most important. LEGO
was running short of funds, due to the major expansion that Ole Kirk
had insisted on. As Godtfred repeated at meetings with the three travel-

ing salesmen, "It's very important—vital to our survival, actually—that we bring money home as quickly as possible. We have less liquid capital this year because of the construction work, so we need to achieve a higher turnover."

The first time Danish toy retailers heard anything about LEGO's new building system was thus the same autumn they received *LEGO News*. The leaflet listed six points that distilled the company's philosophy on what constituted good toys. Several of the six points were very similar to phrases used by Danish child psychologists and pedagogy experts in the newspaper articles Godtfred had read and kept. The most ambitious one, however, seems to have come from Godtfred himself, and was about the timelessness the LEGO System in Play strove for: "It has to be a classic among toys, needing no renewal."

The initial presentation of this new system of toys, which would soon be popularly known as LEGO bricks, was remarkable because the company genuinely tried to involve retailers and their staff to make them, essentially, a kind of ambassador for the LEGO System in Play.

> *We believe that, as professionals in the toy industry, you will agree with us that this is more than an ordinary toy, and we believe you are capable of judging the unheard-of potential involved. We have spared no effort or expense in creating something entirely new and extraordinary—and the stage is set for a tremendous success. Would you like to be part of this line?—If so, success is guaranteed!*

The launch presented not only a new toy system, but also a message about children and play that turned out to be incredibly viable and farsighted. Indeed, it's still upheld at the LEGO Group to this day. The drawing on the front of the leaflet literally shouted this message to the retailers and staff from the rooftops. It featured a small, stout LEGO man in work clothes and a bricklayer's cap holding a megaphone to his mouth, broadcasting the LEGO System's humanistic ideas to the whole world.

"Our idea has been to create a toy that prepares the child for life—

appealing to the child's imagination and developing the creative urge and joy of creation that are the driving force in every human being."

Kjeld: *The major new thing about the LEGO System in Play was that there was suddenly a much wider array of different things you could build. This was Dad's fundamental concept, that the whole thing should be a coherent system of elements that always fit together. Different bricks bought in different sets could always be combined. In his older years, when I was running LEGO, Dad became very critical of us introducing too many elements. He thought we were moving too fast, and that his old invention had become too wide-ranging and too diverse. He wanted us to stick to the brick, and only the brick, as the core of LEGO. This was his*

On the first LEGO Town Plan in 1955, children could build their own real city, complete with houses, cars, signs, and trees. Models displayed in toy and department stores showed fully constructed towns to inspire children and their parents.

view from the very beginning in 1955, along with the fundamental peda-
gogical conviction that children develop their creativity through building
with toys.

The position LEGO found itself in was identical to the challenges facing many other companies in 1950s Europe. The firm had profited from
the import ban, which had limited competition from abroad during and
after the Second World War. They hoped now to translate this success
into their export business, but Ole Kirk and Godtfred were repeatedly
confronted with the plain and simple fact that international trade in the
post-war era was hard. It wasn't just a matter of logistics, of transporting machinery from overseas and paying in foreign currencies, but determining which countries would even permit the sale of Danish goods.

Like so many other Danish companies, LEGO needed an injection
of cash. When they expanded the factory from 1952 to 1953, Godtfred
applied for a loan as part of the Americans' broader program of aid,
the Marshall Plan, which was designed to get Europe back on its feet
after the war. Thirty-three million dollars had been earmarked for these
loans in Denmark, and LEGO's Junior Managing Director spent several weeks putting together a thorough, well-argued application, only to
have it rejected. It was not a huge surprise or disappointment that, as
a toy factory, their products weren't deemed high on the list of "necessary consumer goods."

Although they didn't receive any aid, there was plenty of evidence to
suggest that LEGO, and specifically its dynamic Junior Managing Director, drew inspiration from the Technical Assistance Program, which
offered a vast store of new industrial knowledge and expertise. The Assistance Program was a kind of manual, helping European companies
model themselves on American patterns, use American businesses as
templates, including the latest theories about automation, rationalization, sales, advertising, marketing, and management.

Simply put, the plan put forth a model of the American way of doing business, concentrating on three central "S" words: specialization,

standardization, and simplification. For a Danish entrepreneur with ambitions to develop a multipronged system of toys based not only on the best form of play but also on the most efficient business model, it was compelling stuff.

Like most other Danish companies of the era, LEGO was keen to modernize along American lines, to the extent that this was possible for a toy factory miles away from the halls of power in Copenhagen. This was nothing new for Godtfred, who had to acquire all this cutting-edge information about modern business development, sales, and management under his own steam. Unlike other Danish directors and senior bosses, he had never been on a Marshall Plan–funded study trip to the United States, and he didn't sign up for the intensive courses offering Danish managers insight into American business models and styles of leadership.

Godtfred was self-taught, and one of his key skills was gathering ideas and drawing inspiration from the conversations he had with other professionals, not least his employees. Words like "reorganization," previously unknown in a LEGO context, suddenly started appearing in several of GKC's presentations at internal meetings, quickly followed by terms like "productivity," "automation," "product development," and "market analysis."

Kjeld: *I don't remember ever seeing Dad engrossed in a business book. You never saw journals or newspaper articles about management lying around at home either. I think he picked up most of what he knew from conversations with other people. Dad was always open to listening to others, especially people who thought differently from him and could teach him something new. He loved to be inspired by the people in management at LEGO; actually, he expected them to bring something strikingly new to the table, something that would challenge him. They came from "outside," with plenty of new and unfamiliar knowledge and experiences from the international business community. It's clear that something crucial happened to Dad over the course of the 1950s. He developed both as a person and as a managing director and changed his leadership style.*

Godtfred: "Our idea is to create toys that prepare the child for life." As he demonstrated by balancing on top of a small LEGO house, the toys stood up to repeated use.

The concept of public relations didn't really catch on in Denmark until after the war and appears for the first time in the minutes of managerial meetings in Billund in 1955. Up to that point, public relations and advertising weren't an especially prominent line on LEGO's balance sheet, but as GKC increasingly took control over operations and focused the business around the LEGO System in Play, the advertising budget ballooned. Here, too, father and son disagreed. In Godtfred's eyes, spending money on marketing was a crucial investment, while his father stuck to his faith in craftsmanship alone: "As long as the products are decent quality, the customers will find us on their own."

In the pivotal autumn of 1955, when the LEGO System in Play was rolled out and about to be tested for the first time by retailers and consumers, Godtfred had set aside 60,000 kroner for "advertising and display materials." It was a massive investment, and the Godtfred of a few years earlier would never have agreed to it, but now he hoped to snare LEGO a prominent place in toy and department stores over the Christmas season. The goal, of course, was to communicate and inculcate the basic idea behind the LEGO System in Play. As GKC repeated over and over at sales meetings, "It's not enough that *we* know it—the whole world has to know it!"

One example of LEGO's advertising strategy, in a decade when many young families were enjoying additional leisure time and were dreaming of buying their own home, was a colorful leaflet, addressed to parents and distributed in stores. Initially circulated only in Denmark, it soon expanded to Germany as well, rapidly demonstrating that the message had international appeal: the new LEGO System in Play not only offered a healthy, creative family hobby, but also allowed you to plan and build your own dream home.

The leaflet featured a compressed, illustrated, multigenerational saga about everything that happened to one family after they purchased some LEGO bricks. It all began on Erik's third birthday: "He got a box of LEGO Bricks, and he built the first towers." This was followed by a few snapshots of family life. Then, his little sister Lene wanted to play with LEGO, too, "and of course she built dollhouses." By the age of six, Erik was building large, grand houses that turned into towns with streets, model cars, signs, and trees. Lene was allowed to join in, and "Erik and Lene learned a lot about traffic." As a twelve-year-old, Erik was so handy with the bricks that he could build "a giant skyscraper with twenty-four stories," and at sixteen, LEGO was his favorite hobby. A few years passed. Erik got engaged, and soon he and his fiancée were building their dream home out of LEGO, "using the same bricks Erik was given on his third birthday." Some years after that, the young couple moved into a modern house "identical to the one they had so often built with LEGO." They then became parents, bringing the ad's pleasant little tale full circle. "The boy is only three, but he's already playing with LEGO—just like his dad, because LEGO can be used again and again, generation after generation, far into the future."

The story illustrated Godtfred's grand plan to market the plastic bricks, previously rather modest sellers, as part of something bigger. The LEGO System wasn't just a toy but a whole universe of play that could grow, become a part of family life, and be passed down to the next generation. As he explained in a newspaper interview, "You might say that from a business perspective it's illogical to make a toy that's meant to last a lifetime; but we believe our idea is the right one, and that we've created a toy that isn't just a passing entertainment but can be a meaningful part of children's development."

In the run-up to Christmas 1955, LEGO pushed full steam ahead, almost to the point of chaos, and in January the sales reps reported frustrated and confused retailers who hadn't understood the broader concept of the LEGO System in Play. Over the Christmas season, shop assistants weren't sure whether the LEGO Town Plan was supposed to be an entertaining toy or a sensible lesson in road safety. And wasn't there something contradictory, asked one retailer, about referring to toys as a "system"? Can play be systematized? It couldn't, not according to the child psychologists and pedagogues GKC had been listening to. They would all answer that in order for something to be considered play, it must be free, undisciplined, and unsystematic.

LEGO's new Head of Advertising, Henning Guld, recognized that their initial promotional material was probably a bit too wordy. But GKC was undaunted. He immediately sent his reps back into the field to clarify the idea behind the LEGO System and motivate the assistants on the shop floor. "Our biggest task must be to give retailers a big injection of LEGO vitamins!"

So they wouldn't simply create more confusion, however, they decided to limit the new LEGO System products to some cyclists, a motorbike, a scooter, and a moped, as well as various flags that would create more life and movement on the town plan, which was also significantly improved and turned into a rigid, foldable plate. One half of the back was devoted to an image of the entire LEGO System range: thirty-eight elements in all, plus cars, flags, trees and so on. On the other half was a poster-sized color photo of a blond girl and the freckled eight-year-old Kjeld, wavy-haired and clad in a checked shirt. Kjeld, who would one day follow in his father's and grandfather's footsteps and run the company, now became a familiar face nationwide, appearing on all sizes of LEGO System in Play boxes up until 1960.

Kjeld: *I was used as a model in photographs from when I was very young, and they were shot by a local photographer, but during the second half of the 1950s my dad decided the images should be more professional, so I had to go to Aarhus to be photographed. We made the trips in the Head of Advertising's—Henning Guld's—slick Karmann Ghia sports car. Guld was an important man for Dad in those days. He did all our ad campaigns in Denmark and abroad, and those were the years when the advertising budget just grew and grew. It was also Guld who wrote many of Dad's eloquent speeches when he had to present the LEGO System in Play in a larger public context. I thought the trips to Aarhus in the sports car* *were awesome, of course, actually much more awesome than having to be photographed with some girl my age. It was also on one of those trips that I had my first ever Coca-Cola.*

While the product range was being updated and adjusted after the launch, Godtfred was also trying, with a hitherto unprecedented willingness to take risks, to realize his and his father's dream of selling Danish toys in Germany, the heart of toyland itself. The plan took a bit of a battering when GKC consulted with some export consultants and various other individuals with a knowledge of foreign trade. Selling toys to the Germans would be rather like selling sand in the Sahara.

A persistent trait in the Kirk Christiansen family is a mixture of stubbornness, toughness, and assiduity reminiscent of the characters found in earlier literature by Jutlandic writers such as Steen Steensen Blicher, Jeppe Aakjær, Johan Skjoldborg, and Johannes V. Jensen, who wrote about men and women along the Jutland Ridge battling the heather and the poor soil.

Perhaps it was Ole Kirk's constitutional boldness hereditarily asserting itself, but his son didn't abandon his daring plan to conquer the German toy market. It's unlikely that he conducted much of a financial analysis or overview of the risks. LEGO did turn a profit in 1955, but their turnover was still only 2.1 million kroner, more than 30 percent of which was still accounted for by wooden toys. There was really nothing to indicate that LEGO's plastic bricks were on their way to an international breakthrough, apart from Godtfred's intuition and the kind of self-confidence that can move mountains.

The company "LEGO Spielwaren GmbH" was founded in January 1956, and by now its backstory is legendary. Two months before, Godtfred had been driving home through northern Germany after visiting the Danish Consulate General in Hamburg. He'd been trying to find out more about LEGO's chances of establishing itself in the German market, and had just been given the interesting tidbit of information that if he were to set up an independent German company, instead of

Thobmsems Dym i Hohenwedstedt. et gammelt Hotel [handwritten caption, partially legible]

LEGO's first main office in Germany was located on the top floor of the abandoned railway hotel in Hohenwestedt. From his office inside, Axel Thomsen led the conquest of the German market. *Private collection.*

simply establishing a subsidiary of LEGO in Germany, it would mean lower tariffs, special tax breaks, and better terms for loans.

On his way home from Hamburg, Godtfred looked for suitable locations in Schleswig-Holstein for LEGO to rent as part of their big push into Germany. He also swung by Hohenwestedt to see whether Axel and Grethe Thomsen, good friends of his and Edith's from Sweden, were home. The couple had settled down in the city and started producing dollhouse furniture there, products they'd previously manufactured at Lundby Leksaksfabrik outside Gothenburg.

The Thomsens were home. Over coffee, Godtfred explained his errand in Hamburg and the proposed export business. He then fetched some of the boxes and a LEGO System Town Plan from the car. Axel Thomsen was wildly enthusiastic and saw the potential of the LEGO system idea.

"This toy is fantastic. Why don't I help you sell it in Germany?"

Godtfred hesitated, then said, "What LEGO needs in Germany is a man who can devote himself 100 percent to the job, not someone who already produces and sells other toys." Then he headed home to Billund, leaving Axel Thomsen with something to think about.

A few days later Thomsen phoned Godtfred to say, "What if I let my son take over the dollhouse factory, and Grethe and I work solely for your company and the LEGO System. Could you use me then?"

The answer was a resounding yes. On his way home from Hohenwestedt, Godtfred reflected that Axel Thomsen would be exactly the right person to head their German campaign. He had the energy and the enthusiasm, along with the necessary insight and thorough knowledge of the market.

Not long afterward, LEGO rented the entire second floor of the old railway hotel, Bahnhofstrasse 19, owned by the Thomsens. Dollhouse furniture moved aside in favor of plastic bricks, and as GKC would later recount, "Thomsen became our man, 110 percent. He was fantastically competent, something of a bulldozer. He's the one who laid the groundwork right from the start for the German market to later become our best foreign market."

Meanwhile, the company bought its first truck, a Bedford, with a gigantic red LEGO logo on the white body behind the driver's cab. It was used to transport partially completed LEGO boxes to Hohenwestedt, where they'd be given the final finishing touches and packaged up for sale. This arrangement enabled them to avoid paying a 30 percent import duty on prepackaged toys at the border. At the wheel was the oldest of Ole Kirk's sons, Johannes, who didn't have his brothers' technical talents or gift of gab but was good at driving, and had now been promoted to Export Driver, with his own uniform and cap with the LEGO logo above the brim.

Kjeld: *Johannes drove the truck to Germany when there were goods going down to Hohenwestedt. He loved that job and the responsibility, and he always chatted with the customs officers at the border, who invited him in for a cup of coffee. When Johannes reached Hohenwestedt, he had a great time with the employees while the truck was emptied, and then he'd return to Billund. He kept that job for many years.*

In the beginning, Johannes delivered one consignment per week, later growing to two. Joining him on the very first trip from Billund to Holsten was Axel Thomsen, who was there partly to arrange things with customs and partly to make sure everything was done properly. In Hohenwestedt, his wife Grethe helped with the daily operations, and the couple were in charge of all sales and administration, based at the former station hotel.

At first, it was slow going. Buyers from the German department stores and shops, who met every year at the trade fair in Nuremberg, had dismissed the Danish building toy a few years earlier, when Godtfred tried to promote their LEGO Bausteine, as it was called in Germany. The same skepticism faced them in the spring of 1956.

Kjeld: *At the start it took a bit of time to convince the German buyers that this really was a product that could sell widely. It was odd, actually, that they couldn't see right away that this was a groundbreaking new building system in which children could create the things they wanted to play with. It was a huge victory when Axel Thomsen managed to get a whole chain of German department stores to believe in the LEGO idea, and also to accept that the sale wouldn't go through a wholesaler, who would have to be given a special discount, as was tradition in Germany. Dad and Thomsen stood firm on that issue. It was clever and brave of them, and it set the stage for our success in Germany.*

Present on the maiden voyage of the new truck in 1956 were Johannes, driving, and Axel Thomsen, who came along to deal with the formalities at the German border.

The decisive breakthrough was to come through Godtfred's and Axel Thomsen's painstakingly thought-out PR strategy in the autumn of 1956. They decided to focus their efforts on a single city. Hamburg was a natural choice. A city of more than a million people, it was a mecca for trade, and only fifty miles south of LEGO's German headquarters in Hohenwestedt. As GKC later explained in a speech to his workforce:

> We realized that if advertising and marketing were spread across the whole of Germany, it would simply be wasted. So we concentrated solely on Hamburg. And after preparing the ground with some excellent, pioneering work—exhibitions in specialty shops, influencing owners and sales assistants—we threw fuel on the fire: a film to be played in cinemas.

Showing unwavering faith in the power of advertising, GKC and Guld had produced a two-minute color commercial, "Wir Bauen eine Stadt" ("We Build a City"), which was shown in Hamburg's four biggest cine-

System im Spiel

LEGO Spielwaren GmbH
Hohenwestedt/Holstein

Zur 10. Internationalen Spielwarenmesse in Nürnberg · Wieseler-Haus · 1. Stock · Stand 143

Ad for the "LEGO System im Spiel" at the annual toy fair in Nuremberg.

mas. Hugely appealing, set to a pleasant, jazzy soundtrack, it explained that the whole family—girl, boy, mother, and father—can play with the "LEGO System im Spiel" together.

While the ad was playing in cinemas, Axel Thomsen hired a team of men and women to go around to Hamburg's toy stores, department stores, and major shops to check whether there were LEGO boxes on the shelves. If not, they were told to ask very firmly for LEGO Bausteine, the exciting new building toy that they'd heard so much about.

Kjeld: *Dad often talked about the very first ad he made with Henning Guld and Axel Thomsen. In one of the scenes in the commercial, Thomsen stood on a LEGO house in the middle of the Town Plan to show that the building could easily take his weight. That was something Dad had asked him to do, and he loved doing the stunt himself when there were journalists and photographers around. Dad always emphasized to his employees that it was important to demonstrate and call attention to the*

functionality and quality of the LEGO System, although the bricks were
actually pretty bad at holding together in the beginning.

By January 1957, GKC could safely say that his bold export campaign appeared to be succeeding. In one year, LEGO had expanded its potential customer base to one hundred million people, and the risk he'd run by juggling LEGO's funds, which he'd historically always tried to dissuade his father from doing, seemed to be bearing fruit. Money started rolling in from Germany, partly because German retailers tended to remit payment for their purchases quickly, and partly because GKC, resourceful businessman that he was, had arranged extra-long credit periods for their ever-increasing procurement of plastic powder.

Over the first few months of the year, the LEGO System im Spiel campaign spread to other German cities, along with various other marketing initiatives. In addition to the ad and brochures, there were huge window displays of LEGO models in department stores, and a colorful LEGO magazine for German children soon followed. Meanwhile, Axel Thomsen and his employees visited retailers all over Germany, helping them to understand and experience firsthand what the LEGO System could do and why it was the toy of the future. Thomsen, a fan of systems, set up a directory of retailers and customers, which enabled them to quickly observe any increase or decline in sales of the LEGO Bausteine in a city or region for many years to come, thereby analyzing the reactions of consumers.

One of the interesting things that quickly emerged from Thomsen's data was that German parents believed LEGO was a German product. This fact didn't bother GKC. Far from it; he saw it as a strength, which astonished the newly appointed Head of Exports, Troels Petersen. "Why don't we advertise the fact that the LEGO System in Play is Danish and made in Denmark?" he asked his boss. GKC's answer was typical of the style and tone of his leadership:

If you want to pursue that policy, Troels, then you're definitely Head of
Exports at the wrong company. My strategy is the inverse of what you

want. LEGO's products are international, and the best thing that can happen, in fact, is that the Germans think the company is German, the French think the products are made in France, and so on.

Kjeld: *It was clear early on to Dad that if this company was going to grow, then Denmark was too small a country, so we would need to think internationally. This was ages before anyone was talking about internationalization, to say nothing of globalization and the Single Market. There is an important difference between being a Danish company that exports and an international company with roots in Billund. That way of thinking, which we still have today, originated in the 1950s.*

In a remarkably short span of time, the LEGO System im Spiel was a familiar and sought-after toy in Germany, and by 1958 there were more LEGO bricks per person sold there than in Denmark. Less than five years after German wholesalers and retailers expressed skepticism, almost condescension, toward Godtfred's products at the trade fair in Nuremberg, LEGO's German company brought in ten million kroner in a single year. It was a dizzying sum, especially when you think that three years earlier the entire company in Billund had a total gross revenue of 2.1 million kroner.

One might wonder why the LEGO system became so popular so rapidly on German soil. LEGO's aggressive sales and advertising strategy, in combination with the many qualities and obvious potential of the toy, were, of course, highly significant, but another explanation for their tremendous success was the social demand the bricks seemed to fill. This demand sprang from the national focus on rebuilding not just houses, neighborhoods, and cities all over Germany in the aftermath of World War II, but also family groups and relationships. In 1950s Germany, there was a widespread longing to forge bonds between the old and young, parents and children; people longed to come together as a family. Why not bond over a common, peaceful activity like the LEGO System im Spiel?

Whereas children before the war had played without adult supervi-

Speel ook met LEGO!

Zowel moeder als dochter bouwen van LEGO enthousiast poppenhuizen met meubeltjes. Vader en zoon bouwen vliegtuigen, treinen, schepen, huizen en nog veel meer. Het LEGO SYSTEEM inspireert iedereen - is een uitdaging voor de fantasie, want van LEGO kun je álles bouwen - LEGO is dagelijks nieuw!

Er zijn LEGO-universeeldozen van f 3.75 tot f 21.50 en aanvullingsdozen vanaf 95 cent. Uw speelgoedhandelaar demonstreert u graag het LEGO SYSTEEM!

LEGO - HAREN (Gr.) - NEDERLAND

LEGO's overarching European PR strategy was to use the family unit as the primary context and setting for playing with LEGO. Seen here in Dutch, 1959.

sion, children and their toys were now brought into the living room, into the heart of the family. This trend, which was evident in most Western European countries in the 1950s, was closely observed by LEGO's Advertising Department. The pattern was already established in their first commercial, in which a well-groomed, smiling nuclear family entered the living room and sat down around the table and the LEGO System im Spiel. While the soft jazz fades into the background, the voiceover says, "*Alle bauen mit. Gross und klein, bauen mit dem LEGO Stein*" ("Everybody builds together. Big and small build with LEGO bricks").

The LEGO System in Play moved with the times, profiting from the post-war rise in overall prosperity and the increased focus on the welfare of the family. In Germany, the phenomenon was referred to as the *Wirtschaftwunder*, meaning the country's miraculous economic transformation from rubble-strewn ruin to industrialized nation.

Kjeld: *The post-war period was characterized all over Europe by derelict houses and things that had to be rebuilt, and I think that also played a role in why many families chose the LEGO bricks. They could be used to make something positive—in a sense, to help rebuild. I've often thought about that connection.*

LEGO's progress and success was also reflected in the company's machinery, and by the end of the decade there were more than fifty molding machines in the Plastics Department. There was, however, one nagging issue, and that was the bricks' "clutch power." They simply didn't stick together properly.

Ever since the very first Automatic Binding Bricks in 1949, LEGO's small bricks had been hollow, and in January 1958, when Axel Thomsen headed north to Billund to report on the fantastic Christmas sales figures in Germany, they still were. The only downside in the German market expansion was that a few dissatisfied customers complained that their children's buildings fell apart. LEGO had been aware of the problem for years, although it was rarely brought up at internal sales meetings. Many other customer complaints about the LEGO System

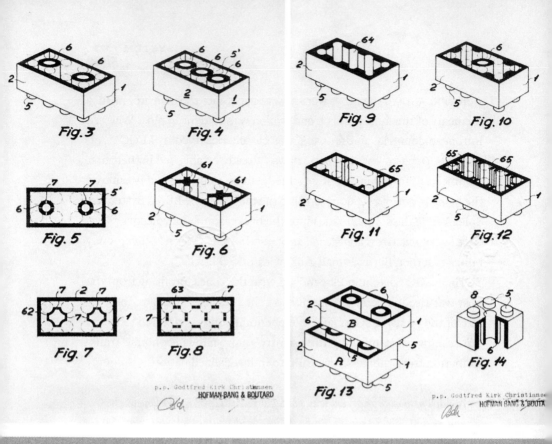

Pat. anm.

In 1958, the modern LEGO brick was patented, featuring tubes and studs. The bricks now interlocked perfectly, expanding the possibilities for building with them. As evident from the top drawings, several other possible solutions to improve the bricks' clutch power were developed, and all the alternative solutions were patented simultaneously in a number of countries all around the world.

in Play between 1955 and 1957 had been discussed, but not this serious, fundamental flaw. As late as January 1957, when GKC introduced a new initiative at a management meeting called the PUK (Produkt Udviklings Komité, or Product Development Committee), a committee designed to "perfect our products," nobody mentioned the bricks' less-than-perfect clutch power. Everyone around the table knew that this obvious quality issue was something the most skilled technicians at the factory, led by the molding workshop's manager, Ove Nielsen, had been trying to solve for years. But amid the overwhelming success of the bricks and the ever-increasing demand, the push to make improvements had stalled somewhat.

The complaints from German customers in January 1958 were a wake-up call. Godtfred reacted instantly, and after a conversation with Axel Thomsen, at which Karl Georg, as head of the Plastics Division, was also present, he sat down that same day and sketched out the various possible options for adding couplings inside the eight-stud brick, several of which had previously been discussed.

The sketch was passed to Ove Nielsen, who was asked to produce a sample of the most recent idea under consideration: placing two cylindrical coupling tubes inside the hollow cavity of the brick. Over the next twenty-four hours they worked feverishly on this solution, and at some point Godtfred suggested trying a third tube.

This turned out to be a stroke of genius. The three tubes ensured that the tubes and studs firmly interlocked when two bricks are combined. It was almost as though the bricks were glued together, but they were still easy to pull apart. Making each stud on the bricks touch at three points gave them the stability and gripping or clutch power they'd been missing for years. At the same time, it proved to be an aesthetically pleasing solution, because the tubes' round shape harmonized with the round studs on the top of the brick.

An engineer GKC knew from previous patent inquiries advised him to patent all the conceivable couplings LEGO experimented with, to thwart any future copycats. During these years, LEGO experienced tough competition from other plastics manufacturers on the toy market who imitated LEGO's bricks, including the Danish firm Puwi, which went so far as to tell customers in their ads that their bricks were compatible with the LEGO System in Play.

They spent a few more tough days in the molding workshop, taking out all the test pieces and coming up with a couple more variants that functioned in a similar way to the inner tube. By January 27 they'd finished, and Godtfred rushed to Copenhagen. All the material was handed over to the patent office, which gave the application the official stamp of approval. January 28, 1958, 1:58 p.m., marked the birth of the modern LEGO brick as we know it today.

With this piece of technical wizardry, the LEGO System in Play was complete. From then on, the bricks fit together differently from any other plastic bricks in the world, and entirely new possibilities for combining and building with them opened up.

Kjeld: *I think Dad was fully aware of the problem back in 1955, when we launched the LEGO System in Play, but we hadn't found a proper solution yet. There were many different, creative suggestions on the table: bricks with cross-shaped couplings, with pegs, with ribs, with all sorts of stuff. All these potential solutions were included in the final patent applications, partly to show that we could achieve the clutch power in several different ways if we wanted, but also to prevent other people from coming up with one of the options we sketched. For a ten-year-old LEGO builder like me, it was absolutely fantastic to suddenly be able to build with more stability—now you could go diagonally upward and diagonally downward, if you wanted. Plus, you could lift a big space rocket off the table without the bottom bricks falling off.*

Throughout the 1950s, Ole Kirk's health was in slow but steady decline, as evidenced by his handwritten signatures on the company records and the minutes from the board meetings at the Billund Mission House. The founder was gradually running out of energy, although even in his final years he and Sofie still went to the North Sea to swim and to Norway to

March 15, 1958. Ole Kirk's coffin was carried out of the Lion House and accompanied all the way to Grene Parish Church by the inhabitants of Billund. *Private collection.*

ski. He had gradually relinquished his control over the running of the company. As he said to a journalist at LEGO's twenty-fifth anniversary in August 1957, "I can't keep up anymore; it's gotten too big for that, and I'm too weak."

A significant portion of GKC's New Year's speech to the assembled staff as the anniversary year drew to a close was directed to his father, who hadn't been seen at the factory since the festivities in August. Ole Kirk sat there quietly, glancing up at his son now and then as he listened to the speech, which was essentially a heartfelt thank-you—and a farewell:

> *Although you can no longer take part in the day-to-day operations, Dad, we very much hope that you are pleased to see the company—which has been your whole life, really—continue to grow. We all know that this company was born during a time of great struggle and adversity, and that its motto has always been "Pray and work."*
>
> *In 1932 your dearest wish was that this company would support you and your family, and we want you and Mom to be happy to see that it now supports several hundred homes and families, directly and indirectly. You have created something of genuine social benefit, Dad! It will be our task to try to keep running the business in the positive spirit in which you and Mom began it.*
>
> *This will get harder and harder as it gets bigger and everything becomes more impersonal, but I think I can venture to say that all of us gathered here will continue to strive to do our best, and that our motto remains "Pray and work."*

A month and a half after the invention of the modern LEGO brick, on March 11, 1958, Ole Kirk died. This milestone in the town's history had to be honored, and the inhabitants of Billund all came out on the street on the day of his funeral. Old and young, they'd come to pay their respects, on his final journey through the town, to the well-liked and respected man who'd taken responsibility for the local community.

The old black-and-white photos in the family album show the coffin being carefully carried out of the Lion House's front door by Ole Kirk's sons, followed by Sofie, Ulla, his daughters-in-law, and grandchildren. Throughout the town and the local area, flags were at half-staff, and the roads out of the town were strewn with spruce twigs. As a precaution, a loudspeaker van had been positioned outside Grene Parish Church, but by putting extra seats and pews on the porch, they managed to find space for everyone inside.

Johannes Bruus, the parish priest, who had known the deceased for three decades, gave a sincere, heartfelt sermon about Paul's First Letter to the Corinthians. "The last enemy that will be destroyed is Death." Standing by the coffin, he summarized Ole Kirk's life with the words, "He remained faithful to the vision he had in his youth, and there can be no doubt that this shaped all of his very capable efforts, life, and work."

In the months leading up to his death, Ole Kirk also communicated extensively with one of his good friends, Johannes Rønberg, the founder of Rønberg Toys in Copenhagen. Once a week during the final months of Ole Kirk's life, Rønberg sent a long letter full of biblical quotations and plenty of shared memories:

> By the way, do you know the greatest and best thing you ever created and manufactured in your entire business career? What do you think it is, and how many people do you think can see it (sadly, far too few)? It was the luminous cross you sent to your clients that Christmas, or was it New Year? They can come out with all the Systems in Play in the world, all the toys in the world, all the mammon . . . in that little plastic cross, which cost perhaps a krone to manufacture, we have the whole of LEGO's history at that time.

When Ole Kirk Christiansen died, the loss was not only that of a diligent, genuine craftsman, with all the integrity that implies, but of a man who'd had a special way of running a company, arising from the close relationships, solidarity and faith of his farming community. As a business owner, Ole Kirk was a patriarchal figure whose tiny factory flourished thanks, in part, to the town and region, and ultimately to their benefit.

In 1954, the entire workforce included about thirty-five women and slightly fewer men, assembled here outside the factory in Ole Kirk's garden, where in the summertime they took breaks during the day. On especially hot days there would be water fights; the family also participated.

In his fatherly way, he always looked after the welfare of his employees. As LEGO's first bookkeeper, Henning Johansen, heard him say during the war, LEGO's employees were always more important than anything else. "Humanity's interests come first, material interests second."

Characteristic of this belief is that Ole Kirk never referred to his employees as "workers," but always "people." The effect of his approach was felt in the work environment and general tone at the factory, too. As Elna Jensen recalled when she retired in the 1970s, remembering the good old days at the factory in the staff magazine, "I won't say that working conditions were better in the 1950s—we did shifts and nights back then, too—but they were good years. They were. Today there's no solidarity. You can't chat with people or confide in anyone."

Kjeld: *Granddad felt a deep sense of responsibility toward his employees; he almost thought of them as family. To an extent this is still reflected in the LEGO Group today, because we strive to create trust and openness between the family owners and the employees. LEGO has always been a "we" organization, where everyone is on informal terms with everyone else. Every single employee uses "we" quite naturally when they talk to people outside LEGO about LEGO. Of course, there also needs to be an appropriate level of discipline. We need a hierarchy, we need people to follow the rules of the game, but on a day-to-day basis we must never forget that feeling of closeness—and we must remain human beings at play—just like my granddad.*

Until Ole Kirk's death in 1958, and for a handful of years after that, religion played an important role in the daily management of LEGO, although the company never tried to dictate its employees' relationship with God. The Christian faith was involved in the processing of every single job application in the mid-1950s, when either Ole Kirk or Godtfred asked about or investigated a potential employee's religious beliefs. One example among many is that of bookkeeper Orla Jørgensen. Originally hired in 1948, he was still there to celebrate LEGO's fortieth anniversary many years later, and throughout all that time, he remained one of Godtfred's most trusted employees.

Orla Jørgensen had responded to a job advertisement in the *Kristeligt Dagblad* that was titled "A devout bookkeeper." He was doing the accounts for a grocer's shop in Hørsholm, north of Copenhagen, where the Kirk Christiansens happened to have some family connections. They received a letter one day from Ole Kirk and Godtfred, inquiring about Jørgensen and in particular about his spiritual convictions. "Is Jørgensen active in the kingdom of God, and is he known as a man of strong faith?" He was, and he got the job.

One established feature of community life at the LEGO factory, which in the 1940s and 1950s included summer excursions, Christmas parties, and Shrovetide entertainment, was a regular morning church service, which Ole Kirk instituted in 1952, when LEGO's new lecture hall first opened. All employees who wished to take part met in the hall at half past seven, after a short blast of the siren, to hear the Word of God and sing a hymn or two. Ole Kirk invested in a larger supply of the Inner Mission's songbook, *Hjemlandstoner* (*Homeland Notes*), which was bound in gorgeous blue leather and printed with the words "LEGO Billund" on the cover in gold lettering. He also acquired a piano, to add greater sonority and rhythm to the morning hymns. He and Sofie, as well as their four sons and their sons' wives, often participated themselves.

Kjeld: *The morning services continued until I was thirteen or fourteen, and on an ordinary morning in the 1950s, you could easily have seventy or eighty employees who sang, put their hands together, and prayed the Lord's Prayer. The whole thing probably lasted about twenty minutes, then they'd go to work, each person to their department and their place. In the early 1960s, this morning routine was discontinued by LEGO's first personnel manager—a former priest, by the way—who'd concluded that the time for religious services at a modern factory had passed. Fewer*

Ole Kirk and Sofie on a car trip through Denmark. *Private collection.*

and fewer people were turning up, and many of them probably felt it
wasn't really all that voluntary.

Ole Kirk Christiansen was never much interested in words, unlike
his son and grandson, who wrote down their goals for how they wanted
people to play with LEGO products, but his respect for the needs of
children was forever enshrined in the origins of the company name—
"*leg godt*," meaning "play well"—as well as in the many stories about the
spontaneous joy Ole Kirk found in children and his perpetual impulse
to give them toys.

One of these stories dates from the summer of 1952, when Sofie
and Ole had gone on a trip to Zealand by car. One day, on the road
from Korsør to Skælskør, they stopped near the village of Boeslunde. A
woman was weeding in a turnip field nearby, accompanied by two small
boys. Her name was Ottomine Andersen, and she lived on a nearby farm
called Ly. She always took her boys to the field because, as a mother,
Ottomine felt that children needed to be with their parents when they
were little.

On that summer's day, when a large, magnificent car pulled up at
one end of the field, she was singing to John and Niels while they played
among the turnips. An older man got out, glanced around, then suddenly walked into the field toward Ottomine and the boys. He paused
and said, "It's good to see that a mother can sing while working so hard
in such heat!"

Ottomine answered that it made the time pass more quickly for the
boys, and the work pass more quickly for her. The man nodded and
smiled, then went back to the car, opened the trunk, and came back with
two small round boxes in each hand. Inside the boxes were some spinning
tops you could twirl between your fingers, making them come to life.

"Are you bored, boys? There you go, now you've got a top each to
play with! And if anyone asks you where you got them, say they were
from me. I live in a little town in Jutland called Billund, and I've started
making toys out of plastic. They're called LEGO."

Many years later, in 1975, a grown-up Niels went to LEGOLAND with his children. He brought the spinning top he'd once been given by a kindly man. By now the man's son was Managing Director of LEGO, but unfortunately he wasn't available at LEGOLAND, so Niels went home to Zealand without having met him. His aging mother, Ottomine Andersen, sent Godtfred a long letter in which she recounted the whole story, concluding with the words, "I know that man is no more, but we don't remember him as the great creator of a very famous toy, but as a simple, warm-hearted man who was kind to children, a man whose acquaintance we made on a hot summer's day so long ago. We honor his memory."

LEGO's first international conference for directors and leading salespeople took place in Billund only four months after the death of its founder. The conference opened with a eulogy commemorating Ole Kirk, in which GKC said that his father's Christian faith was never about being narrow-minded but rather about seeing the joy and happiness in life. "It is on this basis," he told them, "that LEGO is founded."

The question that LEGO's now undisputed leader carefully avoided mentioning in the welcome speech was one that would have inevitably occurred to all the staff members since the founder's death: would GKC change course and put an end to the parallel production of wooden and plastic toys, which had defined the LEGO image over the past decade?

Godtfred had given the matter a lot of thought and consulted with the closed circles of shareholders—the family—about his opinion on the Wooden-toy Division, which he believed should be wound down in the not-too-distant future. However rational his point of view and however diplomatically Godtfred expressed it, it was an extremely sore point. The company's history was built on Ole Kirk's former trade as a woodworker, and LEGO would never have produced the plastic bricks and the LEGO System in Play without the wooden toys.

The issue was further complicated by the fact that Godtfred's younger brother, Gerhardt, had invented a new building toy by the name of BILOfix, which he was now ready to launch on the toy market. Inspired by classic English Meccano sets, Gerhardt combined wood and plastic into an ingenious and original system of toys that consisted of wooden blocks with holes and strips of wood of varying lengths, also with holes, that were screwed together with plastic screws and red plastic nuts. This new LEGO product, which Gerhardt had spent several years developing and had only recently patented, was now apparently on the verge of being scrapped by GKC. This, among other things, confirmed a feeling that Gerhardt and his brother Karl Georg had had for a long time.

> **Kjeld:** *Over the years, the two brothers could see that my father was relying on them less and less, even though Gerhardt was head of wooden-toy production and responsible for all sales in Denmark and Karl Georg was Director of the Plastics Division. After their father died, the two of them must have talked about regaining some control over what Godtfred was doing, and at least having more say in the company. There would definitely have been some conversations that ended with Dad saying, "It's either you or me!"*
>
> *At that point my dad wasn't very inclusive, and he didn't really put himself in his brothers' shoes. Dad was just obsessed with the System in Play! From 1957 to 1960 they pushed insanely hard to grow and develop the company, and they held lots of meetings, including some to which Gerhardt and Karl Georg weren't invited.*

These disagreements only intensified after Ole Kirk's death, which was likely the last thing he would have wanted. The children's inheritance was split into five equal blocks of shares, four for his sons and one for his daughter. At first glance this seems like a fair-minded and loving decision, but it ended up exacerbating the already tense relationship between the siblings, particularly between Gerhardt and Godtfred. Karl Georg, too, felt that the way their father apportioned the shares meant they should be more involved in the running of the company and included in important decisions, which for the last five years Godtfred had made on his own.

> **Kjeld:** *While Granddad was alive, my dad said to him, "I want us siblings to inherit on equal terms, but for me to be at the head of the table at the*

company!" He regretted saying that, about inheriting on equal terms, because it ended up meaning that some of his other siblings felt that LEGO
was just as much their company as his, even though my father had been
running it for many years and had shaped it into what it was at the end
of the 1950s.

He should have said to his father, "You know what, I've been working
on this ever since I was a boy, and I'm the one who's going to run the
company going forward. Of course, my siblings should also inherit, but
maybe they should have a smaller share of the company and then something else on the side."

The distribution of their inheritance must have seemed fair to Ole
Kirk; and he evidently didn't think that the conflict simmering between
three of his sons was rooted in the decision he had made in 1950, when
Godtfred was named Junior Managing Director on his thirtieth birthday,
ahead of all his brothers. The chosen son received his father's blessing
via the congratulatory telegram mentioned earlier, which his brothers

Gerhardt Kirk Christiansen (second from
the left) along with a number of colleagues
around a table with various BILOfix model in
1959. The following year BILOfix was a huge
success domestically and abroad. *Private
collection.*

were also asked to sign: "In appreciation and gratitude for what you have done for the company to date. With total confidence that you will continue to do your best for LEGO's interests, you have been chosen today—Saturday 8.7.1950—as Junior Managing Director of A/S LEGO and A/S O. Kirk Kristiansen. Numbers: 6, 24–26."

This obvious favoritism had been repeated the following year on Ole Kirk's sixtieth birthday, when in the middle of the festivities on April 7, 1951, a photograph was taken in the sitting room of the Lion House. It was later enlarged, framed, and hung on the wall, public testimony to the order of succession in the family business. At the top of the image, enthroned among all his gifts and flowers, was LEGO's founder. Beneath him was Godtfred, and, at the very bottom, his three-year-old grandchild, Kjeld.

Godtfred's promotion didn't appear to put an immediate strain on the brothers' relationship, however. On the contrary, in the first half of the 1950s it seemed as though the four Kirk sons complemented each other extremely well, especially at work. Both Gerhardt and Karl Georg were happy to let their brother deal with the sales, administrative, and financial side, so that they could stretch their technical muscles in production. All four worked together seamlessly day-to-day, and they also got on well in private, often spending Sundays and holidays together, and taking summer breaks in Hvidbjerg near Vejle Fjord, where they had each built a holiday cottage near Ole Kirk and Sofie's cabin.

In the second half of the 1950s, however, the relationship between the brothers became more strained. Their differences weren't just about their father's inheritance and its implications, but also about LEGO's sudden shift from a small, family-run factory to an international export business with huge ambitions. Not least, it was also about Godtfred's transformation from a coveralls-wearing foreman to a businessman in a stylish suit. As he himself later explained:

My brothers felt I had been given too much authority, and that we should be a bit more egalitarian about the whole thing. While these things were all coming to a head in terms of us working together, there was so much

On the founder's sixtieth birthday in 1951, the patriarchal chain of succession at LEGO was immortalized: Ole Kirk, his son Godtfred, and his grandson Kjeld.

going on at the business—setting up foreign sales companies, the expansions in Billund. Our exports were increasing, and for natural reasons my brothers had no impact on that. It was difficult to alter those facts, and a ship can't have three captains.

Both product development and sales of the LEGO System in Play were proceeding at breakneck pace, and the system was now available in Switzerland, Holland, Austria, Portugal, Belgium, and Italy. Things were moving fast, and Gerhardt warned his brother several times that he thought the pace of growth was spiraling out of their control. In 1959, he wrote in a letter to Godtfred that the LEGO System in Play was heading in an unhealthy direction, that management was planning too many new products, and that instead they ought to be more economical with all these good ideas. "We need to make sure we don't overfeed ourselves and the retailers. If there's too much food brought out when we have lunch meetings at Hotel Australia, it's of no benefit to us, and it's the same if we overfeed people the LEGO System."

What Godtfred answered is unknown, but it was probably something along the lines of his response to one of LEGO's sales reps, who like Gerhardt was worried about LEGO's explosive development. "Okay, well, if we can expand and consolidate at the same time, then so much the better, right?"

In Gerhardt's letter, one senses rising frustration at not being adequately seen and heard in the company their father founded, especially since, back in the 1940s, it wasn't just Ole Kirk who had wanted Johannes, Gerhardt, and Karl Georg to play an active role; Godtfred had, too. Gerhardt's frustration was intensified by the fact that now only Godtfred knew what was happening with the business and so, also with Gerhardt's creation BILOfix, which was hotly anticipated in the industry.

In November 1958, a new limited company, A/S LEGO System was established, and GKC, Gerhardt, and Karl Georg were elected to the board. Three months later on February 9, 1959, at the first board meeting of the new company, GKC asked them to comment on the six-page report he had prepared on the future of LEGO.

It was a clear and thorough document, sketching out a total restructuring plan that would make Gerhardt managing director of one company, while both Gerhardt and Karl Georg, in their capacity as technical directors of the wood and plastics divisions, would from then on, as the report put it, have "free access to development to the fullest extent, subject to their own responsibility and personal satisfaction."

It emphasized that "Gerhardt must be aware that he personally bears a lot of responsibility, the greatest demands." The slightly superior tone this report took toward GKC's brothers, which was probably due to the legalistic nature of the language, became even more apparent in a passage explaining that Karl Georg would have to content himself with remaining a technical director for the time being: "It is not advisable to assign Karl Georg with the primary administration of the factory at the present time, but it is desired that he work toward this goal in the long term."

And what about Godtfred himself? According to the report, he'd be relieved of some of his many duties, but he was also named managing director of the new parent company, which was placed above the two older firms in the hierarchy, leaving Gerhardt and Karl Georg with extremely limited power and influence over LEGO's future. In the future, all matters of production and finance in the Wooden-toy and Plastics Divisions would go through the parent company and be approved by Godtfred. He was the one with "overall administrative control," as the report put it. It ended with the words:

> *It is true that our father has created and started this company, but it is also true that the future must be created by us, and this is dependent on our efforts in our respective roles. A division of labor that allows for the free development of initiative can only give the business more backbone and personal satisfaction. If the board can agree on and approve these ideas, they will be realized.*

The board did indeed agree, because as Jørgensen later explained, "Both Gerhardt and Karl Georg were well aware which of the brothers was familiar with exports and foreign markets. They didn't mind that, actually, but they did want to make some of the decisions themselves."

It didn't work out like that. The new structure set out by GKC was put to the test in 1959, as LEGO was still advancing on all fronts not just in terms of exports and total revenue, but also the number of new foreign sales companies and licensing agreements, molding machines, and employees. In just two years, the number of staff ballooned from 140 to 450. Meanwhile, BILOfix was launched on the Danish market, with great success. Understandably, Gerhardt thought his new toy system,

There's only a year between these two photos of the brothers. At the anniversary in 1957 they were cheerfully riding hobbyhorses, but in the spring of 1958, after their father's death, things had changed and the mood had taken a downward turn. Bottom, from left: Gerhardt, Johannes, Godtfred, and Karl Georg.

which was praised to the skies by Danish and international educationalist and toy experts, was ideal for export.

GKC didn't think so. He was worried it would dilute their focus on the LEGO System in Play. Two different toy systems from the same company would create unnecessary confusion among foreign retailers and customers. The two brothers couldn't reach an agreement, but found a compromise; in future, all the wooden and plastic toys they made that had nothing to do with the LEGO System in Play would be called BILOfix.

How would GKC handle this double-edged sword? We never found out. In the beginning of the new year, fate came knocking once again on LEGO's door.

EXPANSION

THE 1960s

Train, 1966

Late at night on February 4, 1960, LEGO's boiler operator headed to the factory to check the central heating, which was supposed to keep the night shift warm. The first thing he saw was smoke coming from windows on the first floor, at the opposite end of the Plastics Division. He immediately alerted the fire stations in Grindsted, Varde, and Vejle, and with help from people in the town, the boiler operator and the night shift workers retrieved a large stockpile of flammable liquids and brought them to safety. Despite the snowdrifts and slippery roads in the open landscape around Billund, the fire engines arrived, and before dawn the blaze was under control.

The following day, no one could explain how the fire started, and several members of LEGO management were left red-faced, because an engineer from the fire insurance company had just been for his annual inspection. His report had pointed out several issues in both the Wooden-toy and Plastics Divisions, including several things that had been mentioned on previous visits. As an internal LEGO memo noted immediately after the inspection in December:

> Engineer Steffensen was of the opinion that if a fire broke out in the Plastics Division, it would be difficult or impossible to curb, because there are no divisions such as fire walls, and he therefore strongly recommends—not least for LEGO's own sake—that we be very careful about keeping adequate fire safety equipment and keeping it in good order.

Luckily, the fire was limited to the Wooden-toy Division and parts of the roof. The painting workshop had gone up in flames, along with a storeroom containing lots of wooden toys, several machines, and various other items. All told, the damage was estimated at 250,000 kroner.

The fire wasn't as large and destructive as the ones in 1924, 1925, and 1942. It did, however, have a crucial impact on the future production and ownership of LEGO.

GKC decided on the spot that LEGO would have its own fire engine, and the following year they acquired a used model from the Vamdrup Fire Station.

Ten days after the blaze, LEGO A/S held an emergency general meeting at which the four brothers, Sofie, and a newly hired director, Søren Olsen, were present. GKC had prepared a statement in advance, announcing that the Wooden-toy Division would now be shut down and that in future the business would focus solely on the LEGO System in Play. He requested the board's support.

Since the fire, everything had come under review, and "the conclusion has been reached," as Godtfred wrote, that concentrating LEGO's energies on the System in Play would yield the greatest benefit. If the Wooden-toy Division was closed, there would be more room for plastics. Moreover, the head of the division, Gerhardt, would now be able to channel all his efforts toward the LEGO System. BILOfix, which had only just entered production and was selling very well, was referred to only as "the item," and was described in the past tense.

Director Gerhardt Kirk Christiansen had been tasked with getting the best out of the Wooden-toy Division by focusing specifically on that. He later constructed an item that had potential for export and also, by restructuring operations, made it possible for the Wooden-toy Division to take a step forward. This would, however, inevitably lead to a degree of competition between the companies, which would mean that, in the interest of external customers, we would have to separate out the factories and the name.

Unsurprisingly, the dispute between the two brothers ended with Gerhardt resigning in the spring of 1961, when Godtfred bought him and Karl Georg out of the company, although not before offering them his own shares in the family business. As he later explained, they turned him down. "And I understood why they didn't want to, actually. Because by that point they were both too removed from the decisions that were being made at the top level of the company. The whole thing ended with me buying their shares, for what was a very high price at the time."

Kjeld: *Gerhardt thought the LEGO wooden toys were a sensible thing to keep making, even after the fire. BILOfix seemed to be a new success, both for LEGO and for Gerhardt himself, and then my dad came along and said, "We won't be bothering with that anymore!" That was probably the main reason why not just Gerhardt, but also my other uncle, pulled out of the enterprise. Johannes kept out of the rows and stayed in Billund with my dad, where he kept driving the big truck back and forth between Billund and Hohenwestedt. I don't know how much Gerhardt and Karl Georg were paid when they sold their shares to my dad and moved to Kolding, but certainly they had enough that they could each get something new up and running. Gerhardt was successful with BILOfix for a number of years, and he also founded a chain of toy stores, while Karl Georg had his own plastics factory. It was a bitter breakup for all concerned, and it was more than twenty years before the four brothers were back on a reasonably good footing. But they were never truly united, the way they had been while my granddad was alive, ever again.*

In the ten years after the war, Ole Kirk and his four sons had run LEGO's day-to-day operations, working with only Orla Jørgensen and a couple of regular sales reps. In the second half of the 1950s and early 1960s, a parade of new faces came through the doors of the System House. This stylish new administrative block had been built on the corner of Hovedgaden and Systemvej using a modular design.

These were people like Helge Torpe (Sales and Marketing), Ole Nielsen (Legal), Henning Guld (Advertising), Arne Bødtker (Sales), and Søren Olesen (Organization and Personnel). And unlike Ole Kirk and his sons, all these new hires were experienced, professional managers drawn from numerous different areas of the Danish business community.

In other words, there was a paradigm shift in management. Godtfred, especially, had been looking forward to this influx of new people, all of whom were familiar with the rules and the new form of business culture typical of a modern company. As the managing director and owner he could consult with them on a daily basis, asking them for advice and

The brothers' disagreements led them to finally part ways, and in April 1961, *Vejle Amts Folkeblad* announced that Gerhardt and Karl Georg had each decided to start their own company. Both moved to Kolding, while Johannes remained in Billund with Godtfred. Vejle Amts Folkeblad, *Jysk Fynske Medier.*

drawing inspiration from them. Meanwhile, his most loyal senior employee, Orla Jørgensen, had been promoted after ten years in accounts, and could now act on the firm's behalf.

Kjeld: *One of the absolutely key people in my father's development of the business in the 1950s and 1960s was Orla Jørgensen, who was hired shortly after I was born. I remember him giving a speech at my confirmation and saying he had come that day on "the Pig," as they called the local train between Vejle and Grindsted, while of course I had come by stork. His daily reports on LEGO's financial situation ensured that my dad was always up to date with how the business was doing and gave* *him a clear basis on which to make decisions in the moment. Some of the new managers were more self-important than others and often ended up squabbling. It was a bit of a balancing act for Dad, I think. How much weight should he put on what his German director said as compared to the Danish one, for instance? That was the price of pushing the business to develop dynamically, he knew. And it all became part of the pioneer atmosphere.*

GKC demanded a lot of his senior executives. They were expected to act decisively, seize the initiative, and not be afraid to fail. It was almost a fundamental law of LEGO's still-evolving personnel policy, a cardinal rule that Godtfred learned from someone close to home, as he later explained in an interview. "My father was a fantastic teacher, and he was always active. As a boy I was very cautious, and Dad always used to say, 'Just do something!' I learned from that, and I like it when people take initiative. If an employee makes a mistake, I usually congratulate them, because it's something to learn from."

GKC also demanded familiarity with, and total commitment to, the philosophy behind the LEGO System in Play. He also looked for executives who were able to inspire and motivate the people under them. As he said in one of his characteristic pep talks at a management meeting around 1960:

We only need managers who know how to motivate people in the right way, and who always put the issue before the person. It is your job to spread this spirit all the way through the ranks, and it is crucial to this company's future that we have managers who really understand this as a priority, and who also have the ability to develop it further.

One of the loyal, dedicated executives close to GKC was so inspired by him as a leader that he later wrote a business book partly about what he learned while on LEGO's management team. Helge Torpe moved to Billund in 1958, and had been hired to deal with sales, marketing, and other commercial activities. The boss Torpe grew to know was a man who thought simply and logically, who invited dialogue and prioritized decisive action. In fact, LEGO's Senior Managing Director and owner was unlike anyone else Helge Torpe had ever met at the top level of business in Denmark:

The way Godtfred led the company during those years of expansion and through the 1960s was actually quite similar to the Japanese style of business management. He wasn't some authoritarian leader who simply trotted out clear, concrete guidelines that everybody had to conform to. Rather, he came out with proposals—constantly. He asked questions. He wanted answers.

Kjeld: *Dad changed his style of leadership and his methods to keep pace with the people he employed and spent time with, not just at home in Billund but also in the foreign companies, where he became really close friends with people like Axel Thomsen in Germany and John Scheidegger in Switzerland. There were some areas in which Dad never became a very good leader. For example, he was very spontaneous and sometimes much too preoccupied with whatever was most important to him at that moment. So it could be difficult for other people to get their ideas across. He also had a tendency to play favorites periodically, preferring certain employees and leaving others slightly out in the cold. A lot of people noticed that, I think. One of the things he was incredibly good at, however, was bringing especially highly qualified, competent people to LEGO, and they all had a tremendous impact on the company's development.*

Fifty-three-year-old Søren Olsen, who was hired as a director shortly before the fire in February 1960 and soon got involved with the major restructuring of production, proved incredibly important for the sense of spirit and community at LEGO during the 1960s and early 1970s. He'd come from a senior management position at the Bjerringbro Sawmill and Furniture Factory, and was known as a firebrand with a broad base of skills and knowledge that ranged from rationalization, produc-

International flags wave outside on the roof of the System House during a meeting at LEGO. The world really had come to Billund!

tion management, and personnel policies to psychology, philosophy, and art. In short, Søren Olsen was a man with expertise in the field that would later be known as human resource management but in 1960 was still emerging only as a concept.

Olsen's expertise and LEGO's terrible growing pains were a large part of why GKC was so eager to hire him. Turnover gross revenue had increased nine-fold over the previous three years, and the constant stream of new hires at Billund resulted in a large, nonhomogeneous staff at the factory and in management. This meant that far too many people were getting too little information and instruction, and there were frequent conflicts over roles and responsibilities.

Eloquent and deft, Søren Olsen introduced a number of new concepts

Søren Olsen came up with LEGO's first HR policy and had a major impact on the culture during the thirteen years he spent in Billund. Regularly supplying the employee magazine with words of wisdom, he was a champion of the LEGO spirit, and shortly before his death in 1982, he wrote to Edith and Godtfred, "Those rich in talents must be simultaneously as stingy with them as a miser and as extravagant with them as a king."

and terms to LEGO, one of the most important of which was "personnel policy." Over the next ten years, he formulated a document capturing in detail what that meant. Drawing on his Inner Mission background and years of friendship with the Kirk Christiansen family, Olsen also took on the difficult task of reminding employees, new as well as old, of the values and culture on which LEGO is based. The multitalented Olsen also explained to workers at the factory, in the most undramatic way, that they didn't need to be afraid of the word "rationalization," because "when done right," Olsen said, "you realize that it actually just means 'common sense.'"

This was Søren Olsen's first foray into the toy industry, and as such he ticked one of GKC's most important boxes when recruiting executives. As he later explained in an interview, "As far as possible, we never employ people from the industry, because they're usually bound by tradition, and that will hamper our development."

Olsen's hiring process was classic GKC. First, there was a long face-to-face conversation, then several follow-up phone calls as well as a monthlong exchange of letters in the summer of 1959, during which GKC threw a brand-new Volvo Amazon into the mix. As a company car, it was a dream, and the car-loving Godtfred decided he had to test-drive it himself before ultimately choosing one in beige for Olsen.

When Olsen retired in the 1970s, he described the company he'd joined fifteen years earlier.

> There was no formal organization at all. No human resources department, no liaison committee, no works security service, and we ran production entirely without schedules and inventory management. On Monday we talked about what we had to do before Friday, and then we did it! The whole thing was very flexible and straightforward. And it wasn't as though this apparent lack of a system entailed any confusion. No, we discussed things together, we stuck together, and the tasks were accomplished along the way, without too much red tape. We communicated almost completely without organization, bureaucracy, or paper!

A couple of months after his hiring, the fire, and the closure of the Wooden-toy Division, Søren Olsen began to show his mettle as a leader at the inauguration of LEGO's new first-floor canteen. At the end of the long staff table, the affable, smiling man, still an unknown quantity to the factory employees, got to his feet. He thanked GKC, as the owner of the company, for "being willing to give the workers such lovely surroundings." He thanked the tradespeople, the manager of the renovation project, and the manager of the canteen. Then Olsen delivered an animated speech of the kind that GKC had been wanting someone other than himself to give. It was a beautiful, heartfelt appeal, touching on the pride and sense of community symbolized by the two plastic bricks that each and every employee was given as they entered the canteen.

You probably think you know these eight-stud bricks like the backs of your hands. But I want you to take another look. I'm not sure you realize what's behind them. This is the most ingenious toy in the world. It's going

Godtfred's ambitions were sky high. LEGO's seemingly limitless success in Europe was contagious.

to conquer the globe. Just think of how much thought, research, experience, molding work, and experimentation went into this little thing to produce such a high level of quality. It's on this little thing that the whole of LEGO's business, both in Denmark and abroad, is based; this is what earns all of us our daily bread.

But we need to move forward. LEGO in Billund must be transformed into a model factory that can be the template for all the LEGO factories that will be built around the world in the years to come. You all have a share in whether this succeeds, and it is this community and collaborative effort that I invite you to join.

The founder of this company, the late Ole Kirk Christiansen, gave the factory its motto: "Only the best is good enough." This still holds true, and we must stick to it going forward. Godtfred has rephrased the motto for 1960 as follows: "Still moving forward, just a little better."

As early as the autumn of 1958, GKC began turning his attention to the English-speaking part of the world. As he put it in his annual report at the LEGO A/S General Assembly, "Our success in Europe is catching. We must tap the American market." But there were several big, unanswered questions involved in this proposal, including whether to look for an American partner or whether future exports to the USA should go via the UK.

LEGO had hired a consultant to conduct various surveys and market analyses, and he reported that the consumption of toys by the USA's sixty million children, from newborn to age fourteen, was promisingly high. Meanwhile, they were also trying to get a clear sense of the market and their potential licensing partners in the UK, which was Europe's second-biggest toy market, known for quality products such as Airfix, Corgi, and Meccano, not to mention William Britain, which had been making toy soldiers since 1893.

The English Kiddicraft bricks had been haunting Billund ever since Ole Kirk first held the small plastic bricks in his hands. GKC dreamed of one day launching the LEGO System in Play in the UK, but he also knew from his investigations at the Danish Patent Office that Hilary F. Page's original patent was probably still in effect, preventing the sale of LEGO bricks in Great Britain.

The patent came under discussion at the negotiating table in December 1958, when Courtaulds Ltd., an international textile company with sixty thousand employees and various subsidiaries, including the plastics factory British Celanese, showed great interest in collaborating with LEGO. Courtaulds wanted to shift production at British Celanese in Wrexham to making plastic toys, and the British chose the Danish LEGO System in Play as the right product to invest in.

The negotiations dragged on into the spring of 1959, largely because LEGO was uncertain. Should they opt for a licensing deal, or try to export the product themselves? While GKC and his closest associates vacillated, Courtaulds had the patent issue regarding Hilary Page and Kiddicraft examined by British lawyers. They eventually came down in favor of LEGO, in large part because of LEGO's further original development of the brick in 1958, when they added the three tubes inside and improved its gripping or "clutch" power.

Godtfred still hesitated. Was now the right time to venture into such a large market? After the most breakneck period of expansion in LEGO's history, shouldn't they take a moment to breathe, consolidate, and concentrate on the markets they already had? Godtfred's advisers, however, were unequivocal, writing in a memo, "Companies of Courtaulds' size and positive outlook don't grow on trees."

It was a huge company with a lot of capital, an international concern with plenty of industrial experience. It could be an invaluable ally for LEGO, not just in Great Britain but also in places such as Australia, Ireland, and Hong Kong. And maybe—who knew—it could be a golden ticket into the USA.

Again, Godtfred showed himself to be a man of action. He struck while the iron was hot, setting up a sales company in July, British LEGO Limited. The contract with Courtaulds took the shape of a licensing deal for production at the factory in Wrexham, and in January 1960 LEGO appeared for the first time in the UK at the annual toy fair in Brighton.

Sales were strong right from the start, and their partnership with

Courtaulds was going swimmingly. Only one year later, in 1961, they also found a solution to the question of sales in North America. LEGO entered into an agreement with Samsonite Corp., known across the world for its trendy suitcases, beauty cases, and briefcases made of hard plastic.

The partnership, though it got off to a good start, was not a success. As Godtfred later concluded, "It's never a good idea to join forces with a company whose primary interest is in another field, and they were incredibly good at suitcases." Samsonite also turned out to be incredibly good at striking lucrative deals. The one they entered with LEGO meant that the Americans had exclusive rights to produce and sell LEGO on the American market for ninety-nine years, in exchange for paying royalties to the Danish company. LEGO ended up taking a tremendous financial hit ten years later, when they wanted out of the binding contract and their unsatisfactory partnership with the suitcase company.

Kjeld: *It was actually our Swiss director, John Scheidegger, who had previously worked for Samsonite, who persuaded my dad to give the suitcase company a license to produce and sell the LEGO bricks on the American market. That agreement wasn't just expensive, it was also difficult for us to get out of, since it didn't go anything near as well as we'd hoped during the 1960s. The contract still had ages to run, and it was virtually impossible to negotiate it back. It wasn't actually like my father to sign such a bad deal, but at that point, when LEGO's exports were spreading so quickly across Europe, he must have thought it would be much too complicated and difficult to set up an independent company on a continent like North America, which in those days seemed so far away. "We've got to have someone to help us there, whatever the cost!"*

In 1962, however, the future of LEGO's American adventure with Samsonite still looked bright. A single photograph from the opening of the big LEGO exhibition in New York in March, when the LEGO System in Play was launched, speaks for itself. A short Danish man with a huge grin was doing a balancing act, standing on a little house between a

LEGO and Godtfred in Manhattan in 1961.

couple of skyscrapers made of LEGO bricks, to show what the toy could withstand. On the wall hanging behind him, the words "LEGO now at last in the USA" were painted in big, bold letters. The Vikings had come to town, and the American press flocked to see them. Thirty or forty journalists from newspapers and TV channels covered the event, and the following day the whole back page of a section of the *New York Times* was devoted to LEGO, as Godtfred wrote in a letter to the company's Danish lifeline, the managing director at Vejle Bank.

One year earlier, before signing the contract with Samsonite, GKC and his legal adviser, Ole Nielsen, had gone to Chicago to remove a serious obstacle: the American toy brand ELGO, which since 1947 had been known for its "American Plastic Bricks," which were very similar to the Kiddicraft bricks and LEGO's very first version in terms of their look and quality. In the 1950s, the American Plastic Bricks were still sold on the American market in boxes and tins, and ELGO ran a major campaign halfway through the decade—"Plan and build your *own* city"—which featured colorful drawings of streets and towns reminiscent of LEGO's town plan from 1955.

The name ELGO wasn't a copy of LEGO, but rather a contraction of the first two letters of the owners' surnames (Harold Elliot and Samuel Goss). They had begun trading under the name in 1941, well before anybody outside Denmark had heard of LEGO. But Godtfred felt that the two might easily be confused, and so for several reasons they were an unfortunate competitor to have on the American market.

His meeting with representatives from the toy company Halsam, which owned the rights to the name ELGO, took place at a hotel in Chicago, and GKC later explained that the Americans initially demanded $250,000 to sell the trademark, equivalent to just over three million dollars today. Negotiations were slow, but over the course of the night the Danes knocked the sum down to $25,000. Still, the Americans wouldn't sign anything until they had the money in hand. That was a tall order in 1961; as a Danish person abroad, you couldn't just wander down to the nearest bank and take out a huge sum of money, nor could you get it transferred from home, because of Danish currency exchange restrictions.

The situation was desperate. First, GKC called the Managing Director, Holm, at Vejle Bank who knew better than anyone that the Danish currency regulations were utterly inflexible. His next call was to LEGO's director in Switzerland, John Scheidegger. Through his personal contacts in the more accommodating Swiss banking world, he arranged to wire twenty five thousand dollars to Godtfred, clearing a major hurdle on LEGO's road to the American market.

The process of internationalization was proceeding apace, and the LEGO family soon got a foothold in Japan and Morocco, as well as the USA, Canada, Australia, Singapore, and Hong Kong. The residents of Billund noticed with increasing frequency the meetings and conferences

Eleven-year-old Kjeld watches the strangers. From left: Mario Mitrani and his wife (Italy); Hans Grohe (Austria); Rene Frankfort (Belgium); Ragnar Lyngra (Norway); K. Lameris (Holland); John Scheidegger (Switzerland); Bror Åsberg (Sweden); Sales Manager Aage Jørgensen (Norway); and Exports Manager Troels Petersen from LEGO. Many years later, in a speech to her fifty-year-old son, Edith remarked, "When I see this picture, Kjeld, I always think of the biblical story about the twelve-year-old Jesus in the temple, where he listened to the wise men talking. It looks like that's what you're doing here!" *Private collection.*

happening in the System House, at which foreign flags were hoisted on the roof and languages never heard in Grene Parish were spoken all day long.

LEGO's owner found it a challenge. "I barely learned to speak Danish in school," he remarked in an interview, explaining that he was constantly surrounded by multilingual employees, and that the language difficulties had occasionally been to his advantage. In important negotiations abroad, it gave him a little extra time to make decisions if the communication was slow.

Godtfred got a chance to go back to school when his fruitful partnership with Courtaulds in Great Britain developed into a friendship with several leading executives at British LEGO. In 1962, a Mr. Stimson offered to arrange a long, intensive language course at Wrexham, and one of LEGO's correspondence secretaries replied that the managing director was definitely interested in "two or three weeks in Wales in order to brush up [his] English" but that sadly he was busy with a trip to the USA, and would return to the matter sometime in the spring. But the idea never went any further.

Kjeld: *Dad never learned any languages at school and didn't know English, but he did learn a little bit of German, although not enough to carry on a conversation. He joked about it a bit, but if he had to give a speech he could start with a few words in English or German before switching into Danish. So it was quite a lengthy business, giving speeches and lectures at the international meetings in Billund. Some of the foreign managers didn't speak English or German, either. Behind the participants at the meeting they'd have three or four professional interpreters and simultaneous translators.*

As they became more international, LEGO needed employees to deal with correspondence, contract management, and so on. The first new hires were taken on in 1958, and housing was built for them at the bottom of Godtfred and Edith's garden, which later became known as the "Jomfruburet," an old-fashioned Danish word that literally means "Maidens' Cage," but was used to refer to a room belonging to a young, unmarried woman. The building was intended as accommodation for English-, German-, and French-speaking young women, who rented lodgings in the shared block for 90 kroner a month.

Kjeld: *Obviously, they couldn't just live in rooms in town or the local area, Dad thought, so they needed a decent place to stay near the System House, where they were much in demand during the daytime, what with all the correspondence from across the world. The first secretaries who came to Billund from the business school in Aarhus were named Eybye*

and Ehlers. We addressed each other quite informally at the company
even in those days, but we still used people's surnames, so the two secre-
taries were called Eybye, not Inge, and Ehlers, instead of Lisbeth.

Right from the start of his adventures in exports, Godtfred's plan
was to build an organization that gathered the foreign sales departments into a family-style community rooted in Billund. The idea was
that they would all be working in line with the same principles as their
parent company in Denmark, although each would be able to adapt to
the vastly differing situation in their local country, and no one from
the Danish team would undermine the foreign managers' initiative and
zeal. This became a fundamental and global principle of management,
which in Godtfred's words was about "always working diplomatically
so that we guide without stripping the senior executives in the various
countries of responsibility."

At the core of the organization was the LEGO System in Play, or, as
Godtfred put this shared idea, "We are one big LEGO family. We consider it our life's work to create toys that have long-term potential and
afford the best opportunities for play."

The physical center of this global business was the System House,
which today, after a long and tumultuous period as LEGO HQ and Billund's town hall, is home to the history of the LEGO company, in the
form of a company museum. The System House was built in two phases
in 1958 and 1961, situated on a contested corner of the town where the
local barber had owned a house for many years, refusing to sell to the
"high and mighty" LEGO company. In 1957, while Ole Kirk was still
alive, a local paper described the protracted feud with immense relish.

The barber's house and back garden are wedged into the factory site.
Ole Kirk has been able to purchase the other neighboring properties for
LEGO, and the manufacturer has offered the barber a new villa with
central heating and a modern barber's salon in exchange for the old shop.
But the barber won't sell!
"I'll show you there's something you can't buy with money, little Ole!"

The barber is sticking to his guns—and the smith is on his side. And now Ole Kirk is wondering whether to build a stretch of wall from the factory site to the barber's house!

"All right, then I'll tell you what," some mischievous little voice has popped into the manufacturer's head, "I'll build that bit of wall so that the barber has to carry his fuel from the street and through all his rooms and kitchen to get it to the back of the house . . ."

In 1958, LEGO was granted permission to buy the corner plot after all, and for many years it marked the entryway from the town to the factory site on Systemvej. Speaking of the new System House building, which functioned as LEGO's central hub in Billund, GKC remarked, "It's the mother house where senior employees and their staff, to a certain extent, will come to get inspiration and guidance and where ideas can be gathered and coordinated."

The System House was also the place where the management and administrative staff had their offices and meeting rooms. This was where the modern and tastefully designed conference room known as the System Hall was located, featuring a wall-to-wall map of the world, serving as a symbol of LEGO's global ambitions. Every year until the beginning of the 1970s, the whole international LEGO family convened here for a few days' constructive conversation.

Kjeld: *It was a fantastic space. We were thinking big even then, and the goal was clearly defined: We're going global! We wanted our own setup everywhere, run by local talent, people who were close to their markets and knew everything about them. We specifically didn't want to be working with Danes we'd sent out there from Billund, but with citizens of the individual countries. First, Dad had a nice corner office in the System House with a little group of sofas at one end and then a big desk by the corner windows with a view over Hovedgaden and the factory. Later he moved upstairs and got an even bigger office with a meeting table and its own access to the flat roof. When I visited him, I loved going out there. It was up there that we raised all the flags when we had visitors from* *abroad. It became a tradition that the executives from the various countries went up onto the roof and raised their national flag the first time they came to Billund. The flags fluttering in the wind were an extraordinary sight. The whole world had come to Billund!*

The meetings at the conferences consisted of presentations, plenary sessions, and group work, with these deeply committed men speaking, listening, and smoking like chimneys. Orla Jørgensen remembered their shared enthusiasm about the new ideas that were put forward, in particular. "There was a genuinely pioneering spirit, and a high degree of cohesion across the various national mindsets."

An important part of the LEGO conferences in the 1960s was about strengthening this sense of social community. When people of different nationalities got to know one another well, it was like being part of a

The "System Hall," the large meeting room with a map of the world on the back wall, where the first international conferences were held and where the air was thick with different languages and the smoke of the various cigar- and cigarette-smoking LEGO executives.

big extended family and meeting distant cousins for the first time. The foreign bosses' spouses were invited on the trips to Denmark, too, and while the gentlemen (which they all were at the time) put the world to rights at LEGO and discussed "how to realize its potential," as Godtfred loved to call it, the ladies were escorted by Edith on excursions to Aarhus, where they went shopping in the city center and sailing in the bay. On the final evening of a conference, all the couples would be invited to a cocktail party at the family's architect-designed, single-story mansion, which boasted a sea of bedrooms and four large living spaces arranged around a central atrium.

> **Kjeld:** *Our new house, which was down a long driveway behind the old one, was finished in January 1960. At that time there weren't many places to stay the night in Billund—only the Inn, in fact, which maybe wasn't the most respectable place, now that we were getting all these visits from abroad during the year. So Dad built our house large enough that there was always room for overnight guests. It might be Axel Thomsen from Germany, John Scheidegger from Switzerland, Bror Åsberg from Sweden, or one of the other foreign distributors and directors. They'd stay one or two days with us, so in that sense they weren't just part of LEGO, but also of our family. All of that helped shape me. I mean, I was only an onlooker, at twelve or thirteen, but I could see and hear, and in that sense I grew up with the company and knew all the people who were driving this incredible progress.*

LEGO's main challenge in the early 1960s was to get a grip on the company's internal affairs. Innovative ideas poured out of the workshops and offices; there was a strong pioneering spirit. Growth was felt everywhere in LEGO HQ, which was constantly having to be expanded to accommodate more employees in the factory and offices. In short, everything ballooned at once, and it soon became apparent that something had to be done to stop the company careening off track. As the virtuoso wordsmith and director Søren Olsen put it, "Can we keep the plow in the furrow?"

One of the management devices GKC used was a system of communication that consisted of various differently colored A4 folders, which were distributed to all senior executives. In his presentation, he explained that the purpose of these was "to promote loyalty in the company through internal information." The communication system was named "LEGO Internal," and it housed all the most important information and decisions from top-level management, as well as summaries of presentations and discussions.

Around the same time, GKC introduced a special forum he called "Worth Knowing." These evening events, which explored issues related to work, the company, and the LEGO System in Play, were aimed at staff at a certain level of seniority, who were expected to attend lectures, film screenings, and other forms of educational content once a month.

The purpose was also to reinforce a sense of cohesion and make LEGO's growing cohort of middle-managers even better at motivating their teams. As GKC said, if you wanted to create something of quality, you needed motivated employees who understood the demands being made of them. "In a modern organization, it is not enough to hand out orders; the person who receives the orders must understand why they are given, and why they must be carried out in a particular way."

At their core, the Worth Knowing meetings were about general education, very much in the spirit of college-level studies, and were given an additional boost when Søren Olsen took charge of the evenings. His motley list of speakers featured everyone from the head of Danfoss, a family-owned Danish thermostat maker, who talked about organizational structure, to local police officer Qvist Sørensen, who dropped by the factory one evening to discuss town planning, and the lack thereof, in Billund. Also on the program was psychologist Sten Hegeler from Copenhagen, who taught the LEGO managers about the importance of play for children. Another evening, Pastor Philipsen from Fredericia discussed the question "Does God have a hand in everything that happens?" Strøjer Sørensen, a senior staff member at Vejle Bank, had the honor of wrapping up the final Worth Knowing season in 1963 with his lecture "Does Money Make the World Go Round?"

When the new wheels were produced, thirteen- or fourteen-year-old Kjeld could finally build proper models of cars. "I wrote little stories about each of the cars. The size of the engine, how fast they could drive, and so on. I also priced them so that people would want to buy them."

It was a good question, especially if you were the managing director and owner of a company that had outdone itself for eight years in a row. In 1963, gross revenue reached a dizzying 35 million kroner, and LEGO bricks were flying off the shelves, particularly now that some had been given wheels.

The two-by-two stud wheels with rubber tires were invented by model maker Knud Møller way back in 1958, and it was an idea that had been taken back out and put into production. The product was an instant hit, and when it was followed up with gear wheels in 1970, new, more technically elaborate possibilities opened up for all children who dreamed of being an engineer or working in construction.

Kjeld: *I have always loved cars, and as a boy I built countless different models. Especially when we invented the wheel—the LEGO wheel, that* *is! I called my big collection "LECA," which, of course, stood for LEGO CARS, and actually I even made a LECA garage for the whole fleet. There were big American cars and small English sports vehicles and whatever else I could think of. Building on the commercial success of the LEGO wheel, in 1963, for the first time in the company's history, we began selling sets, which were LEGO building sets that included the instructions. In the beginning they were pretty small sets—a truck, for example, which could turn its wheels with the help of a knob on the roof of the cabin. There was also one with a white off-road vehicle, which I had designed. Otherwise I was mostly building big cars in those days, and with the cogs I could now also build whole gearboxes for them, with gears you could shift and moving cylinders.*

Two other landmark LEGO products saw the light of day in the early 1960s. One was the Scale Model line, which contained a handful of new, flatter LEGO elements that let the user plan and build more detailed models and homes. Just as radically, these new white, gray, and black LEGO bricks were aimed at adults.

The other product was Modulex, that had smaller bricks conforming to a standardized system known as modular coordination. A one-stud brick measured five millimeters [0.196 inches] on each side. This product was intended for the professional construction industry, the idea being that these small elements could be used to build very detailed models of various projects.

Like so much else during this period, initiative came from the unflagging GKC. He hoped not only to tempt more adult hobbyists into playing with the LEGO System, but also to persuade architects, engineers, designers, and developers to use these new, smaller LEGO elements as tools for 3D design and planning in the construction industry, a sector that was undergoing profound transformation. Over the course of the 1950s, architecture and old-fashioned construction methods were revolutionized with the advent of simple, standardized components and modules, which could be mass-produced in factories and later installed on-site.

The Scale Model line was an ambitious attempt to bring the LEGO brick into the adult world, enabling not just hobbyists and model builders, but also architects and engineers to design modern houses like Godtfred and Edith's villa from 1959. For Edith's ninetieth birthday in 2014, some exclusive building sets were produced in the LEGO Architecture series called "Edith's House" and were given to family members. Note the recommended age on the box: 90+.

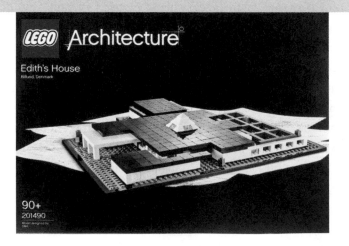

An example of this technology in action was Godtfred and Edith's hyper-modern one-story white house, which they decided to build in 1958 on a large plot behind the old house on Systemvej. As they mulled over various suggestions on architect Åge Bundgård's drawing board, Godtfred got an idea.

Kjeld: *At the beginning of the construction process, Dad was irritated by the fact that we couldn't build a model of our house with ordinary LEGO bricks. That gave him the idea for a completely new system of smaller bricks that would enable people to model a potential project in great detail. The idea grew and grew within my dad, who was imagining that his idea could become even bigger than the toy business. Imagine if they could get not just architects and engineers to use the two new systems, but also all the adults in the early 1960s who were dreaming of a detached house that they themselves had played a role in designing? It would be a massive new market for LEGO!*

At no other point in his life had Godtfred ever thought so radically, or so completely shifted his focus from the LEGO System in Play, the importance of which he constantly stressed to his employees. He called the foundation and potential of his vision the "LEGO Column," entailing a four-step development process he presented to his staff for the first time at a meeting in the System House in 1959.

Step One was the familiar LEGO System for children. Step Two was "the product refined and reworked on another scale, as a hobby for adults." Step Three was for engineers, architects, and other professionals in the construction industry. And Step Four was an almost philosophical superstructure that looked toward a world, as GKC explained, in which playing with LEGO would lead to a global shift not just in the way we build and construct but also the way we think and behave as human beings, almost along the lines of an evolutionary shift.

His vision traced a line from the abstract games of childhood, played using small plastic bricks, to concrete construction work executed by adults using regular bricks and modules. Every vision mixes reality and imagination, and GKC saw it all in his mind's eye as he outlined the concept in broad strokes to his employees. "In the future, more and more houses will be built entirely of standard elements according to our modular system, without significant labor on the building site. Using all our experience so far and through systematic research, we will give something good to humanity that no one else has dreamed of."

Not all the staff members around the table were able to follow the full trajectory of GKC's soaring idea and imagine LEGO becoming a tool in the building trade. But the plan of action that GKC's presentation put forward was easy to grasp. It was about expanding LEGO's target audience, not simply beyond children to adolescents and adult hobbyists, but also to millions of professionals in the construction industry worldwide.

A considerable increase in revenue would happen almost of its own accord, explained GKC, when the adults of the future, who used LEGO either as a hobby or in their working lives, gave their children LEGO bricks. Someone who was enthusiastic as a child would instinctively understand as an adult that good, imaginative play could carry over to real-life construction. The idea sounded financially promising, and an enthusiastic Axel Thomsen from LEGO Germany exclaimed spontaneously at the meeting, "We can become rulers in the field of toys!"

For a while, the tireless entrepreneur side of Godtfred was completely preoccupied with the human and social aspects of this further "grown-up" development of the LEGO System in Play. In a LEGO internal communication file to senior employees, he described it as almost an evolutionary process:

> The LEGO idea involves the pedagogical task of educating people in a simple, appropriate, rational, and well-thought-through method of construction. Through a generation of children brought up with the LEGO System, the thought will inevitably be pushed into the subconscious of millions of people: "Why make something difficult, when it's so simple with the LEGO System."

GKC was so convinced of this "evolutionary" concept, that at a senior management meeting in the spring of 1963, while discussing the potential for confusion between the familiar LEGO products for children and the two different lines for adult hobbyists and professionals, he remarked that, "We aren't a toy factory, we are a LEGO System company with a special purpose."

Kjeld: *The sets for adults that we launched in 1962–1963 as the Scale Model line never had much success, but Dad's overall concept—that you could build more realistic things with smaller bricks—ended up producing something extremely valuable for the LEGO System for children: a new type of brick, the flat and thin one, the one that's a third the height of a regular brick and is an incredibly important part of our building system today. This flat brick in all the LEGO colors immediately afforded a ton of new and completely different possibilities. Suddenly, as I discovered for myself, you could build much more realistic planes, ships, cars, and space rockets . . . Sputnik, Saturn, whatever they were called.*

Modulex was taken off the market after a couple of years, and in 1965 Godtfred's idea of revolutionizing the construction industry was shelved as well. Yet the fundamental idea wasn't abandoned; a new company was set up called A/S MODULEX, where instead of being a working tool for architects, the small bricks were developed into modular signage and wayfinding.

It was the first but far from the last time that Godtfred ignored his own injunction never to take the focus off the LEGO System in Play. His ideas and initiatives continued to be developed, sometimes at breakneck speed. GKC was a dynamo, working all day long and often late into the night. At home, however, in one of Jutland's most modern one-story houses, with huge windows, eight bedrooms, four living spaces, a hobby room, atrium, sauna, and a gorgeous modern kitchen, he was sorely missed by his family.

A teenaged Kjeld built increasingly large and more complex systems incorporating LEGO. LEGO pit stops and stands were added to his Scalextric racing track, while a gigantic LEGO bridge was developed into a total work of engineering. *Private collection.*

Kjeld: *In a way, Dad was more ambitious than my grandfather. He was much more about "work, work, work." He often came home accompanied by some colleague or other. They'd just have to keep working on some problem, and then the guest had to have a bite to eat, and in many cases my mother wouldn't have been given any advance warning at all. That was my dad's way; he was straightforward and spontaneous. When I think back, I really didn't get much time with him as a father. He was always busy, either physically absent or sitting by himself, absorbed in his own thoughts. The only way I could really reach him was by showing him my LEGO buildings. Then he lit up, and we'd have a conversation,*

while he asked for my opinion, for example about my Scalextric racing track, where I had built stands and pit stops around the track out of LEGO bricks.

In 1963, the Billund Mission House celebrated its fiftieth birthday. The national secretary of the Inner Mission, Stefan Ottesen, came all the way from Copenhagen with his gift, a new Bible, bringing greetings from the governing council. In his speech, which was about the importance of having God's blessing, he said, "There are differences in the conditions for spiritual growth, but we must admit that God has blessed this town in a special way."

That was safe to say. Like the rest of Danish society, Billund in the 1960s was in a state of flux, swept along by the historic rise in prosperity, which meant, in turn, that LEGO became ever richer—and increasingly unmoored from its once unshakable religious basis. The secularization of the business was a symptom not just of the spirit of the age, but also reflected the many new employees who arrived from all parts of the country, as well, of course, as becoming a more international company.

The prelude to this spiritual shift took place in 1960, when the trade union movement wanted LEGO to abandon Ole Kirk's old agreement with the Kristelig Dansk Fællesforbund, the Christian Danish Federation (today known as Krifa), and encouraged the workforce to organize into a union that would fall under the Landsorganisationen, the Danish Confederation of Trade Unions. Since the 1930s, the old agreement had meant that if a new hire wasn't already in a union, it was his or her duty to join the Christian Danish Federation.

During the initial phase of the negotiations with the unions, LEGO's management tried to stand firm, arguing on the basis of the company's history. They pointed out that their connection to the Christian Danish Federation had great symbolic significance for LEGO's founder. It was no use. The foundation of the old LEGO spirit, Ole Kirk's sincere commitment to his faith, was crumbling, and when in the autumn of 1960 the employees were allowed to choose which union they wanted to belong to, there was a mass exodus from the Christian Federation.

It was a new era at LEGO. The Worth Knowing meetings, at which attendees would always have sung a song or two from the Inner Mission LEGO hymnal, grew fewer and further between, and the decision was eventually made to put an end to the daily morning services. Paradoxically, the decision was made by a priest, Gustav A. Højlund, who'd been appointed as LEGO's first independent Head of Personnel in 1962 and quickly realized that Ole Kirk's morning ritual had run its course.

The decision to hire fifty-one-year-old Højlund, who had over twenty years' experience in the church, was made by both Godtfred and Søren Olsen. They knew him from the Christian community, and realized instinctively that Højlund, whose résumé included such varied jobs as hospital orderly, farmhand, digger and concrete laborer, ship's minister in Hamburg, and embassy priest in Stockholm, would be able to deal with all types of employees and handle personnel challenges from a "socio-Christian point of view," as an internal memo noted.

Godtfred, however, was somewhat apprehensive. What would the other managers, with their multiyear backgrounds in business, say about a theologian suddenly appearing in the meeting room? Godtfred wrote point-blank to Højlund that several of them expressed astonishment; that astonishment had made Godtfred wonder whether the question of who should be appointed head of personnel was, in fact, fully settled.

Dear Højlund!

I heard a talk last night at the Rotary about the importance of making sure us human beings are properly placed, and I can't help but say to you: if you are happy being a priest and it can continue to fulfill you, then you should stick to it. Then it would be wrong of us to try to tempt you away. Only if you can be happier and find even greater fulfilment by taking on a role in personnel, should you renounce your ministry. And it is clear to me that a mixture would not be right. It should be by virtue of your capabilities as Head of Personnel that you pursue a Christian calling.

In the summer of 1962, Pastor Højlund made the front page of several Danish newspapers, through headlines like "Removing the cassock and collar and going into business" and "Priest takes job at toy factory." Godtfred had already asked his new executive to keep any communication with the press to a minimum, determining that he'd be the one to publicly defend the controversial hire, and on July 26 he explained in the *Aarhus Stiftstidende* that LEGO was motivated by humanistic concerns, despite appearances. "In a big industry, a lot of money is invested in machines, but usually very little in the people who look after them. This, for us, is the crucial issue. The machine age requires a radical shift in the treatment of personnel, if humanity is to survive."

Two or three decades before words like "HR Department," "performance reviews," "satisfaction surveys," and "personality tests" were to become a generally accepted part of Danish working life, LEGO launched into an experiment to tackle the challenge that was increasingly attracting attention in post-war offices: employee well-being in the workplace.

Højlund set about his task with enthusiasm, approaching the job in his new congregation with great commitment and plenty of zeal, but despite his good intentions, the experiment didn't work. The cultural divide proved too great, both for Højlund and for LEGO, and in 1964, after two years at Billund, he returned to the priesthood. News articles about him and LEGO splashed across the front pages yet again, and even a tabloid paper from Copenhagen, hardly the most spiritual publication, wanted to know what Pastor Højland had learned from his two years in Billund. Højlund replied in a somewhat revealing way, that hints at what his experience must have been.

"The worker is supported by a community of fellow employees and supports them in his turn. They are aware that they are capable of performing their task; they have a sense of security and a harmony of which there is no trace among those in the more exposed roles close to the top."

Although the influence of the Inner Mission had significantly weakened in the 1960s and the first sentence of the draft personnel policy ("LEGO shall be led according to a Christian outlook") had been removed, Godtfred never made a secret of his religious beliefs. His faith wasn't nearly as strong and vibrant as his father's, but it accompanied him throughout the arc of his life. After Ole Kirk's death in 1958, Godtfred regularly mentioned that he missed the sound of church bells in the town, which was something his father had often talked about when he was alive.

During one of his stays in the USA, Godtfred was inspired by a small town center where the church, library, theater, cafeteria, kindergarten, and other cultural spaces were all assembled under one roof. Coincidentally, the bishop of the Diocese of Ribe, Henrik Dons Christensen, had made the same observation during a trip to the States, which Godtfred learned one day during a conversation the two of them had. The next question seemed inevitable: could the bishop imagine a similar religious and cultural center in a rapidly growing town like Billund, which didn't have a church? Godtfred certainly could, and he set out to realize his idea with the same enthusiasm, stubbornness, and analytical flair with which he pursued every project pertaining to Billund and LEGO.

During this period there was a serious shortage of housing for the influx of new staff. Building on his father's idea of offering people at the factory not just a place to live, but also the chance to have their own house and garden, GKC built a series of single-family homes on Fasanvej, Bogfinkevej, and Solsortevej in Billund between 1958 and 1962. He purchased an agricultural property and subdivided the land, making space for twenty houses, each intended for LEGO employees. An assistant did all the paperwork, and each house ended up costing 56,000 kroner, with a deposit of 5,000, for which GKC personally acted as guarantor.

LEGO's tremendous growth had left its mark on the small town, which had swelled from eight hundred to two thousand inhabitants over ten years, and now faced major challenges in virtually all areas of civic administration. As Officer Qvist Sørensen pointed out at his Worth Knowing lecture in LEGO's canteen, the town council hadn't really managed to keep up with the company's staggering expansion. In a sense, this was understandable, if one considers that, until 1954, the local government had no offices in Billund other than the council members' private living rooms. The chairman had been in charge of all correspondence, while the treasurer collected the taxes and did the accounts.

In traditional Jutland fashion, the town council had been hesitant and skeptical about LEGO's success for far too long. Was it worth investing in new homes, drainage systems, water supply systems, better infrastructure, and more public buildings? Apart from a newly constructed assisted-living facility for the elderly, which housed the council's first offices in the basement, and the Billund Housing Association's residential block on Lærkevej, no major public works were carried out until Ole Kirk's sons, led by Godtfred, appealed directly to the town council.

Godtfred had big plans for LEGO and Billund, and around 1960, he
struggled to get the town council to see the benefit of new housing,
more facilities for children, and better infrastructure. He is seen here in
conversation with Town Council Chairman Hans Jensen. Top: Billund from
the air in the early 1960s. The System House, the Lion House, the factory
building from 1942, the Molding Division, the exports warehouse, single-
family dwellings for LEGO staff, and, to the far right, Godtfred and Edith's
new house.

10 VIGTIGE KENDETEGN FOR LEGO	
1	LEGO = ubegrænsede muligheder i leg
2	LEGO = for piger, for drenge
3	LEGO = begejstring til alle aldre
4	LEGO = leg hele året
5	LEGO = sund og rolig leg
6	LEGO = de fleste legetimer
7	LEGO = udvikling, fantasi, skaberevner
8	LEGO = mere LEGO, mangedoblet værdi
9	LEGO = let supplering
10	LEGO = gennemført kvalitet

"The Ten Most Important LEGO Characteristics," which Godtfred presented internationally in 1963, were the basis of the development of LEGO products for decades to come:

1. Unlimited play possibilities
2. For girls, for boys
3. Enthusiasm at all ages
4. Play all year round
5. Stimulating and harmonious play
6. Endless hours of play
7. Imagination, creativity, development
8. More LEGO, greater play value
9. Easy to supplement
10. Sustained quality

In a long letter, the family set out a plan to develop Billund, dangling a carrot in front of the passive council members' noses. The company offered to gift the town roughly eighteen acres of land for a park or recreation center, something Billund sorely needed. And to make the bait truly irresistible, they also promised that LEGO would cover the construction costs, estimated to be roughly fifty thousand kroner.

The donation mentioned in the letter has to be seen in the context of the future residential areas LEGO envisioned in the town. Billund could become an oasis, particularly for LEGO employees, who didn't have farming in their blood.

In time, at relatively little cost, we can create a beautiful, remarkable layout in which the heath serves as an exceptionally lovely contrast to all the new construction. Eventually we can add a swimming pool, tennis courts, a playground, and lots of other things, which will help accomplish the goal of making Billund a town that is attractive to talented people, valuable members of society who will take initiative and build a future. Why not make Billund a town of which people say, "It's the leading rural town" or it's "an oasis in the heath" or "the town with that fresh new

initiative"? LEGO would love to help with this task, to make this prospect
a possibility.

Lastly, they specified that a church should be included into the prospective town plan: "When the new recreational area comes, we will
recommend the old facility as an excellent location for a church." The
council could count on LEGO providing support to build that, too.

If you asked Godtfred, the council's decision-making was far too
slow. In 1962, running short of patience, he sent another letter, this time
rather sharper in tone. LEGO was on the verge of another major expansion of its factory, but the town's development still hadn't advanced
one bit. Something needed to be done now, wrote Godtfred, rattling
his saber. "I would go so far as to say that if we're not able to make
this development proceed hand in hand, in earnest, it would be better
for LEGO to cease its activities now and plan to build its new industry
somewhere else."

This is language that even the most reactionary forces on the town
council could understand. In February 1963, the Council Chairman
Hans Jensen informed the papers that they'd hired a town planner
from Copenhagen, who was to come up with a "development plan" for
Billund's future, which would include homes, a town hall, a shopping
center, a hotel, and public buildings. The chairman acknowledged that
LEGO, which by now had seven hundred employees, would be the back-
bone of this new plan. It was clear, however, that he'd had his hands full,
convincing everyone on the council that the more children across the
world play with LEGO, the less the citizens of Billund will have to pay
in taxes. "We want to stay grounded. Out here on the old Jutish heath,
we don't usually get ideas above our station, but it's the council's duty
to look into the future, insofar as that is possible. We must, in our own
interests, pave the way for steady development, which cannot be hap-
hazard."

The older people on the farms, who hadn't forgotten Ole Kirk's modest, unselfish efforts at the Mission House and in the town in general,

remarked that his son was playing rather more fast and loose with the Christian commandments, especially when it came to the one about remembering the Sabbath and keeping it holy, which was something LEGO's founder had never neglected. But Godtfred, who as a young man wrote to an acquaintance during an existential crisis, "I know only one way—turning to God," more often returned to his office as soon as Sunday service was over and lunch was finished. On his many lengthy trips away, he worked in his hotel room on the Sabbath, preoccupied with his thoughts and calculations. How could LEGO keep most shift workers and molding machines going round the clock, all week long, including Sundays?

"Big words rarely do pious deeds," as the old Danish saying goes. This was how some of Billund's inhabitants viewed Godtfred's vision in the early 1960s. Not only did Ole Kirk's son want every child and adult on earth playing with LEGO bricks, but there were now rumors that he was getting local governments and councils on board with the crackpot idea that Billund should host the largest airport in the region.

The almost Hans Christian Andersen–esque fairy tale about Billund Airport began in 1961, when LEGO assumed part-ownership of a small propeller-driven aircraft. At that point there was nowhere to land a plane in Billund, so GKC often had to be dropped off in Esbjerg, which had an excellent grassy field, but no electric lighting. That could quickly have been remedied if the relevant official on Esbjerg Council had been as savvy a businessman as Godtfred. As GKC later explained, "I made an offer to Esbjerg Council that we would pay for half the lighting system. We would also build a hangar at our own expense. But I was told it couldn't be done. Private and public sectors couldn't work together like that . . . end of discussion!"

After having been given the cold shoulder in Esbjerg, Godtfred took matters into his own hands. He bought a large plot on the outskirts of Billund and built a grass landing strip with the aid of his first pilot at LEGO Airways, Hans Erik Christensen, also known as HEC. The landing strip was ready in the spring of 1962, and a few months later Godtfred bought a Piper Aztec, which HEC and his cousin, in the style of

The new Piper Aztec, just landed after a long trip across the Atlantic. Edith and Godtfred thanked two tired pilots, Hans Jørgen Christensen (left) and his cousin Hans Erik Christensen, also called HEC, who was later tasked with constructing Billund Airport and became the first Airport Manager.

the famous American aviator Charles Lindbergh, flew home to Jutland across the Atlantic from the American East Coast. The plane landed in Billund after a twenty-hour flight over Newfoundland and Ireland. A very long trip, recalled HEC, during which the two pilots had to urinate in empty Thermoses they later emptied over the Irish coast.

One month later, a hangar was added to the small airfield, and the landing strip was lined with colorful LEGO bricks of mammoth proportions so they could be seen from the air. The Piper plane was immediately used for business travel, and Johannes was put in charge of providing the necessary landing lights for when the plane returned home at dusk. Lighting was accomplished with the aid of some employees' private cars and Johannes's big truck, which were positioned along the runway between the huge bricks, with their headlights on.

Johannes was also the one in radio contact with the pilots as they approached Billund. HEC, who had been promoted to airport manager in 1964, remembers the crackly sound of Ole Kirk's oldest son when the pilots in the cockpit asked about the visibility in Billund.

"How far can you see, Johannes?"

"I can see quite far, Hans Erik—all the way to the forest, actually!"

"Fine, then we're coming in now, Johannes!"

Stationary lights were soon added along the landing strip, which was also improved so that other, smaller aircraft could make use of the facilities at Billund. And before long there was talk that Denmark's second-biggest airport could well be located in Grene Parish.

A number of large and mid-sized West Jutland towns had already put in their bids to build a provincial airport. Officials in the Ministry of Transport in Copenhagen couldn't quite picture how the project would come together in Billund, not in such a small town on a boggy heath with only eight hundred inhabitants, and with no major access roads or train connections since the line between Vejle and Grindsted had closed in 1957.

But Godtfred could picture the whole thing clearly and, with his irresistible faith in his own energies and power of judgment, he flung himself tirelessly into lobbying, setting up an endless parade of meetings with local and national politicians, administrative officers, mayors, and ministers. In February 1964, the first shovelfuls of earth were dug up, preparing the ground for a 1,660-foot-long asphalted take-off and landing strip on the fields behind LEGO's factories. In November of that same year, Scandinavian Airlines (SAS) would operate a regular, daily route between Copenhagen and Billund.

Kjeld: *Dad managed to get support from administrative officers, local authorities, and ministers to make the airport. He helped to finance it himself, and he was supposed to get his money back if it did well, but he was also willing to eat the loss. After it opened, it was incredibly important to get more traffic than just one SAS flight per day. What could be more obvious than to contact the priest in Tjæreborg, Eilif Krogager, who* *at that time was highly successful with his travel agency and Sterling Airways? Pastor Krogager was very interested in starting package holidays to Mallorca from a destination in Jutland, so he and Dad came up with a mutually beneficial arrangement, and that's how we ended up with so many Danish package tourists at Billund Airport, right from the start.*

The opening of Billund Airport on November 1, 1964, was met with great fanfare, attended by the Minister for Transport, Kai Lindberg, as well as a number of mayors and national politicians who arrived in an SAS plane from Copenhagen. Time had also been set aside for a tour of the LEGO campus, which was crowned by a reception at the System House. There, these powerful men were given a sneak preview of Billund's plans for the coming years and made aware of a completely new idea designed to lure even more people to the region: a family park. Offering something different from both Disneyland and Tivoli, it would be based around the world-famous LEGO bricks. The idea had come out of the ever-increasing stream of people, now up to twenty thousand a year, who visited LEGO and asked to be shown around the site.

Kjeld: *Year after year there were more and more people, from schoolkids and high school students to retirement clubs and housewives' associations, asking for a guided tour of the factory and to see our model production. After a while it got a bit too much of an inconvenience for the people building with the bricks to have to talk about what they were doing. In 1963, my dad bought a farm with a lot of land from an elderly couple, and he got the idea to build a little hall with a more permanent collection of the big LEGO models that were so popular, and which we had started to display abroad. That way the farmer could keep an eye on things while his wife made coffee and served cake to the park's guests. Well, that was how it started.*

Godtfred noticed that the highlight of nearly every visit to the LEGO factory was the collection of huge buildings made out of bricks in the model design department. Visitors flocked to see the models, chattering enthusiastically about how builders were limited only by their imagina-

The inauguration of the airport in 1964 became a local festival, involving planes flying overhead, fifty thousand people on the ground, visits from ministers and mayors, and a cart drawing the town council chairman and the eldest citizen in Billund.

tion. Much of the credit for this was due to Dagny Holm, Godtfred's creative cousin, who spent her time building models with the experienced Christian Lasgaard. She revolutionized their design. Whereas they'd previously featured mostly houses, transportation, and roads, they now also showcased fairy-tale characters, animals, and landscapes.

> **Kjeld:** *It was a fantastic place, the model workshop, and as a teenager in the early 1960s I often went to see Dagny and Lasgaard after school. I had my own corner there with a table and chair, and access to mountains of bricks, and I'd sit there all afternoon, till the end of the workday, actually, building my huge models of cars. At the same time, I was incredibly inspired by others' fantastic projects.*

Lasgaard was the model builder who, in 1961, tried to teach Dagny the fundamental ground rules of building with LEGO. But right-angled, rule-bound buildings weren't suited to Dagny, who'd been working with clay for much of her life. As she'd later explain in the staff magazine: "I had a hard time getting used to the rigid bricks, but the more you worked with them, the more possibilities opened up."

Dagny Holm was employed at LEGO for a brief period in the 1930s, but then she moved to Copenhagen, where she remained for nearly three decades, drawing, making busts and sculptures out of clay, and taking classes with the sculptor Harald Isenstein in her free time. In 1961, Dagny returned to Jutland and to LEGO. A couple of years down the line she was to play a crucial role in Godtfred's plans for the family park, but already upon her return, she began to employ a new, more abstract way of using the LEGO bricks.

"In the beginning I steered well clear of houses, because Lasgaard was so good at that. I made dolls and characters, and Godtfred really liked those. I put a lot of effort into bringing them to life. That's why I always started with the dolls' eyes and later with the windows in the houses, because for me they're a mirror of the soul."

Dagny's artworks, big and small, were initially intended for exhibition all over the world, but she was soon given the title of Senior Designer, the first to hold that role in the company's history. She was also the first woman at LEGO with a title above that of Canteen Manager. Dagny had first one, then three, then five, and, finally, nine women working under her, whom she called "my girls." They helped her create the large animals, houses, and characters that were used for various purposes, including to depict Hans Christian Andersen's fairy tales.

As the LEGOLAND project began to take shape in 1965–1966, and continuing through later periods, when it had to be revamped every other year with new buildings and scenes, Dagny was a traveling model builder. She jetted off to Italy, Holland, England, and Norway to look at landscapes and towns, houses and buildings, which she studied and photographed and then reconstructed back home in Billund. Over almost two decades, millions of bricks went through the hands of Dagny and her girls.

"We shared each other's sorrows and joys. We were girls in a man's world, and that brought us together. Honestly, for many years I felt that it was a problem being a woman in that world, because you had to be twice as good as the men in order to be accepted for your abilities. But we supported one another, and they were splendid years."

What Godtfred envisaged with the family park wasn't just a practical solution to the problem of coping with too many visitors to the factory. He had also glimpsed a new and exciting form of marketing. In a letter to a close friend in retail, he later described his LEGOLAND idea as "a bold step toward finding new promotional strategies within the Danish toy industry that will benefit all distributors."

At the same time, GKC hoped to burnish the company's educational pedigree, arguing that the aim of the park is "to illustrate the right kind of play and make clear its significance for the child and the child's development, not only for the children themselves, but also for their parents, teachers, and others who deal with children."

From the very beginning, this was both an idealistic and commercial project, but Godtfred had to use all his rhetorical gifts to get the other senior executives on board with his concept of "a children's paradise like nothing seen before." In the late summer of 1962, when he presented to the directors the idea of a park "where the child is king, and where children forget they ever need to grow up," he was met with a certain skepticism.

Wouldn't they be biting off a little more than they can chew? Hadn't they already strayed too far from their core business, with projects like the Scale Model line and Modulex? As one of the more skeptical managers pointed out, LEGO had plenty of experience producing and selling bricks but absolutely none running a family park.

Godtfred stubbornly maintained that his idea was not only squarely within the fundamental concept of the LEGO System but that it offered new and unexplored potential for growth. They wouldn't be trying to create a Danish version of Disneyland, he explained, but making an outdoor showroom that focused on the LEGO System in Play, displayed as many products as possible, and also encouraged children and adults to play and build with LEGO.

His regular financial backers at Vejle Bank didn't see the genius of the

Dagny Holm and her female team left a very special mark on LEGOLAND. As Kjeld observed, "Dagny refused to use special elements. Everything had to be made out of our classic system bricks, but she used them in this very special way we'd never seen before. She was more of a sculptor and an artist than a designer."

project, either, when Godtfred asked if he could count on them to bail him out if the project, against all his expectations, ran into the ground. The chairman of the bank's board inquired how many people Godtfred expected this family park in a field might expect.

"Three hundred thousand a year" was GKC's confident response.

The chairman stared at him and shook his head. This was a risk that GKC would have to run alone. He did exactly that, unmoved by the bank's trepidation and LEGO's apprehensive management. As he would later remark about his intuitive gift, "In many ways it's an advantage that I only went to a village school. Good ideas are often simple and straightforward. I'm impulsive, and that means I'm often at odds with all the rules. I don't let myself be stopped by cold logic."

On his trips by plane to Copenhagen in the early 1960s to sort out the various issues around the proposed airport in Billund, Godtfred always spent the night at the Hebron Mission Hotel on Helgolandsgade in Vesterbro, which was rented by Ulla's parents-in-law. Late in the evening, Godtfred would usually take a walk before bed, and outside the main entrance of Tivoli amusement park he loved gazing across the street toward Anva, the department store, whose themed window displays had become something of a tourist attraction.

On one such night, Anva had transformed its windows on Vesterbrogade into a Danish springtime paradise featuring woodland and lakes. He found it magical, and sent a big bouquet of flowers with a thank-you card to the store's head window dresser, whoever that might be. It was a typical GKC thing to do: spontaneous but not without purpose. Imagine if all the imagination and creativity behind the fantastical tableaus in Anva's windows could be let loose on the fields on the outskirts of Billund . . .

From the back of the LEGOLAND train, Arnold Boutrup and Godtfred saw their idea come to fruition in 1968. One hundred forty thousand square feet of flat heath had been transformed into an undulating, thrilling miniland where children and adults could nurture their impulse to play (and to buy more LEGO).

After several telephone calls with the window dresser, who turned out to be named Arnold Boutrup, and who made it clear from the start that he would never move to Jutland, Godtfred invited him to Billund to show him the vast canvas and infinite possibility of his as-yet-unrealized plan to build a park. Boutrup never forgot that trip. As he later recounted in his article about the founding of LEGOLAND:

> *After meeting with GKC, I was convinced. He was incredibly fascinating, wore a pair of unusually eye-catching braided-leather shoes, and radiated an optimism that got me on board with the idea of an "adventure park," as it was being called at that point. Dagny Holm had drawn a sketch that depicted a circular park a little over 100 yards in diameter.*

Godtfred managed to bring the capital's most coveted window dresser to Billund, but Boutrup still refused to move permanently and ended up getting his way on that point. For the next twenty-five years, first as a consultant on the construction project and later as director of LEGOLAND, he flew back and forth to work, either with SAS or LEGO Airways.

Initially, Godtfred was eager to get the park ready to open in the summer of 1964 or 1965, so the project team met every two weeks in Billund or at Boutrup's home in Bagsværd, a little outside Copenhagen. As early as October 1963, the talented designer had a plan laid out, with an exhibition hall, restaurant, kitchen, and a LEGO train on rails that would carry the guests around the whole park. But then the project ground to a halt. Godtfred was distracted by his other big plan for the future of Billund and LEGO—the airport—and he'd been kept busy negotiating for several years, all while running a company that was undergoing extraordinarily rapid growth abroad.

Not until 1965 did the plan get back on track, and Boutrup was then officially handed creative responsibility for developing and setting up the LEGOLAND park. He immediately brought in his two most talented colleagues from Anva to help build models and come up with ideas for additional activities in the park. It was a job that mainly took place in the basement of Boutrup's home, where he'd set up a workshop. He and his colleagues built their designs with bricks, cut things out, glued and drew. In the autumn of 1966, Boutrup got some unexpected help from the youngest branch of the LEGO family tree.

Kjeld: *When I passed my final school exams in 1966, I didn't know what to do, and I had no clear ideas about my future at all. Music, horses, and LEGO were still the only things I was really into. My cousin in Copenhagen was studying chemical engineering at the College of Advanced Technology, as DTU (the Technical University of Denmark) was called in those days, and I thought that actually sounded pretty exciting, so in August 1966 I rented a room with my cousin and his wife in Lyngby. It turned out that my marks in mathematics, physics, and chemistry were so bad that they would only accept me if I did an introductory semester, which finished with an exam in those three subjects.*

I couldn't stand it, so I dropped out and, instead, started helping Arnold Boutrup, who was powering ahead at his home in Bagsværd, planning and designing the LEGOLAND park. I turned up every day, helped out with whatever he happened to need, and was allowed to participate in some of the concept development. Even at this early stage, they were talking about maybe doing something involving pony rides at the park, and in those days I used to do a lot of riding, so I was immediately onboard with that idea.

But shouldn't there be something more than horses, I suggested, for example, some carriages that the ponies could pull?

"Yes, good idea!" said Boutrup, and he let me design the horse-drawn carriages. That was my contribution to LEGOLAND.

Down in Boutrup's basement, the park emerged from one of Dagny Holm's original sketches and had now evolved to covering an area of ten acres of land, slightly more than half the size of Tivoli in Copenhagen. In addition to the various permanent exhibitions of LEGO's large-scale models, the plans included a doll museum and a stage, as well as a "construction site" with enormous bricks and huge tubs filled with small LEGO bricks that people could use as they pleased. And in the center of

the park was Dagny Holm's mini-sized models of cities, buildings, and scenes from Denmark and the rest of the world.

Several permanent attractions were planned, including a driving school where children could earn a LEGO license for small electric LEGO cars. They also entertained the idea of a canal ride in little boats, and a few vintage cars to take children on a safari past various wild animals built out of LEGO bricks. There would be a playground where you could ride giant tortoises and swing off LEGO giraffes, while slightly older children could follow the Native American chief Playing Eagle over to his camp, which was to feature wigwams, a totem pole, free feathers to wear, and a bonfire in which you could bake twistbread.

In 1968, LEGOLAND opened its doors, and families streamed in from near and far, in private cars and tourist buses, filling every single space in the parking lots in the surrounding fields. From the very start, the new tourist attraction in central Jutland was a huge success, drawing in four hundred thousand visitors within the first couple of months.

The entrance to LEGOLAND in 1968. Opposite page: Even King Frederik IX of Denmark dropped by. The king, who was interested in trains, was allowed to test LEGO's first experiment with electronics, a train that could be operated with a whistle. One whistle meant "Go," two meant "Stop," and one long one meant "Reverse." Queen of Denmark Ingrid, Princess of Denmark Benedikte, and Godtfred watched the royal train driver play.

Throughout the summer, the lines were twice as long as expected, and on some days during the heatwave of 1968, the crowds were so massive that the executives at the System House were asked by Godtfred to fetch their wives and head to LEGOLAND to help out in the understaffed cafeteria. There was a severe shortage of people to wash up and take orders of sausages and soft drinks.

By the time they finally closed for the season, 625,000 children and adults had been through the gates, and there was no longer any question that LEGOLAND was a brilliant idea. Once again, Godtfred had proved himself to be a gifted creative mind and entrepreneur, always working on new concepts, with a Monaco cheroot in one hand and a cup of coffee in the other.

But this perpetual success came at a price. Even a hardworking dynamo like Godtfred, who lived and breathed LEGO, couldn't be everywhere at once. While he'd been sucked into time-consuming projects like Billund Airport, LEGOLAND, or Billund Center, there'd been a vacuum in the day-to-day management of LEGO, which meant that in the second half of the 1960s, despite mushrooming sales figures, there was a sudden slump in the development of new product lines, and the organization began searching for a new vision for the future.

Kjeld: *Dad did love launching new projects, and you saw that in the 1960s especially. First LEGO had to have planes, and then Billund had to have an airport, and then there was the LEGOLAND idea, which kept him so busy for a few years that he virtually forgot all about the company, until several of our foreign directors began tugging at his sleeve. They thought they could handle a lot more than our LEGO building system and wanted to sell other products with the LEGO name. So why not start making some small plastic cars, for instance, alongside the bricks?*

Dad really had to fight to hold his ground, and luckily he did. First he got the LEGO train underway, which gave the whole business fresh impetus. And in 1969 LEGO came out with DUPLO, the big bricks for little hands. He was good at that stuff, my dad. When he met with resistance among his closest colleagues, he always reacted by coming up with something new.

In 1966, Godtfred made his first countermove in response to LEGO executives who wanted to expand the core business by introducing an entirely new super-product, the first motorized LEGO train. Model Set 113 was attractively packaged; it featured blue rails that formed an elliptical track, a blue locomotive, blue mail carriage and blue passenger carriage, as well as a 4.5-volt motor and a battery compartment, marking the first use of electricity in the LEGO System in Play.

One million sets were sold, and the train was adapted in the 1960s for various international markets. All sets sold on the European mainland had the passenger carriages with signage featuring destinations of Hamburg, Basel, and Genoa. The sets sold in Great Britain, Ireland, and Australia had trains running to London, Manchester, and Glasgow, while the sign on the mail carriage read, of course, "Royal Mail."

In the second half of the 1960s, things started to move fast. The West was becoming increasingly affluent, and traditional norms and values were suddenly disappearing as more and more young people rebelled against what were perceived as earlier constraints and limitations upon their individuality. Sons let their hair grow, daughters burned their bras, some called themselves flower children and devoted themselves to expressions of peace, free love, psychedelic music, and experimental drug use.

The cultural shock waves eventually reached Billund, too, where the son of LEGO's managing director let his own hair grow slightly and launched his own small-scale revolt against his old-fashioned high school teachers and their boring curriculum, which he often only managed to glance at on the bus in the mornings on his way to Grindsted. Instead of studying, Kjeld spent his free time building technically advanced LEGO models, riding horses in Vejle, and most of all, listening to the Beatles, the Animals, the Red Squares, Van Morrison, and Jimi Hendrix. Seventeen-year-old Kjeld thought his sleepy little village needed to be shaken up by something other than the noise from the factory and the airstrip, and he got permission to open an all-ages club every Saturday night in the old canteen, the same place where Ole Kirk had gathered people to pray and sing before they went about their day in the 1950s.

Kjeld: *I thought we were missing somewhere in Billund where we young people could get together, and so Dad gave me permission to outfit the old cafeteria with a stage in the corner and a counter along the wall. It was supposed to look like a bar in a nightclub, even though we weren't*

In June 1966, Kjeld graduated from high school, but just barely. When he left for his final oral exam at Grindsted High School in the morning, Edith and Godtfred weren't sure if they would be celebrating that night. Kjeld passed, and the rest of the summer he slept late in their summer cottage in Hvidbjerg with posters of the Beatles on the wall. *Private collection.*

allowed to serve alcohol. It quickly became a place for young people to hang out. Small local bands from Grindsted came and played, and we would dance. "Club-A-Go-Go" I called that place, after the old Animals hit. It ended up becoming a little too popular. There would often be up to a hundred youngsters in the old factory building on a Saturday night, including some from farther afield, who'd bring beer. Then my dad said, "Enough is enough, Kjeld. The club's getting a bit too rowdy!"

After Kjeld left school and spent six months in Copenhagen, eventually dropping out of university to help Arnold Boutrup with LEGO-LAND, Godtfred suggested his son try something completely different. What about business administration at the business school at Aarhus University?

Yes, why not? thought Kjeld.

Then Godtfred had another bright idea; what about spending six months as a trainee in LEGO's German sales division in Hohenwestedt? Yes, why not? thought Kjeld, and headed south.

Kjeld: *I was nineteen years old, curious and absolutely ready to learn something new, so those were six exciting months that had a big impact on my future. One of the employees at Hohenwestedt took me under his wing and made sure to arrange a program for my stay. That meant I got to see all LEGO's departments in Germany, and for the first time I experienced the world outside Denmark on my own and spoke a bit of German and English. Plus, the German sales company had an absolutely fantastic IBM computer system, which I learned a bit about and got to practice on. I found that unbelievably exciting.*

The Kjeld who returned home to Denmark in the summer of 1967 had more grit and a greater appetite for life. He looked forward to moving permanently to Aarhus and starting his course at the business school, but for the moment he was most thrilled to be reunited with his Billund friends and old classmates in Grindsted. This was the famous Summer of Love, when young hippies from across the world met in parks to play music, dance, and celebrate love.

One August Sunday in Grindsted Park, current and former students of the local school—including the LEGO heir, wearing colorful sunglasses, a broad-brimmed cowboy hat, and a big leather coat—agreed to meet down by the lake at the fountain.

"They wanted to draw attention to the fact that the world cannot be saved through war," one of the local newspapers wrote a few days later, further explaining that the word "Love" was painted everywhere on the young people's clothes and bodies, while any and every flower that could be found in the park was woven into garlands on their heads or tucked behind their ears. The correspondent also delved into the deeper meaning behind their dancing, performed in a chain to "the ear-splitting music of the age."

"They want to get rid of status symbols and authorities. They don't want to make trouble or use violence; they'd rather teach young people to realize the importance of being good members of society and of practicing love of one's fellow man. One way to do this is to give each other flowers."

This is the philosophy Kjeld brought with him to Aarhus in 1968. There he lived a bohemian lifestyle full of contradictions: by day he was a diligent student at the business school, immersed in discussions about company administration, while in the evening he'd meet up with friends, talking more about yin and yang, Lao Tzu, and Transcendental Meditation than accounts, sales, and financial management.

Kjeld: *I really came into my own at the business school. I told myself I had to prove there was something I wanted, and something I could do. And also, I just enjoyed being a student. We were all hippies in those days, more or less. In my mind I've probably always had an inclination toward Eastern philosophy. I started going to Transcendental Meditation (TM) in 1968, in any case, and the following year Maharishi Mahesh Yogi visited Aarhus. At that time he was world-famous for having taught the Beatles. Along with lots of other people who were also into TM, I went to get my mantra, which is a kind of passport to another world that you're never allowed to reveal to anyone. I also brought a flower to give to this tiny Indian man in a white robe with long hair and a beard, which made a huge impression. I really found meditation very enjoyable. It was a fascinating way to get back in touch with oneself and feel an inner stillness. That's how it was back then. We looked for answers that could not be supplied by established religion, our parents, or material things.*

**Tiny fingers.
Big blocks.
LEGO
DUPLO®
from 18
months.**

Launched in 1969, the DUPLO brick was twice as tall, twice as long, and twice as wide as an ordinary LEGO brick, designed for children between eighteen months and five years old. It wasn't the first time these kinds of bricks had appeared on the toy market. In 1964, Samsonite was selling LEGO Jumbo Bricks on the American market. They were somewhat larger than the later DUPLO brick.

CHANGE

THE 1970s

Minifigures, 1978

In late October 1969, Edith and Godtfred looked forward to celebrating their silver wedding anniversary with a big party to be held at the restaurant in LEGOLAND. On Wednesday, October 22, the couple lunched there with Edith's sister, Ellen, and her husband, Einar and they arranged some details about the menu, service, and table settings with the staff. A waiter inquired about Gunhild, Godtfred and Edith's oldest daughter, who'd recently been in a car accident on her way home from visiting her husband at Varde Barracks and had hit her head on the windshield. Luckily, Gunhild had recovered from her fractured jaw; they assured the waiter that it could have been much worse, promising to pass on his greetings to their daughter.

Back home at the villa on Systemvej, eighteen-year-old Hanne who, like Kjeld had just started studying in Aarhus, had a visit from her friend Jørgen, whom she'd met at school. He was from Esbjerg and had borrowed his parents' car. Hanne and Jørgen asked Kjeld if he wanted to come to Give to watch *Death at Owell Rock*. Loving Westerns, he readily agreed.

They decided to drive down Båstlundvej, which offered an unobstructed view of the Billund Airport, and at the end of the runway they'd pull over to enjoy the sight of all the planes. Then they'd drive on toward Give, with Jørgen at the wheel.

Kjeld: *I've never been able to recall many details of the accident, but I do have a lot of small, fragmented images in my memory . . . a few miles after the airport, on the narrow stretch of road near Båstlund, the road was blocked on the left-hand side by some construction. Suddenly, there was someone heading directly toward us, pushing a bike. We saw him way too late, tried to get out of the way, but veered too far out onto the edge, skidded, and hit something hard, which made the car whirl around and slam into one of the big trees alongside the road. The roof was crushed down over the front seats, and my sister and her friend died instantly. I was in the backseat and got thrown out of the car, breaking my collarbone, getting a minor skull fracture, and spending a week in hospital in Grindsted, unconscious.*

"Two young people killed when car hits tree near Billund" was the headline splashed across the front page of *Vejle Amts Folkeblad*, above gruesome photographs of the crumpled wreck. That anybody emerged alive from that accident had to be considered a miracle, the newspaper wrote, and reconstructed the moment of the crash:

A few feet before the car hit the tree it swerved onto the side of the road, where there were still the stumps of some trees that had been cut down to thin out the forest. A wheel, or the bottom of the car, must have caught on one of these stumps, knocking the car completely off course and flinging it

**o unge dræbt,
a bil ramte et
æ ved Billund**

ren blev overrasket af vejarbejde
ene af de dræbte er datter af
ktør G. Kirk Christiansen, Lego,
Billund

ulykke nord for Billund kostede i aftes to unge mennesker livet,
tredje i dag ligger kvæstet paa amtssygehuset i Grindsted. De
r den 18-aarige Hanne Kirk Christiansen, datter af direktør G.
istiansen, Lego, Billund, og den 22-aarige Jørgen Thostrup
Gormsgade 93, Esbjerg — Den kvæstede er den dræbte Han-
Christiansens bror, den 22-aarige Keld Kirk Christiansen. Døds-
skete, da en personbil, de tre unge mennesker var kørende i,
og tørnede mod et træ.

bund har grebet fat i en af disse
stubbe, og bilen er slaaet helt ud
af kurs, saa den med voldsom
kraft er slynget mod træet. Mær-
ker paa træet viser, at bilen er

kastet to meter op ad stammen.
Vognen synes at have tippet over
venstre forhjul og derefter at have ramt træet med taget, der blev
(Fortsættes side

Mystik omkring en
hemmelig central

Læs side 10

Billederne viser den forulykkede bil — taget kort efter dødsulykken

Ny Mellemøst-krise

*into the tree with terrible force. Marks on the tree indicate that the vehicle
was hurled 7 feet up against the trunk.*

The accident was also mentioned in the national press: "LEGO
managing director G. Kirk Christiansen's youngest daughter has been
killed and his son seriously injured." About Kjeld, they noted, "Studying
abroad all over Europe, he is training to join the senior management
team at the global company LEGO System."

For one dreadful moment that night, Edith and Godtfred believed
that Kjeld, too, had died, when they called the local hospital in Grindsted and were told that both the young woman and a young man had
been killed.

Godtfred would never recover from Hanne's death. In his grief, he considered selling the company, but chose instead to set in motion a generational handover that would last most of the decade. *Private collection.*

Kjeld: *I only faintly remember the doctor sitting by my bed, saying that I didn't have my little sister anymore. When I was fully conscious, my parents came and told me Hanne had been buried. I wasn't discharged from the hospital until a month after the accident, and it took me a long time to get my strength back. I had to redo the entire year at the business school, but of course losing Hanne was the worst thing of all. Back home, we all went into her room, sat down by her bed and cried, clasped our hands, and prayed together. I often drove to see her grave. It was really difficult, and it still is, when I think about it. Hanne was an incredibly lovely little sister. We always had fun, even though there were three years between us. She and I did all sorts of things, and in particular we shared a passion for horses. I started riding again because she got a horse. They were unforgettable, those years we had together.*

The loss of his youngest daughter was a terrible blow for Godtfred, who was overwhelmed with feelings of guilt. He viewed what happened as a judgment, a punishment directed toward him and no one else; the price he'd had to pay for working nonstop while the children were little, while they grew up and bonded with Edith. As he wrote many years earlier in a Christmas card to a friend, "It's always interesting to work on something being developed, but in the moment you can often forget what's really most important."

Kjeld: *For a long time, Dad completely stopped. He didn't know what to do, and he blamed himself for all sorts of things, mainly that for far too many years he hadn't given himself more time to spend with his family.*

Godtfred was shaken to his core. He was ready to sell LEGO, cut all ties to his former life, travel to Switzerland, and live there permanently with Edith. He got in touch with Incentive, a consultancy that specializes in helping companies in crisis, including during transitions from one generation to the next. Maybe they could help him, and LEGO, move forward?

Kjeld: *There were many meetings in 1970, some of which I was allowed to attend. It was there I got to know Incentive's managing director, Vagn Holck Andersen, and at one point I couldn't help saying to Dad, "We shouldn't sell the company; we should just get that Vagn guy on board." My dad had evidently had the same thought, and it was one of those moments—well, probably the first one, actually—where he and I felt that we were really on the same page when it came to a decision about the future. Vagn Holck and I quickly became extremely good friends. He ended up being a bridge between me and my father at a time when Dad was very much in doubt about LEGO, himself, life . . . everything.*

These meetings went on for the better part of a year after Hanne's death. Incentive's advice took a long-term view, looking toward the rest of the decade, since Godtfred had said during the conversations that he would like to give up some of his power without being completely cut

Vagn Holck Andersen became a key figure in LEGO's history in the 1970s. A skilled, highly professional businessman, he led the company through a difficult period and created a solid foundation for Kjeld's assumption of management in 1979.

off. At the same time, he wasn't sure of the best way to go about handing control over to the next generation.

Vagn Holck Andersen soon realized that he was dealing with an owner and managing director who had an extraordinarily detailed understanding of how his company was run; he knew every inch of it. For instance, Godtfred had direct interactions with a surprising number of employees, given the size of the company. As Holck later explained in LEGO's staff magazine: "Godtfred had his fingers in every pie and had so many people who counted him as their manager that anyone else would have buckled under the pressure."

The conversations ended with Godtfred hiring Holck. Both he and Kjeld sensed that Holck could be a major asset in LEGO's restructuring. On February 1, 1971, Holck joined LEGO as a director and swiftly set about building a more flexible organization and preparing for the handover Godtfred had vocally envisioned. As Holck later recounted: "The organization was very much shaped by Godtfred's personal style of management and his direct participation in a range of decisions. That left the organization with a lot of bottlenecks and made it ill-suited to expansion."

Two key points in Holck's plan were decentralization and delegating responsibility, but the main, all-important task was to find a new managing director to replace Godtfred, a director who could bring everything together, and in whom both father and son would have confidence. Vagn Holck Andersen took the position in 1973, making him the first managing director in LEGO's history who wasn't a member of the family, and he soon found himself faced with an unforeseen challenge. As they liked to say in Billund, you never know what's going to happen when GKC is around.

"Godtfred was busy all over the place and on the go at all hours," Holck would later say. "As managing director, I wanted to know what he was doing, what he was promising and what he wasn't promising, who he was talking to and what they were talking about, and what he decided. It was demanding work, because Godtfred was absolutely synonymous with LEGO."

A key element of Holck's multipronged plan for the generational transition were his advisory conversations with Kjeld, who, because of the car accident, didn't complete his studies at the business school until 1971. He immediately enrolled in the master's program, imagining that he'd need to spend some time in the business world and get a little experience before potentially getting more involved with LEGO.

Hanne's death, his father's profound grief, and his encounter with the empathetic managing director of Incentive made Kjeld change his plans. Holck advised him to abandon his master's degree and travel to Switzerland to do a one-year diploma at the International Institute for Management Development (IMD), which wouldn't simply mature and motivate Kjeld, Holck thought, but would also be highly significant for the generational transition at the family company.

Twenty-four-year-old Kjeld was thrown to the lions during his IMD course in Lausanne, but he clung on and eventually felt he had found his path in life.

Kjeld: *I joined the IMD in Lausanne, although I had nothing like the same business experience as the others in the course. Several of them were much older than I was, and tough, hard-nosed management executives. I was only twenty-four, and all I had to boast of was six months as a trainee, although that had given me a bit of insight into how a sales organization is built and run. Doing the master's in Switzerland really made me realize that I could do this, and that I wanted to. Suddenly I knew I didn't have to go out and get experience at a different company. As Vagn said to me, it was much better to be thinking about LEGO at LEGO than thinking about LEGO somewhere else. He was absolutely right about that.*

■　■　■

While Kjeld grappled with management and organizational issues in Switzerland, the final touches were being put on a new landmark back home in Billund, a complex near the town center that would house a variety of cultural institutions and a church, but no supermarkets or clothing stores or bars.

The path toward creating Denmark's first complex with both a church and a cultural center, financed with six million kroner from Ole Kirk's Foundation and three million from the local government's coffers, had been long and arduous. Bringing together so many different ventures under one roof required the cooperation of many separate offices, including the town council, the mayor, and the bishop as well as religious, cultural, and housing ministries. Several teams of architects had taken turns during the protracted project.

Meanwhile, the citizens of Billund were tentative. Only a few responded to the survey the council had distributed to each household in an attempt to involve the local community. A few critics did pipe up, making it clear that they weren't remotely interested in "local democracy." Others sneered at the makeup of the building committee and cast further doubt on a project already beset by strikes among the construction workers.

Throughout the arduous ten-year process, Godtfred did what he could to speed things up. The commemorative volume compiled for the twenty-fifth anniversary of the Billund Center in 1998 described how, when the committee was faced with one particularly large stumbling block, GKC came up with unorthodox but constructive ideas, such as a trip to Finland on LEGO Airways to take a look at similar buildings. And when, in the final phase of the project, they were searching for workshop space to paint the church furniture and fittings, he immediately made areas available at the LEGO factory.

What began as a sudden flash of inspiration in 1962, when Godtfred visited a combined community center and church facility in the USA, ended up as Billund's latest landmark. And for many of Billund's older residents, the church in the middle of town was a memorial to the man who had laid the groundwork for the town's industrial revolution.

The Billund Center, inaugurated in 1973, fused church and culture in a broad sense that Godtfred had first seen in the USA. From the very start, there were plenty of activities on offer, including lectures, concerts, children's theater, and film clubs. An art exhibition featuring images of nudes wasn't to the town's taste, however, and provoked much debate. *Private collection.*

For the family, and Godtfred especially, the building was also part of Hanne's legacy, and the large sum of insurance money that was paid out to her siblings was donated in its entirety by the family to the center, which was inaugurated on Sunday, April 15, 1973.

In his capacity as mayor, Jens Bach Pedersen accepted this gift to the town with the words, "In memory of Ole Kirk Christiansen and little Hanne, I gratefully accept the Billund Center, and express the wish that it must always celebrate their memory and never come to stand as a lifeless monument."

The chairman of the town council, Søren Olsen, another LEGO executive, also gave a speech, concluding with words directed to Godtfred, Edith, Gunhild, and Kjeld. "You have suffered a great loss and given a great gift!"

Thereupon the doors of the Billund Center were thrown open, leading into a kindergarten, a library with a reading room, a language lab,
an area where the public could come and listen to records, a square
for people to stop and chat that featured a wading pool for children, a
church, a town hall, and an auditorium for viewing films, lectures, and
plays. All incorporated the very latest staging technology. There were
also exhibition arcades for sculpture and painting, playrooms for both
quiet and noisy creative pursuits, as well as a small cafeteria with a view
over the church, where people could sit and reflect on the past and the
future. Godtfred too, reflected in a newspaper interview around that
time. It was the most difficult part of his life to date, and he suddenly
found himself longing for the tiny little town and the tiny little factory:

*I'm philosophizing about all the dissatisfaction we feel in this coun-
try, even though materially we're better off than ever before. I wonder
whether the reason is that we're increasingly isolated in our fast-growing
urban communities, so we become mistrustful of anyone not in our own
age group. We create prejudices on the basis of ignorance. In villages like
Billund used to be, everybody knew everybody else. It promoted a sense
of well-being, to be on such familiar terms, right down to the marrow.
We're still on those terms; at least, I am with everyone at the factory. But
I can feel it myself, how unsatisfying it is that I don't actually know every
single person and their family like I used to. There are so many people in
town now, because of the factory, that the bonds between us need a shot
in the arm. We hope the center will help preserve the best of these village
traditions.*

On behalf of his family, Godtfred stipulated that the gift came with
certain conditions. The citizens of Billund were to decide what the center would be called, just so long as it didn't contain the word "culture,"
he said, because then some people would immediately be intimidated
and think it's too inaccessible for them. Nor would there be any limits
on what the Billund Center could evolve into. But even so, when he was
asked if there could be room at the Billund Center for "young social agi-

tators singing protest songs and carrying Mao's Little Red Book like the Bible," his answer was: "Certainly they can do so. I just don't think we have teeth-gnashing rabble-rousers like that in Billund. I know there are a lot of us in the town now, two thousand five hundred or thereabouts, but we still know one another so well that we can grumble directly without taking it to that extreme and getting into battle formation."

Although Godtfred sounded like himself in cheery statements such as these, the loss of Hanne and his constant grief had broken something inside him. His indomitable will, stubbornness, and self-confidence seemed to have vanished.

Kjeld was home for the opening of the Billund Center just before Easter in 1973, but it was only a fleeting visit. Work was piling up, and soon LEGO's crown prince was back on the road, carrying out various tasks for the firm. His intense year at the IMD in Switzerland had been wrapped up with an eighty-page thesis that Kjeld wrote with Torsten Rasmussen, a fellow Dane who'd become a good friend and source of support abroad. They titled their dissertation "Formulation and Implementation of the Business Policy of LEGO A/S," about the company that Kjeld was born into and would soon helm.

> **Kjeld:** *You couldn't help seeing that LEGO's growth, as early as the late 1960s, demanded a little more than the background and training my father had, and I felt convinced that with my newly acquired skills, I was up to the task. Torsten's and my dissertation, in which he could only see LEGO from the outside, of course, while I knew the company from the inside, was quite theoretical. We used all the phrases our talented instructor, who had just trained at Harvard Business School, liked. But what was most on my mind was something more between the lines. It was about LEGO's soul, about our most fundamental concept, and about what we wanted to do with this company.*

Kjeld's dissertation was an analysis of the challenges that were then facing the LEGO Group, building on conversations with nine managers, from his father and Vagn Holck Andersen to the heads of marketing and production. The analysis began with the words:

It has become apparent that the informal and creative organizational structure that has primarily been created by the company's entrepreneur and leader is insufficient to guiding the firm's future direction. The company management has therefore come to the conclusion that the informal structure must, to a certain extent, be replaced by a more formal structure to underpin planning, supervision, and decision-making processes.

In a way, the two young MBA students' thesis was a reflection of the process Vagn Holck Andersen had already started, an implicit critique of Godtfred's old-fashioned management style.

Kjeld: *Dad relied heavily on just a few people. He had his select group of key people in whom he had a lot of confidence, and they didn't necessarily have to be senior managers. They might be people further down in the organization, on the technical side, for instance. That wasn't always exactly easy for Vagn to handle. Or for me, when I was hard at work on the construction of LEGO's new factory in Switzerland in 1973 and 1974. I had to pick up the phone several times, sort the whole thing out and say, "Dad! That decision is up to Hans Schiess down here, not such-and-such a person in Billund." That also meant that I knew for sure that when eventually I came home to take over, I would very quickly bring a much broader and younger management team to LEGO. I don't think my father ever read Torsten's and my thesis, but that doesn't mean he never listened to me at all. The fact that the transition took so long also shows that my dad was aware that I really had to get deeply involved.*

The years he spent in Switzerland were profoundly formative for Kjeld as a manager. For a long time, Godtfred had been planning to open a factory and tools division there, and in 1973 Kjeld was provisionally made director and given the task of starting and running LEGO AG in the city of Baar, not far from Zurich. The idea was that Kjeld would

A young, long-haired executive heading a management meeting at the
new factory in Switzerland in 1974. Around the table are Laboratory
Manager Werner Pauli (left), Technical Director Hans Schiess, Production
Manager Walter Schmocker, Finance Manager Peter Kilgus, and Head of
Development Per Randers.

be responsible for the administrative part of setting up the organization, while Hans Schiess, who'd been at LEGO since 1962, dealt with
the technical side of the molding and tools. Production was based on
entirely new principles of molding, and would eventually supplement
the factory in Billund with consignments to the European market.

Starting an entirely new LEGO company—doing technological research and development, employing new people and buying machines
and tools—was an immense challenge for the newly minted MBA gradu-
ate. The twenty-five-year-old director was still very green, and suddenly
he was sitting at the head of the table, chairing meetings in German and
English in front of much older, more seasoned executives.

Kjeld: *I was conscious of my age in the sense that I listened a lot to what other people said and thought. That meant the meetings did sometimes run on, because I wanted to find a broad-brush consensus. I had learned that from my time at the IMD, where we discussed things a lot, and for a long time. I also brought that habit home to Billund, to the displeasure of some coworkers, who thought we spent too much time in meetings. As one of them said, "You're really keen for us to agree as much as conceivably possible, aren't you?" And another one said I was "much too inspired by the Japanese on that issue." There was probably some truth to it.*

Alongside the huge responsibility for the rapidly growing factory and workshop in Switzerland, Kjeld was also involved in setting up a new independent American sales office in Connecticut. After extricating themselves from their deal with Samsonite, which had offered nothing but disappointment, LEGO now looked to go it alone in a market equivalent to all of Western Europe and would begin independent production of the LEGO bricks in the USA for the foreseeable future.

From time to time, Kjeld also returned to Billund to take part in board meetings, as well as brainstorming in the department about which he was most enthusiastic: product development, which also went by the name LEGO Futura. And amid this turbulent but also exciting period in Kjeld's life, he met a woman named Camilla Borg and fell in love.

Kjeld: *Camilla's paternal uncle was my uncle, and her aunt was my maternal aunt, and it was through this family tree that we met in the summer of 1973. She was finishing up her law degree, and we both soon realized that this was something we just had to figure out. We got married in 1974, and by that point Camilla had already moved in with me in Switzerland. Our three years down there were a wonderful time, with plenty of opportunity to do what we wanted and what we felt like. There was never anyone we had to ask first. I can well understand why, these days, Camilla occasionally thinks back to that time and says, "Why didn't we ever take more time to travel around Switzerland and experience that together?"*

Thirty million children around the world and twenty-five thousand toy retailers in Europe can't be wrong: LEGO was a phenomenon. There seemed to be no end to the bricks' success and no corner of the world they couldn't conquer. In the early 1970s, expansion grew by 155 percent, and Vagn Holck Andersen continued working steadily and confidently on his plan to decentralize the company and increase efficiency. Among other things, this involved setting up a number of new limited companies, which in 1976 were collected under the umbrella of a parent company named INTERLEGO A/S.

Initially, Vagn Holck ran the parent company, but the role was intended to go to Kjeld once he and Camilla returned to Billund. Sometime earlier, Godtfred had made sure to reserve a large single-family home in Skovparken, the fashionable and expensive part of Billund where the LEGO directors and executives lived. Although Godtfred rarely mentioned the impending transition or his retirement when he was with Kjeld, he'd given him several signals.

In 1973, Kjeld met Camilla Borg, a law student three years his junior. She would soon move to Switzerland. *Private collection.*

In 1974, Kjeld and Camilla got married in Nørre Nebel Church in West Jutland. Left: Nora and Kaj Borg; right: Edith and Godtfred. *Private collection.*

Kjeld: *I don't recall Dad saying to me directly at any point, "Do you want to take over LEGO, Kjeld?" But I couldn't be mistaken about his stance. In the early 1970s, while I was still in Switzerland, we rejiggered ownership of the shares so that I had a nominal majority in the company while Dad had a smaller holding, although on the other hand he had a bigger vote. That was how he laid the groundwork for me one day coming in and taking over the company. That technique, transferring the shares like that, was obviously something we discussed. "Is that okay with you, Kjeld, if we do it this way?" We were in total agreement about that.*

Although the annual sales figures remained strong in the early 1970s, the company seemed to have lost some of its former spirit and verve. Naturally, the oil crisis of 1973 and the global economic recession played a role. Demand for toys was waning, and even LEGO's products were no longer flying off the shelves. It wasn't just the transition that had stagnated; product innovation and development had, too. The infectious echo of GKC's voice saying, "Let's go, let's go!" was no longer to be heard on the factory floor, where the workers were building, molding, and packing.

> **Kjeld:** *Dad's spirit had vanished. In the 1950s and '60s, he was the one who really got things moving and was virtually unstoppable, but suddenly in the '70s he was the one holding back, and he didn't really want to do much.*

GKC, once so dynamic and willing to take risks, was now suddenly advising caution. In the employee magazine, he explained that during a period of stagnation, it was tempting to venture into dangerous, complex territory, releasing too many new and insufficiently thought-through products:

> *During several periods over the years, I have been put under pressure, including from parts of this organization. People have suggested that we spread our resources across more products. This has been a natural mindset for those who don't fundamentally know LEGO. It is my personal conviction—and Kjeld's, as co-owner of the firm—that we should continue to focus on the idea and philosophy behind LEGO.*

So there was little to report from these years. Since the late 1950s, LEGO had been inspiring not only retailers, consumers, and millions of children, but also the company's employees, creating a pioneer spirit and a very special sense of community at the factory in Billund. But in 1976, for the first time in over twenty years, not a single new LEGO element was introduced. And an attempt to reproduce the success of LEGOLAND on German soil, in Sierksdorf, north of Lübeck, had to be abandoned that same year. After three years' poor performance, the doors of the park were permanently closed.

LEGO's former enthusiasm and remarkable will to venture into new and unfamiliar territory seemed to be on the decline, and more and more employees felt that the current management was too conservative and passive. Was it time to give the LEGO spirit a thorough revamp? That's what the staff magazine, now called *Klodshans*, said, at any rate. In 1975, it asked, "Tell us, is there a LEGO spirit, and can you describe it?"

The question prompted a reaction among many employees. The old-timers cast a nostalgic look back at the 1950s, and at one point the pining for days of yore all got too much for Torsten Rasmussen, employed in LEGO's Logistics Department. In March 1976, Kjeld's friend and cowriter of the IMD dissertation attacked the fabled LEGO spirit, which he viewed as a moth-eaten ghost that was overshadowing the future. In his contribution to the magazine, which could also be read as an attempt to pave the way for his former classmate and future boss, he didn't mince words:

> *I find it unfortunate that we are gradually whipping up a ridiculous longing for LEGO's past. Casting Ole Kirk and GKC as geniuses and infallible people. Insisting that the spirit of those days must be instituted everywhere. Making the history of LEGO into a shining fairy tale that we should all be groveling before. Well, it makes for a good story, but we can't keep flogging that dead horse. We should exorcise this "LEGO spirit" as soon as possible, so it won't keep haunting us!*

In the mid-1970s, the company held its breath, waiting for some signal about the huge, looming power shift and changing of the guard that had been at the top of Vagn Holck's agenda. What would happen to LEGO in the long term? Or, as the inquisitive editor of the employee magazine posed the question to Holck Andersen in February 1976: "In Switzerland there's a young executive by the name of Kjeld Kirk Kristiansen. Who is he, and what is he going to do?"

Holck replied that, since October 1975, Kjeld had had full responsibility for production in Switzerland, where he "had been given all facets of a manager's responsibility for people and production, at very close quarters."

Would Kjeld stay in Switzerland?

In 1973, LEGO set up its own sales company in the USA. Two years later, ground was broken for a new packing plant in Enfield, Connecticut, by director Jack Sullivan (left), GKC, Vagn Holck, Kjeld, and Governor Ella T. Grasso (center), who remarked in her keynote address that the future of the state, the nation, and the whole world depended on how well children's talents were developed. For adults, she said, toys were something to play with. But for children, they were developmental aids.

"No. The plan is for Kjeld to come home to Billund in a few years, to work for the LEGO Group here, and gradually relieve his father of his duties," came the answer.

The factory in Switzerland grew rapidly. The "LEGO Aktiengesellschaft" expanded from roughly 50 employees in 1974 to between 500 and 600 three years later. When Godtfred and Edith came to visit, Kjeld sensed his father's approval, especially when he got the chance to walk around the large factory, chat with Hans Schiess, and discuss technical solutions with Manfred Müller, who showed them how to make tools down to a thousandth of a millimeter's [.03 inches] precision in the molding workshop.

During one of his visits, Godtfred noticed the large computer terminal on his son's desk. Kjeld explained that it was connected to a Honeywell machine with enough storage capacity to run their database, which was located in Houston. Godtfred was probably aware that this was the future of any sizable company, although he personally preferred to keep his eye on the finances with the aid of Orla Jørgensen's daily paper balance sheets.

Kjeld learned to program at the business school in Aarhus, and he was very enthusiastic about it, because it was like building with LEGO bricks. He continued to develop his IT skills at the IMD, where the future MBA professionals were each given a terminal and asked to calculate the outcomes of the various decisions a company might make, learning how to make the right decisions at the right time.

Kjeld: *One of the first things I did when I got my new office at the factory in Baar was to get a Honeywell. I used the computer in my day-to-day work in Switzerland, but on the side I started experimenting with long-term strategic planning for LEGO. How many users could we expect in any given market per year? How would that affect our marketing? What could we earn? And so on. Everything was done in modules as part of a strategic planning system, which I got help with from a young guy back in Billund, and the whole thing was really just a sideline next to my day-to-day work in Switzerland. I had a lot of fun with it. Our Swiss auditor did not. He was used to ledgers, which you sat down and wrote out by hand, so he was very uncomfortable with all our accounts suddenly being on a database in Houston. He had to learn to live with it.*

Things were going well for Kjeld, not just in Switzerland, but also in the other Danish and foreign LEGO projects in which he was involved. The outlines of a new Kirk Kristiansen era at the wheel in Billund were coming into sharper focus more quickly than even Vagn Holck Andersen had calculated. As early as the summer of 1977, Kjeld and Camilla moved back from the Alps to the flat, bare landscape around Billund. With them was seven-month-old daughter Sofie. She had been born in Switzerland, and Camilla Kirk Kristiansen, a fully qualified lawyer, became a stay-at-home housewife in Billund, where much was expected of the young couple, right from the start.

> **Kjeld:** *It was an abrupt transition for us, of course, but most of all for Camilla, who was born and brought up in Virum, north of Copenhagen. Now, suddenly, we had to navigate everyday life in Billund, first with one and soon two small children. There were lots of people around us who knew me and my family, but they didn't know Camilla, and I don't think it was always exactly easy for her, going down to the supermarket and bumping into people who wanted to chat with her about this or that because she was "Kjeld's wife" and "Godtfred and Edith's daughter-in-law." In her own quiet way, she coped magnificently.*
>
> *As for me, I was just "back home," as they say, and I didn't feel remotely afraid of the task before me. Far from it. At that point we weren't yet a giant, global company, so it was an easy organization to join. I already knew many of the people I was going to be working with, and for the most part I was accepted in the role. Even by the older executives, in time, although I had to have a few dustups along the way, because they listened more to my dad than to me.*

Vagn Holck Andersen was now dealing with a much more intense version of the generational shift. When Kjeld had been busy in Switzerland and GKC was on a relatively short leash in Billund, Holck had been in charge of making the decisions and navigating the choppy waters between father and son. Now they were both at close quarters, and he found himself reluctantly drawn into all the disagreements between them:

Godtfred was looking forward to bringing his son and daughter-in-law home to Billund, and made sure to get them a house and garden in Skovparken, which he had reserved and made ready for them. *Private collection.*

One day I had to discuss with Godtfred whether I thought what Kjeld was doing was the right thing, and the next I had to listen and talk to Kjeld, who was asking for my opinion on his father's latest schemes. And one thing I was clear about: I couldn't "compete" with them on the weekend when I wasn't there, and they both had the opportunity to discuss things on Saturday and Sunday, or at private get-togethers.

Kjeld: *When I came home in 1977 and was given responsibility for marketing and product development, I had some clear ideas about various new ways of developing the company. Things hadn't gone as well as expected in 1976. The American sales, especially, which we had great expectations for, weren't making much progress, and, in fact, there was a dip in revenue over there. Something similar happened in West Germany, for various reasons, and apart from the exciting Minifigures, LEGO's product development had almost ground to a halt. I felt like I knew exactly*

During Kjeld's first year as CEO, no one was as critical to his success as Vagn Holck Andersen, who became a kind of father figure and managerial role model.

what we needed to do, because there was so much more we could do with the company if we pushed development of the LEGO products that were related to children's needs in different age groups. It would also make it more challenging for our development people. Overall, my dad supported my ideas, but he also thought I wanted to do too much. That led to the first major confrontations, where Vagn sometimes felt like a monkey in the middle.

In 1978, Holck Andersen decided that his mission had been fulfilled; he'd successfully ensured that the company would remain family-owned. The legal path had been laid out, the finances were reasonably stable, and the organization was ready for Kjeld to assume his role at the top, rallying a new generation of executives.

When Holck decided to leave LEGO, his official reason was that he'd accepted a job offer from the Danish supermarket chain IRMA. He informed Godtfred and Kjeld in a long emotional letter that described, among other things, how the need to shuttle back and forth between Copenhagen and Billund for eight years had taken a toll on his family. Holck also addressed the letter to Edith and Camilla, thereby including the whole clan. Holck had become fond of them and felt like a part of the family.

The letters were placed discreetly in their mailboxes on Systemvej and Skovparken. Both wives read the letters with their husbands, and they grasped Holck's true motivations more clearly than Godtfred or Kjeld did. Godtfred was completely silent; Kjeld deeply disappointed. The loss of Vagn, a well-liked, exemplary managing director and a modern kind of leader who was capable of listening, motivating, appreciating, and implementing, was almost unbearable.

Kjeld: *In some respects he was like a father to me, and also an outstanding manager. Fantastically good with people, great at organizing and inspiring, and always positive. I don't think I ever heard him in any situation say, "Good Lord, what are we going to do now?" Calm was his great strength.*

There was never any question of a divorce between Vagn Hock Andersen and LEGO; it was more like a separation, because the future managing director of IRMA had been given permission by his new employer to remain on the board of INTERLEGO A/S and LEGO System A/S. This proved highly significant over the coming years, because Vagn was still able to support Kjeld, offer his management experience, and help persuade Godtfred to accept that his son was now the person in charge.

Kjeld formally took over his mentor's role as managing director in 1979, but in practice he'd been in the driver's seat since the prior year, around the same time as the first crop of LEGO Minifigures entered the market, dressed as everyday heroes: police officers, firefighters, doctors, and nurses.

Over the course of the year, Kjeld had gradually been introduced to Holck's routine, and the two were essentially a twosome until the latter definitively left LEGO's senior management team. Matters between father and son were reasonably settled. Godtfred told a newspaper that he didn't want to be 100 percent active again, preferring instead to remain in the background, taking on ad hoc tasks and supporting Kjeld, who'd already started making decisions.

Going forward, Kjeld wanted to spend as much time as possible in LEGO Futura, the product development division, which would now be given the highest priority. This was the key to growth: dynamic product development. Godtfred supported this view, but not if it meant launching "too many" new products into the market.

His son couldn't promise that, however, and GKC got confirmation of this on Tuesday, March 7, 1978, when Kjeld walked onstage in the auditorium on Aastvej and gave his first full-length speech as head of the company, in front of a hundred LEGO executives, about market segmentation. Kjeld argued that, in consumers' minds, LEGO shouldn't be simply a building toy, but a "high-quality toy that promotes creative development." They'd have to encompass a broad range of products, adapted to different age groups and their varying needs. Godtfred's original idea and concept, the LEGO System in Play, had been watered down over two decades with too many identical-looking sets, Kjeld argued.

Kjeld: *At the March conference, when the directors of all LEGO's European sales companies were present, and where the mood was initially a little despondent, I got up and explained the future development model for the company. It was a model I had had in my head for several years, and it meant that, more than ever before, consumers would be able to buy LEGO that suited the ages of their children. That was LEGO's new strategy and vision.*

Going forward, the name LEGO would be a broad umbrella covering a number of smaller umbrellas: toy universes like DUPLO, FABULAND, LEGOLAND Town, Castle, Space, LEGO Technic, and LEGO Scala, which was a jewelry series for girls. This clear delineation between the product lines would give consumers a general overview of the possibilities of the LEGO range. Kjeld ended his speech with words that made his listeners' eyes shine.

"We *have* to move forward, grow, be top of mind among consumers as well as retailers, and we *can*, not just because we have the best toys in the world, but because together we're the best toy company in the world."

The speech proved a turning point. Nobody had any lingering doubts that the third generation of the LEGO family wanted to reinvigorate the company. At the same time, it seemed as though thirty-year-old Kjeld had inherited his father's intuitive grasp of what would serve the business best in the long term, as well as his grandfather's unshakable faith in the importance of quality, and the quality of their employees. But he was also his own man, spelling the family surname with a "K" and refusing to be called "KKK." Kjeld would be Kjeld.

Unlike his dissertation, Kjeld's big speech was only indirectly critical of the way GKC had led the company and the methods he used when there were signs of crisis. Certainly, a significant part of LEGO's challenges in the 1970s could be ascribed to two separate oil crises, a stagnating global economy, Denmark's falling birth rate, and a declining toy market abroad, but, as Kjeld saw it, the fact that his father had scaled down—indeed, almost eliminated—product development hadn't been to LEGO's benefit.

He intended to take the opposite approach, and immediately set about putting his words into action by presenting so many new products that 1979 witnessed LEGO's widest new selection ever. It was a veritable cornucopia of new LEGO sets, fifty-three of them, all of which fell under the lines set out in Kjeld's development model.

And what did Godtfred think of his son's powerful speech on the first day of the conference? He was proud, even if he hid it that day; that very night he sent Kjeld a written message:

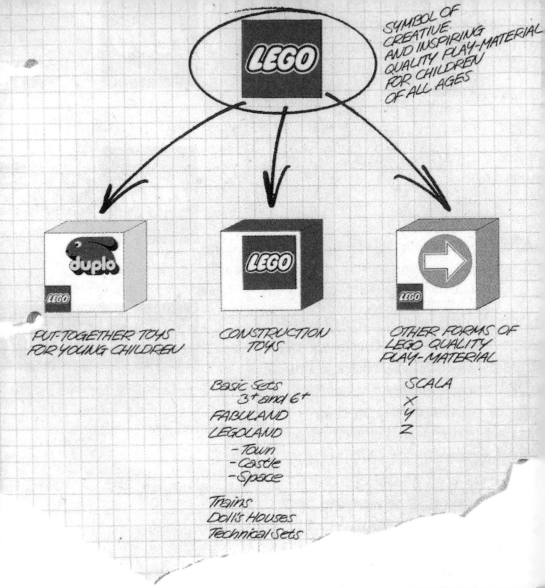

SYMBOL OF
CREATIVE
AND INSPIRING
QUALITY PLAY-MATERIAL
FOR CHILDREN
OF ALL AGES

PUT-TOGETHER TOYS
FOR YOUNG CHILDREN

CONSTRUCTION
TOYS

OTHER FORMS OF
LEGO QUALITY
PLAY-MATERIAL

Basic Sets
  3⁺ and 6⁺
FABULAND
LEGOLAND
  - Town
  - Castle
  - Space

Trains
Doll's Houses
Technical Sets

SCALA
X
Y
Z

In March 1978, Kjeld introduced a new
LEGO development model, which created
a "system in the system" by dividing up
product lines by age group. One of the
most important things he introduced was
to separate the bigger bricks, creating an
independent product line, DUPLO,
which was aimed at children between one
and five and would be recognizable by its red
rabbit logo.

Dear Kjeld,

I feel the need to express how happy I am inside!

With skillful thinking, rock-solid faith, diligence, and the ability to express yourself articulately, you have managed to accomplish something infinitely important at and with this conference—and for the future. You have strengthened and expanded your standing (or respect for yourself) in this organization, both internally and externally, and what is more important for LEGO and us—and especially now—you deserve sincere thanks, which I don't usually dole out.

Your old man

Kjeld's ideas were particularly inspired by the new LEGO Minifigures, which had been in development for nearly ten years. The figures' "evolution" made him realize that while LEGO had in the past always been a building toy, they now also embraced the possibility of boundless role-play. It was a revolutionary prospect for LEGO, and one which ought to have been actualized long ago, Kjeld thought. Instead, a combination of hesitation, uncertainty, and overly passive management had allowed Playmobil's somewhat larger plastic minifigures, which hit the toy market in the 1970s, to stake out that ground. Now, however, LEGO needed to look forward, and their countermove—nimble little figures with moveable arms, legs, and hands that could grip things—would take playing with LEGO to a whole new level.

Kjeld: *The idea for the Minifigures was originally my dad's, and in a sense it goes right back to the twenty-fifth anniversary in 1957, when they did a drawing of what they called a "Lego Man": a chubby little worker in overalls and a cap. Back then, the drawing was used as an illustration in the materials LEGO distributed to retailers, and it became a bit of an icon in the late 1950s.*

That sowed the idea in Dad's head, I think: "Could a figure like that possibly be an element in the LEGO System?" The thought wasn't real-

ized until around 1970, however, when designer Jens Nygaard Knud-
sen, the one who also came up with LEGO Space and LEGO Castle, was
experimenting with some tall "Building Figures." There was actually a
whole family, and a set that sold really well, in 1974. The following year,
Nygaard developed the Minifigures, which were three and a half centime-
ters [1.37 inches], or four bricks, tall. They fitted the scale of the LEGO
bricks, but that version didn't have moveable arms or legs, so it was nick-
named the "Pillar of Salt." That wasn't good enough, and Nygaard, Dad,
and I spent ages discussing it. Something had to be done about these fig-
ures. They at least had to have moveable arms and legs. Back then I was
a 100 percent sure that we would do incredibly well, very quickly, with a
figure that size. That came out in 1978.

In LEGO's Analytics Department, which was responsible for studying children's habits of play and their reactions to LEGO's products,
among other things, there were numerous key discussions in the late
1960s, many of which related to the development of the minifigures.
These debates mainly revolved around the company's constant challenge: girls. Girls had never embraced LEGO with anything like the
same enthusiasm as boys had, even though LEGO had been marketing
to them heavily since 1953. Outwardly, they tried to sell the LEGO System as a game for both sexes, but internally they'd known for more than
ten years that there was a fundamental gender gap in terms of boys' and
girls' interest in the LEGO System in Play.

A long memo from 1969, written by Olaf Thygesen Damm from the
Analytics Department, described the urgent need to create some humanoid figures for the LEGO universe. Girls wouldn't accept a toy that
only consisted of *things*, whether they were furniture, houses, or cars,
the memo argued. For girls, these things only existed and had purpose
in relation to human situations and activities. Boys, on the other hand,
were happy simply building houses, cars, and trains and making them
work.

He also pointed out that, while LEGO had tried to sprinkle a few
female-related issues into certain production lines over the years, at the

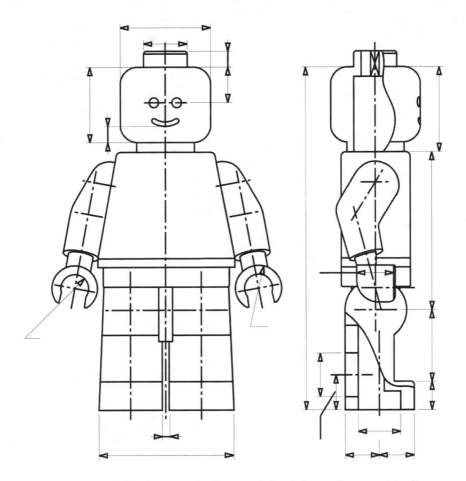

Jens Nygaard Knudsen was the designer behind the revolutionary Minifigure. Drawing on more than fifty sketches and prototypes, he found the figure's final shape, which fitted with all the standards of the LEGO System. When Knudsen died in 2020, a dedicated LEGO fan wrote on Twitter that the designer left behind "a wife, three children, two grandchildren, and eight billion Minifigures, filled with life from children's imaginations."

moment they found themselves in the middle of a period of upheaval that wasn't just about young people rebelling against authority, but also about women's liberation and the toppling of old-fashioned gender norms. LEGO's male-focused product development was no longer good enough. The company's male-dominated management had to recognize

When LEGO presented its 1978 assortment in the employee magazine, it stated that "girls have always been a special problem at LEGO." Five products were created to address this, including a dollhouse with hinges that could open and close, which was filled with knickknacks and allowed girls to role-play.

that it was time to take the imagination and creativity of both sexes seriously, not so much for noble, gender-political reasons but for financial ones, as Thygesen Damm noted.

"If we don't take into account that girls are different and play differently from boys, we cannot tap the immense potential of the girls' market."

At the meeting, attended by GKC and four other male executives, Thygesen Damm emphasized that the LEGO System in Play was crafted to suit stereotypically masculine traits much better than feminine ones. It was a question not just of materials (the hard, angular bricks) but also of the building process itself, and of the objects children expect to make with LEGO: trains, ships, cars, and houses.

The houses, in particular, symbolized the crux of the problem, and LEGO's dilemma, in a nutshell. Houses made of LEGO bricks were "outward-oriented." The focus was on the exterior, while the interior was always a closed, empty space with some windows and doors that couldn't be opened, Thygesen Damm observed. When children played with LEGO, they could only interact with the outsides of the buildings, never the insides. This meant that LEGO offered only limited scope for games involving living, personal, human, and emotional play. Thygesen Damm continued:

> In the future, girls will not accept toys that consist only of objects. They want life. Girls require objects to be humanized, and they have to have some naturalistic symbols for people that they can incorporate into their games. These figures or dolls cannot be rigid and angular. They must be able to sit and stand and be suitably proportional. The family mentioned above can gradually be expanded to include grandparents, more children, and so on.

This was precisely what transpired over the course of the 1970s, first in the shape of some doll furniture and a dollhouse in 1971, then three years later the "Building Figures," which were the first humanoid figures in LEGO's history, if you disregard the small, static plastic figures

After returning to Denmark, Kjeld bought a sailboat with three friends and participated in the Fyn Rundt boat race several times over the following years. It was like being back on the water in Vejle Fjord, where, as a boy, he had his own rowboat and learned to use oars before a sail and motor. *Private collection.*

on bikes, mopeds, scooters, and motorcycles driving through the LEGO Town Plan in the 1950s. But the members of the Building Figures family in 1974, although they were well received and sold respectably, were much too large compared to the things that could be built with LEGO, and were therefore scaled down twice to produce the final Minifigure in 1978. Over the following decades, these Minifigures reached cult status, and today there are nine billion of them spread across the globe.

In Billund, expectations of the LEGO Minifigure, and of the future managing director, were high. A slightly shy but always smiling young man, Kjeld dressed and styled his hair according to the fashions of the day: shoes with chunky heels, flared trousers, fitted shirts, well-groomed long hair, and bushy sideburns. He also had no intention of copying his father's style of management. He wouldn't be sauntering around the company during the day to chat and mingle. Nor would he prowl around after work, checking to see what was in production or currently underway on some model maker's table or shelf.

Instead, Kjeld was to follow in Vagn's professional footsteps, guiding LEGO into the future with a number of new, ambitious young executives who would each be in charge of their own area of expertise. Kjeld's personality and his visibility in the company would be de-emphasized, including management of the employees. Still, the young senior executive couldn't refuse when, in late 1978, the employee magazine asked him to talk about himself, his style of management, and the future of the business:

> I think for the most part, I'm an open and democratic leader, although it can be hard to dissuade me once I've made up my mind on something. I think of myself primarily as someone who has to help set some long-term goals for the company and lay out some strategies for how we get there. I particularly want to make time to work on the products and marketing-strategic side, so it's important that I'm freed as much as possible from day-to-day management.

Back home at the villa, there was another development in the pipeline. Camilla was expecting their second child. LEGO's employee magazine commented that the couple had divided up their roles at home in a good, traditional manner. LEGO's future top executive left the care of two-year-old Sofie and the housework to his wife, saying, "Um, cooking has never been much of a hobby for me, let alone washing up. I must admit, I'm pretty good at getting out of that."

And Kjeld wasn't out of the spotlight long. A couple of months later, in February 1979, he made a sudden appearance in *Billed-Bladet*, along-side another crown prince of Danish business, Peter Zobel, who, like Kjeld, was the third generation in a family that had built a major corporation. Peter was also about to become managing director of the insurance firm Codan. "Both are typical father's sons, born to take the helm," wrote the weekly magazine, adding, "They have one thing in common—their talent—which makes them obvious candidates for the job."

For many years, Kjeld would do more or less everything he could to avoid appearing in the media, but the magazine did note one or two things about his private life. He was previously a keen rider, they observed, but had now gotten into sailing and the previous year had bought a sailboat, moored in Vejle. He also played a little golf, but it'd been a long time since he'd played with LEGO, his great childhood passion. Kjeld's all-consuming interest continued to be cars, and while he was in Switzerland he bought a metallic green Porsche 911 Carrera Coupe, which had now been assigned a Danish license plate.

Billed-Bladet also shared with its readers that Kjeld wasn't fussy but didn't particularly like boiled cod and *øllebrød*, a traditional Danish dish made of rye bread and beer. He wore a European size 41. Personally, he wasn't a big spender, and friends described him as "thrifty without being tight-fisted." Only in one area, apart from cars, did he have expensive tastes, and that was when it came to whiskey. He preferred it neat, favoring twenty-five-year-old Chivas Regal. Beyond that, Kjeld still loved pop and rock music and had started listening to Bruce Springsteen, not least the songs about the relationships between fathers and sons.

PLAY

THE 1980s

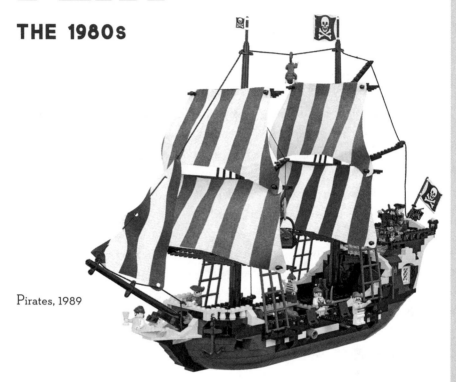

Pirates, 1989

When the world's biggest restaurant chain opened its doors for the first time in Denmark in the spring of 1981, it gave LEGO an idea. The thought first came from the American sales division in Enfield, Connecticut, but Kjeld in Billund, who'd often grabbed a bite at McDonald's on his many trips to the USA in the 1970s, seized upon it. Munching on a Big Mac with a big cup of Coke in front of him, he'd realized that the secret to the fast-food chain's success wasn't just having the right mixture of good mayonnaise, mustard, vinegar, garlic, onion, paprika, and relish. Its success was just as much about the toy that came in every single Happy Meal.

> **Kjeld:** *McDonald's wasn't massive in Europe at that point, and it was mostly a place for teenagers to hang out, while in the USA it was just as*

much for families with children. That was my experience on my trips to America, so I had nothing against the burger chain, which many people in Europe at that time thought was awful. There were also several critical voices raised when we entered a copromotion deal with McDonald's. How could we do such a thing! My directors weren't particularly keen on the initiative either.

Copromotion was a new form of LEGO marketing, one that was to grow over the course of 1980s, resulting in collaborations with several other famous brands, like Kellogg's, Colgate, and Pampers. These co-promotions raised eyebrows among some of the older, seasoned veterans in Billund. They asked, "What, we don't think the good old LEGO bricks can sell themselves anymore?"

Of course they could; the young executives Kjeld had brought together didn't doubt that. The team members were nearly all in their early thirties: Torsten Rasmussen, Niels Christian Jensen, Stig Christensen, and Christian Majgaard, alongside older, more practiced hands such as Finance Director Arne Johansen. This was the team that would bring LEGO even wider global recognition, and they knew that they needed to do something extra, ideally something new, so that they could keep optimizing sales—so they could sell more to people who already owned LEGO and make first-time sales to people who didn't.

The deal with McDonald's was signed in the USA in the autumn of 1983, and it stipulated that the Americans would be responsible for advertising, promotion, and TV spots for the months-long campaign the following autumn. Six thousand five hundred McDonald's restaurants in the USA and Canada would be the backdrop for millions of North American families' first encounter with the colorful construction toy.

LEGO was obligated to produce and deliver no less than 25 million transparent little bags of bricks, as well as 6,500 large-scale LEGO-brick models of Ronald McDonald, which would be placed in all the burger chain's restaurants. They were also to supply the same number of glued-together models for the countertops, to show what kinds of things chil-

In the 1980s, LEGO dared to claim that thirty-five million North American children would leave McDonald's hungry . . . for more LEGO toys! Three successful copromotional campaigns with the American burger chain helped LEGO enter the world's largest toy market.

dren could make out of their bag of LEGO or DUPLO bricks, while their parents chatted and ate the rest of the kids' burgers and fries.

The campaign was followed up with similar efforts in 1986 and 1988, and over the course of the decade, LEGO produced nearly a hundred million bags of bricks for McDonald's. Finally, they seemed to have found the quick and effective back door into the lucrative American market that LEGO had been searching for ever since their truncated licensing agreement with Samsonite. The LEGO brand was now spreading rapidly all over the USA and Canada through the burger chain's core customers: families with children, who were the best possible LEGO ambassadors. As LEGO's American Director of Brand Marketing, Kerry Phelan, later concluded, "An event of this magnitude accomplished all our key copromotion objectives. It generated incremental brand exposure, encouraged collecting among current LEGO owners, and recruited new LEGO consumers by means of sampling."

The McDonald's collaboration was an example of the kind of approach it took to break into the world's biggest toy market in the 1980s, where huge firms like Mattel, Hasbro, and Tyco didn't play well with others. Tyco, especially, began flexing its muscles once they'd discovered that LEGO's patent had expired. Tyco launched a system of bricks called "Super Blocks," made of the same plastic material, which were a direct copy of LEGO but cost only a third of the price in stores.

In big, aggressive commercials, Tyco informed American consumers that Super Blocks were compatible with LEGO, and in 1985, the company took the extreme step of declaring war on LEGO, on customers' behalf. They released a commercial that featured a fearsome tank built out of Super Blocks, aiming its gun barrel at the enemy in the tiny country on the other side of the planet. "TYCO DECLARES WAR ON LEGO—and you're going to win!" the ad announced. The implication, of course, was that the consumer would emerge victorious.

Tyco believed this type of marketing was justified, partly because LEGO's American patent had run out, and partly because they claimed that the Danish toy company took its original idea for the product from another company back in 1948–1949. Once again, Kiddicraft haunted

TYCO DECLARES WAR ON LEGO.

And you're going to win! Tyco Super Blocks. The Super Value Blocks.

TYCO

Lego is a registered trademark of Interlego A.G.

(Circle No. 88 on Reader Inquiry Card)

Toy giant Tyco went on the offensive, accusing the "enemy" in Europe of plagiarizing its plastic bricks.

the boardrooms of Billund, and LEGO's legal team readied itself for the company's biggest international lawsuit to date. It would go on for several years.

The first stage of the case was decided in LEGO's favor. The case was heard in Hong Kong in 1986, and that was the first time Godtfred told the detailed story of LEGO's development of Hilary F. Page's "Self-

Locking Building Bricks" under oath, admitting that they'd copied the English bricks "very carefully," as was noted in the court transcript. It was a difficult moment for Godtfred. While in strictly legal terms he'd never acted illegally in relation to Page and Kiddicraft, he'd nonetheless always felt twinges of guilt.

During the examination in Hong Kong, Tyco's lawyer turned the screws on Godtfred, recounting a story about a recent visit he'd taken to LEGOLAND in Denmark with his son. During the visit, he was surprised that LEGO made no mention of Hilary F. Page anywhere in its account of the bricks' success.

"People get the impression that the whole idea and design of the interlocking bricks comes from LEGO . . . isn't that a bit unfair?"

Godtfred replied, "Some people might find that unfair, if they know about it. Personally, I haven't thought about it."

Well before that point in 1986, when GKC and his entourage of lawyers and consultants booked their tickets for a three-week stay in Hong Kong, reserving ten rooms at the Hilton Hotel, LEGO was already undergoing plenty of upheavals in Billund.

When Kjeld and his young team moved into the upper-level management offices around 1980, they immediately instituted a radical shift from the more cautious approach of the 1970s, keeping their fingers firmly on the pulse of the future. Enthusiasm, curiosity, and the courage to think creatively and innovatively were once again rewarded in the Product Development Division.

Within a few years, there was a small explosion in the range of products, and the number of sets, which had been stable at about 145 per year throughout the 1970s, mushroomed to 246 in 1983. In Kjeld's first five years as managing director, turnover tripled, reaching two billion kroner. The number of employees increased from 2,500 to 3,300, and new factories were planned in Switzerland, Korea, and Brazil. Progress was obvious in all areas of the company.

Expansion was due not only to some of the new blood on the management team and LEGO's burgeoning success in North America, but also to the flexible, modifiable LEGO Minifigures, which proved adaptable to virtually any realistic or fairy-tale context. Soon there were nurses, police officers, astronauts, knights with shields, pirates with wooden legs, luminous ghosts, and many more. In record time, the Minifigures, dubbed "Minifigs" in the USA, were wreaking havoc, in the most positive way, on the classic LEGO System in Play, which was traditionally devoid of people.

Kjeld: *We were in need of a bit of life in our LEGO universe, and the Minifigures certainly brought that. The combination of building and role-playing drove much of the development, and laid the groundwork for the golden period of growth throughout the decade and into the 1990s. With Town, Castle, Space, and Pirates, we captured the interest of an extraordinary number of children.*

More than ever, it was crucial that LEGO stay alert and on its toes. In the early 1980s, the whole industry found itself confronted with a previously unknown challenge: handheld gaming consoles, which were suddenly disrupting traditional forms of play and changing more than a few wish lists in the run-up to Christmas. In Billund, the situation was initially viewed with supreme calm. When a newspaper asked if the LEGO Group would come out with anything electronic the next year, the Head of Public Relations, Peter Ambeck-Madsen, replied, "We haven't changed our product-development plans because of these irritating electronic wasp stings on the toy market. But the explosive growth that has taken place in electronic games is helping to keep us vigilant."

Kjeld: *Personally, I was fascinated by the first handheld games, and later also by the big gaming consoles with joysticks. I wouldn't say that as a toy company we were afraid of the new competition, however, at least not in the beginning. Of course, we talked a lot about how we might integrate something digital into the LEGO experience, and, having inherited my granddad's curiosity about machines and technology, I really gave it a lot of thought.*

More life and excitement were brought into the LEGO system, and on the front of the 1981 catalog was a whole horde of small figures from various product lines, underlining the endless possibilities for role-play.

It soon became clear that gaming consoles couldn't be ignored. Danish schoolchildren of the early 1980s spent their school recesses enclosed by walls of synthetic sound effects, staring fixedly at the little gadgets gripped in their hands, while their thumbs pressed buttons at lightning speed, issuing various commands. Donkey Kong, Octopus, and Mario Bros. were just a few of the games that could be played on the consoles, which were invented and developed in Japan.

The handheld gaming devices became an existential challenge in record time. Parents and teachers were driven to madness by the beeps and boops, while some toy stores in Denmark initially refused to stock them at all because some critics posited that they undermined good, healthy forms of play. The head buyer for Magasin, a major department store in Denmark, called the games "nothing but beeping," and, like LEGO's management team, believed they'd be just a flash in the pan. Many Danish childcare centers were also somewhat circumspect about the "antisocial" new type of game, and several after-school clubs for-bade children from bringing the electronic handsets. The head of one such center in Kolding explained in the spring of 1983:

> We've had enough now. There was a huge boom in these games just before Christmas, and it was at its worst here before Easter. The games made children eerily passive. They play all by themselves with the handset, so there's never any motivation to socialize with the other children. If any-thing, it can lead to aggression if another child is blocking a player's light.

Today these strong reactions have been relegated to the level of quaint historical anecdote. The truth is that the wave of beeping hand-sets, which were quickly followed by gaming consoles like the Com-modore 64 and Nintendo's revolutionary Gameboy, were merely the harbingers of a tsunami of digital hardware that was to flood children's and teenagers' bedrooms across most of the developed world, all the way up to the turn of the millennium. Over the course of the next de-cade, the way children played, whether by themselves or with others, and especially what they played *with*, underwent a paradigmatic shift.

At first, LEGO's attitude was one of skepticism; they believed the games to be a passing fad. When *Børsen,* one of Denmark's leading busi-ness newspapers, published a special feature on the internationally renowned toy company in the spring of 1983, the former and current managing directors both went on record saying that they didn't con-sider electronic gaming to be a threat to LEGO's continued growth. On this issue, father and son were, apparently, of like mind. Godtfred remarked, "In the toy industry, we're among the most successful com-panies in the world, and we're in no way shocked by the popularity of these electronic games."

Yet the journalist from *Børsen* sensed a rift between the two genera-tions, so he pressed the question, asking the son whether LEGO would start producing electronic toys. It wasn't inconceivable, argued the journalist, since LEGO had recently announced that it would be releas-ing a series of books featuring stories from the FABULAND universe, in

The tension between father and son was palpable in a newspaper interview in 1984, in which Godtfred presented himself as a level-headed, stubborn Jutlander. "I won't stop until my son throws me out, and he can't do that until I'm seventy. But we do also work together wonderfully, just as well as I did with my father." Kjeld made no comment. *Photo: Flemming Adelson.*

partnership with Denmark's biggest publishing house, and there were also rumors flying around about LEGO films. So, would LEGO continue to shift further away from its core business?

Kjeld denied this, but added:

Of course, that doesn't mean we won't use every new technology we may find relevant. But it will be because the new technology can serve our purposes. We won't introduce a new technology into the product for technology's sake. If we use electronics, it will be incorporated in a natural way, just as we have been using motors and other technology as a natural part of our range for many years.

Kjeld, the computer nerd, had already envisaged LEGO finding its own niche in the new technology, in the intersection between play and education—in other words, in schools. As early as 1980–1981, LEGO's designers collaborated with educators and experts from various fields and forms of teaching, and a commercial for DUPLO featured the slogan: "Make learning fun for little hands."

The educational aspect of the toys was further emphasized over the following years. LEGO worked on a range of proposals for technologically enhanced building projects for teachers, students, and young children aged eighteen months and up, for a new product line called LEGO Education. LEGO Technic 1 launched in 1985, followed a couple of years later by LEGO DUPLO Mosaic. The company also set up a learning portal where teachers could download free educational activities, as well as instructions and activity packs for the two sets.

In 1982, in LEGO's official fiftieth anniversary book, Kjeld used the phrase "learning through play," and around the same time he commented to a newspaper: "Instead of reading about technological things in books, the students can build them themselves. We have a lot of faith in that market." Not everyone in the company leadership was convinced, however, when Kjeld tried to explain that a large, important future market for LEGO would be not just schools and childcare centers, but also higher education.

Kjeld: *I remember clearly one of the executives saying, "No, that won't work. If the kids are using the bricks in school, they'll get really sick of LEGO and won't want to play with it when they get home."*
"Oh, come on, don't be silly!" I said.

One evening in late February 1984, after yet another long day at the office, sitting in meeting after meeting, Kjeld was relaxing at home in Skovparken with Camilla. The television set was on, and some schoolchildren appeared onscreen, using a computer to make a little tortoise-like robot do what they asked. The scene changed, and a man with a gray beard came on, telling viewers that he'd made a special programming

Seymour Papert argued that children learned through experimentation, and that there was a synergy between technology and children's creativity. Kjeld was of the same mind, and it proved to be the beginning of a partnership between LEGO and the MIT Media Lab that culminated in the launch of LEGO Mindstorms in 1998.

language that was so simple and intuitive that children could easily master it. The man was Seymour Papert, and he described computers as creative tools in a new kind of teaching, suitable for the digital age, which was just around the corner. "Education has very little to do with explanation. It has to do with engagement, with falling in love with the material."

Kjeld was sold on the spot. Or, the *Wall Street Journal* wrote a few years later, it was well aligned with the ethos of a company that had "made a fortune satisfying children's need to tinker." For the first time, LEGO was seriously looking for answers as to how the simple little brick could find a place in the computer age.

Kjeld: *I became deeply fascinated by Seymour Papert's idea about children learning by playing with a computer and the programming language he had invented, which he called "Logo." The day after the broadcast, I asked some employees to contact Papert, and soon got his* *response. Funnily enough, he'd been thinking of writing to us for a while, because he'd used LEGO bricks in several of his experiments at the Media Lab at the Massachusetts Institute of Technology (MIT) in Boston. Even then, the Media Lab was an interdisciplinary stronghold of technology, encompassing all sorts of interests and widely varying ways of thinking when it came to programming and digitalization. Not long after that, I went to Boston to speak to the man.*

The man Kjeld met was both a firebrand and a big kid at heart, with a diverse range of skills and talents. Trained as a mathematician, computer scientist, and educator, he was deeply inspired by the world-famous Swiss psychologist Jean Piaget. Piaget had sought to understand how children construct knowledge, believing that children developed through meeting challenges. Also, at the most fundamental level, he believed they wanted to further their own development. Papert expanded on Piaget's theories, advocating for the idea that when children built things with their hands, they were building knowledge at the same time. This type of learning was important, claimed Papert, because it lodged more deeply in the child's brain than when the teacher simply told him or her how something worked and how it should be understood.

Meeting Papert and learning about his ideas regarding schools of the future, where the nature of play would also be the nature of learning, and computers would be on an equal footing with pencils and books, was a watershed moment for Kjeld. He was never particularly fond of his own time at school, and he saw potential in a school where the children, as Papert said, took control of their own learning and used the materials around them to explore the world and understand themselves in new ways.

Kjeld: *It was Seymour who introduced me to the idea of the intelligent bricks that you could program yourself, and he gave me the inspiration for how these intelligent bricks could be the third big technological innovation in LEGO's history. Out of the original, groundbreaking building system in 1955, we had created the wheel in 1962, which meant that the* *bricks could move. In 1966 came the electric motor, which meant people could get even more life and play out of their bricks. The next stage Seymour and I pictured was that people could build behavior into our models and program their LEGO robots themselves.*

In May 1985, Seymour Papert visited Denmark. Before heading to Billund to talk to Kjeld, he gave a lecture at Christiansborg to three hundred elementary school teachers about the future of learning for children in a technological society. Papert's message was that computers could be a fantastic tool for suppressing pupils' creativity, if that's what you wanted to do. But machines could also be used to liberate children's creativity and promote their independence.

After the lecture, Seymour Papert mentioned to the journalists in attendance that the Media Lab at MIT in Boston had begun collaborating with LEGO. They were working on developing bricks with built-in sensors—infrared photocells—so that robots could be programmed to react to contact with a wall or other objects. Papert also told them that the project would be ready for the American educational market within a few years; they'd offer the new, technologically sophisticated bricks to schools so that children could build robots, cranes, and vehicles out of LEGO elements, and control them on computers, using the Logo program.

Kjeld: *We established a setup for developing LEGO in Boston, which would work closely with the Media Lab. I really felt an intellectual kinship with Seymour, which sounds strong, but we communicated incredibly well when we met, which we did many times in the years that followed. We never used big, fancy words and long, flawless sentences. We'd just sit together and philosophize a bit. He wasn't really a man of many words, but when he said something, it was nearly always meaningful.*

Kjeld's faith in the concept of learning through play took a big leap forward in the late 1980s, when LEGO and the MIT Media Lab developed software for LEGO's own models in the LEGO Technic line.

With the LEGO TC-1 in 1986, you could build robot-like objects that were controlled via computer. Journalist and computing expert Ole Grünbaum was very enthusiastic but pointed out the limitations of the era: "You need to already have a computer, and that itself amounts to several thousand kroner to start with. So the robot idea is slow off the blocks, and it's mostly only schools that are doing it."

The first tangible result of this overseas collaboration was presented in 1986–1987 and named LEGO TC—"TC" standing for Technic Control. Using different kinds of LEGO bricks, a control box, and software, students could now build a robot controlled with Apple and IBM computers.

These sets were making headway in American schools as early as 1990, by which time the use and demonstration of modern technology had become an obligatory part of the curriculum. Developing children into problem solvers and inventors was a pedagogical objective. As Papert put it in the *Wall Street Journal*: "Computers give our society, for the first time, the choice of deciding whether we want to produce role-learning people who do disciplined routine work and follow orders, or whether we want to produce critical, creative minds."

But Seymour Papert wasn't Kjeld's only inspiration in the 1980s. Back at HQ in Billund, which a business journalist once described as something reminiscent of "an old folks' home on a spruce plantation," there was a rather odd duck roaming the halls of the dark brown brick building. Per Sørensen had a surprising way of expressing himself when it came to management and LEGO, given that he was a highly paid executive in the yuppie-ish, Filofax-obsessed 1980s.

"When Columbus set out to cross the Atlantic, he didn't know where he was sailing. When he came ashore on the other side, he didn't know where he was, and when he got back home, he didn't know where he'd been. We were in no better a position at LEGO when we started talking about developing our management team."

Kjeld had made Per Sørensen a director at LEGO in 1979, putting him in charge of personnel, organization, training, and working conditions, among other things. Handed this rather fluid area of responsibility, Sørensen was essentially given the run of the place for two decades, helping the managing director to broaden his view of himself and his role.

Kjeld: *I'd experienced Per as a very inspiring and highly nontraditional teacher at the business school in Aarhus, where he taught computer science and organizational development. When we were looking for a head of personnel, Per applied, and I arranged a job interview, which my dad absolutely did not want to be part of.*

"Oh no, a man like that has no business at LEGO," he thought. Still, he crept into my office in the middle of the interview, sat down, and was fascinated by Per's ideas. He was very—how should I put it—yin-and-yang-like, and was fond of turning things on their head.

"Okay, but why don't we look at it this way, or maybe that way?"

Dad really liked challenging and unorthodox managers who had never been involved in the toy industry before.

Personnel Manager Per Sørensen (left) had an unusual view of management, and he expressed it when talking to the press. "If customers think the goods are really expensive, and our employees think they're only just getting paid enough, and the suppliers say they can't do business with us, and our shareholders say their returns are too small, we're doing our jobs as managers. All interest groups must be suitably dissatisfied, one might say." *Photo: Erik Jepsen.*

Highly educated and with a clear sense of the LEGO spirit and values, Per Sørensen played a key role in shaping the culture at LEGO throughout the 1980s, just as Søren Olsen had done in the 1960s. He also proved to be a valuable sparring partner for Kjeld and other upper-level executives at the company. Extremely well-read, Sørensen liked quoting words of wisdom from figures such as Lao Tzu and Mao, Kierkegaard, Grundtvig, and Jens Christian Hostrup, whose old song "High North, Freedom's Home" contains three lines Sørensen always used when he wanted to remind people of the conversations and innovation needed at LEGO:

Let it break, let it ferment!
Do not stem the current, endure its roar!
It will bear fruit for a summer's day.

These lofty lines were meant to show that people were welcome to disagree at LEGO, especially if they came out and said so, as long as they could communicate like real people and not just as "roles." So Kjeld's former teacher became the source of inspiration and ideas behind many of the training projects the new managing director launched, projects in which LEGO's young team of managers grew accustomed to working with one another in a company that was barnstorming ahead and occasionally threatening to spiral out of control.

Kjeld: *In the 1980s I really started thinking about management philosophy. It was necessary, I thought, because we were growing so much. We ended up putting on a number of seminars, with external experts on communication who could help us organize and think in a new way, especially when it came to our very diverse styles of management. I have always been a firm believer in collaboration, so we held lots of meetings in those days. I wanted to be sure that I had convinced my close colleagues, and anyone who would be developing my ideas, that it wasn't just my idea but also theirs. I wanted this to be passed on through the organization and spread throughout the company. To a degree, this was a success.*

This success was due, in large part, to Per Sørensen, whose approach to management had always been shaped by the realization that all tasks are dialectical in nature and should be considered from different angles. Building on his Taoist philosophy of management, Sørensen came up with a series of dogmas known as "The Eleven Paradoxes of Management." This set of simple, easy-to-remember rules was printed on top of a huge yin-and-yang symbol and turned into a poster given to all executives at LEGO. The individual paradoxes were formulated as paired statements that initially seem contradictory but, through that contradiction, produce new and deeper insight. For example:

A leader must take the lead—and recede into the background.

A leader must be dynamic—but also thoughtful.

A leader must be visionary—but also keep both feet firmly on the ground.

A leader must be self-confident—but also humble.

Kjeld: *Even though the paradoxes are more than thirty years old, I still like the attitude behind them. And we did get a lot of fun and exciting conversations out of them, back in the day. They actually arose out of a management team meeting where we had started chatting about the requirements of a good LEGO manager. All the usual platitudes were on the table, and suddenly Per Sørensen suggested that we organize it as a series of paradoxes. That maneuver was incredibly inspiring, and one of my good directors at the time contributed to the animated atmosphere with the unforgettable words "Leaders with high-flying visions and both feet on the ground don't grow on trees!"*

For Kjeld, the paradoxes turned into not just a starting point for a new philosophy of management at LEGO, but also a more personal admonition. It was partly about maintaining an accommodating, open, outlook on life, one in line with the company's spirit and culture, and partly about Kjeld's own conviction that most things in life can only be explained by, and develop meaning through, their opposite. It was a foundational worldview and a way of dealing with his surroundings that wasn't without its problems, given that he was the head of a company with five thousand employees who expected their boss to be action-oriented, capable of cutting to the chase, and setting a clear course.

Kjeld: *I have always known that there's more "both/and" than "either/ or" in this world. That was already at the back of my mind, even as a young manager in Switzerland. But as Per Sørensen and I used to joke with each other, we needed both more "either" and more "or"—both at*

THE 11 PARADOXES OF MANAGEMENT

To be able to establish a close relationship to your employees,	– and to keep proper distance
To take the lead,	– and to recede into the background
To show the employee confidence,	– and to be aware of their doings
To be tolerant,	– and to know how you want things done
To be concerned about your own field of responsibility,	– and at the same time to be loyal to the overall goals of the company
To plan your working-day carefully,	– and to be flexible to your planning
To express your opinion,	– and to be diplomatic
To be visionary,	– and to keep both feet firmly on the ground
To aim at consensus,	– and to be able to cut through
To be dynamic,	– but also thoughtful
To be self-confident,	– and humble

"The Eleven Paradoxes of Management," written down by Per Sørensen in 1986, were printed as a large poster with a yin-and-yang symbol and circulated to all LEGO managers at home and abroad. The purpose was to help them understand that all management is full of contradictions.

once, I mean—in the management of LEGO. We had some great semi-
nars, but not everybody was equally enthusiastic and inspired.

Some would say, "We talk almost too much about things, don't we,
Kjeld?" We probably did, but back then I felt it was crucial that we made
decisions as a team, and that everybody felt we were on the same page.
That was pretty much my management philosophy in the 1980s, and it
always has been, really.

When Per Sørensen stepped down after nearly two decades at the
LEGO Group, he was given a gold pocket watch by his former student at
the business school. A representative from the employee magazine was
at the reception, and asked what Per would like to be remembered for.

"Just write that for a number of years I helped to make sure things
didn't get formalized, that it wasn't too much of a symphony orches-
tra with a conductor and sheet music and not enough of a jam session
with ensemble playing and space for improvisations. This is how we
preserved the LEGO culture, or the LEGO spirit, if you will."

Reading through the outstanding annual accounts through the 1980s,
during which period LEGO's turnover and profits skyrocketed, it was
clear why the management felt like miracle workers by the end of the
decade. That's why Godtfred, in his capacity as chairman of the board
of LEGO A/S, asked for the minutes of one general meeting to note that
the young managers should take care "not to let this success go to their
heads."

The company was going nowhere but headlong into the future. In
1988, LEGO was awarded the prestigious Imagepris for the first time, a
prize given by *Børsen* on the basis of votes from Danish business leaders. Throughout the 1990s, LEGO was to take the prize another five
times. Spearheading all of this, although had it been up to him, he'd
have stayed in the background, was Kjeld Kirk Kristiansen, now aged
forty, who'd been selected by the *Jyllands-Posten* in 1989 as one of the
young Danish executives who'd leave his mark on the 1990s. A new
generation was in full ascendance in the world of Danish industry: Jess

Søderberg at A.P. Møller, Mads Øvlisen at Novo Nordisk, Mogens Granborg at Danisco, and Kjeld Kirk Kristiansen at LEGO. All of them represented a break with tradition; no longer were old men hoarding all the power and the money at Denmark's biggest companies.

Kjeld was said to have been something of a kindred spirit with Mærsk Mc-Kinney Møller, another Dane who was an equally unusual executive. One of the things they had in common was their personal, family-based ownership of a gigantic international corporation. Another was the style of leadership they favored, one in which everyone in the company had a singular attitude drilled into them, that people only achieve the things that they do alongside others, and that everyone's contribution counted. A third common trait was that both the older shipping magnate and the young toy manufacturer didn't make a big song and dance of their public image. As *Jyllands-Posten* wrote about Kjeld:

> He almost never raises his voice in ordinary political debates. But behind the scenes his influence is undeniable, not just in Billund, where next year's budget is run by LEGO's senior managers before it's approved by the council. LEGO also has strong ties with government and the Danish parliament. Kjeld Kirk Kristiansen is on the senior board of the Danish Industrial Council, and as a member of the board at Danske Bank, he has close links with several key figures in the business community, including A.P. Møller's Jess Søderberg and one of Denmark's most powerful businesspeople, Poul J. Svanholm, Chairman of the Board and Managing Director of Carlsberg.

But even though LEGO's managing director was considered one of the country's most influential businessman in the late 1980s—he was described elsewhere as "seemingly unaffected by the fact that he's in charge of 5,800 employees and a business that's constantly adding major new factory complexes in Billund"—Kjeld had more to contend with on the personal front than most people realized at the time. Throughout the 1980s, he periodically doubted his charisma and effectiveness as a leader. This insecurity was only exacerbated by the fact that his father

Father and son continued to disagree even more into the 1980s, and Kjeld often found himself wondering about a question asked in one of his favorite Bob Dylan songs: "How many roads must a man walk down / Before you can call him a man?" *Photo: Flemming Adelson.*

was still working behind the scenes, occasionally questioning his son's leadership abilities. It all took a toll on the young executive's mental state and self-esteem.

>**Kjeld:** *It happened pretty much from as soon as I got back from Switzerland in 1977 and lasted until Dad died in 1995, but it was the worst in the 1980s. On the one hand, Dad was proud of me, and he could see that there was a need for me to push through certain initiatives. But he demanded I set aside time for meetings just with him. For example, he wanted us to go to his hunting lodge in the woods at Utoft, between Billund and Grindsted, once a week, to talk about anything and everything involving the running of the company.*
>
>*The result was that I spent far too much time on what my father thought and wanted. He wanted me to ask him for advice more often, and I indulged that. At the same time, I had to constantly think about*

how I could get him excited about the developments ongoing at LEGO with me at the helm. Throughout the 1980s, we had regular showdowns, and I had to make myself pretty unambiguous: "I'm the one who makes the decisions, and you, dear Dad, need to stop going behind my back and talking to this person or that person!"

This also meant, sadly, that we didn't see so much of each other personally, because we always ended up arguing, and, of course, that was something that affected both Camilla and my mother. The children also couldn't help but notice. My dad and I almost invariably spiraled into some kind of stupid debate that neither of us could stop. We were probably equally stubborn in that regard.

Deep down, he wanted the best, of course, and I did too, but we were just two different generations.

In a joint interview with father and son in *Management* in 1981, Godtfred declared that he had entered his "second life as an entrepreneur" and wanted to work on ideas and projects that would benefit Billund and the local area. He'd accomplish this working through a holding company, KIRKBI A/S.

But what did that mean for his role as chairman of the board at the parent company, LEGO A/S, where Godtfred had to make sure his son was up to snuff? inquired the journalist.

Godtfred replied, "I would put it more like this: that if there are things we disagree about, it'll certainly take thorough elucidation of the whole issue to get me convinced."

As chairman of the board, did he like getting involved with the nitty-gritty?

"You never know! You should never stand in the way of new management, of course, but you do have to offer an alternate view, based on experience. Things are being done that I would have done differently, but I can still say that there haven't been any major decisions that I disagree with."

The journalist then asked for more details about how father and son worked together to determine LEGO's future plans.

Kjeld replied, "We agree that continued, healthy growth is important for the future, but we probably don't entirely agree on what healthy growth is. We can't just expand through new markets; we need to ensure healthy growth in the markets that already exist."

But what would their strategy for the future be based on?

Godtfred answered this question, emphasizing that the most important thing was controlled growth. "We have to be the ones running the company, and not the other way around!"

Kjeld listened and added, "I completely agree with that."

Kjeld: *I had a lot of respect for my father, and I still do. Luckily, there were also a lot of good times when we were able to be close. It was nearly always something to do with running the company that made us argue. But it was his life's work, after all. LEGO truly was his life in every respect, so it was tough on him to be pushed out. I can certainly see and understand that, but it also meant that I often saw a more negative side of my father.*

People frequently told me that Dad was visibly proud when he talked about me and what I did for LEGO, but that wasn't my experience of him at all when we were together. There was rarely any praise, even when things were going fantastically well.

In August 1982, LEGO celebrated its fiftieth anniversary. That celebration became, to a significant extent, Godtfred's show. He appeared in newspapers and on TV, and on the anniversary day itself, he was the one who gave the signature speech on the lawn outside the company headquarters on Aastvej, where rows of chairs and a platform had been set up on the grass. The weather, however, didn't cooperate. LEGO Airway's three planes, a Cessna and two King Airs, circled in heavily overcast skies, partially drowned out by the events in LEGOLAND Garden, where a marching band assembled on the damp ground, while Godtfred prepared to give a welcome speech to the 150 invited guests, journalists, and photographers.

Rain started pelting down, with the entire Kirk Kristiansen family

Godtfred addresses the family and employees at LEGO's fiftieth anniversary in August 1982. The umbrella is held by Peter Ambeck-Madsen, Head of Public Relations. *Private collection.*

gathered under umbrellas in the front rows. In the middle was eighty-five-year-old Sofie, surrounded by her and Ole's five adult children and their spouses, reunited for the first time in two decades. Godtfred began by thanking them warmly:

> *I'm so glad the whole family can come together. And a special thanks to you, Mom. you played a large part in keeping Dad going through those difficult years at the start. In 1932, many people wondered about Dad's toy business: will this actually work out?*
>
> *Today, in another period of crisis, it seems appropriate to ask a similar question: "Can we keep going?"*

We can only guess what his two brothers, Gerhardt and Karl Georg, who had allowed themselves to be bought out of LEGO twenty years earlier, were thinking at that moment. Fifty-six-year-old Gerhardt had never turned BILOfix into the world-wide sensation that the toy was predicted to be. Eventually, he sold his invention and put all his energies into a chain of toy stores, GK Toys, which did very well for many years. When the chain celebrated its anniversary, Godtfred turned up to offer his congratulations, and the *Jyske Tidende* seized the opportunity to ask about the relationship between the brothers.

Gerhardt answered, "We get on well in the family, but we run the businesses as though we were strangers. Those things need to be kept separate."

Sixty-three-year-old Karl Georg came back to LEGO in 1982, taking charge of manufacturing the many millions of wheels for cars and trains. Production took place in Kolding, where Karl Georg had once run his own plastics company with more than fifty employees. The company had to shut down in the 1970s, however, after which Karl Georg ran a trading company before accepting the job at LEGO.

Godtfred concluded his anniversary speech under the umbrella by saying that the company had reason to be optimistic. "We have a focused and dynamic management team, led by you, Kjeld!"

Godtfred repeated this rare praise to a journalist that same day.

"Everything has gotten a bit of a boost since Kjeld took over leadership. He has a bolder disposition than I do, but to be completely honest, I would have preferred the company not to get so big that I don't know all the employees by their first name."

And to another journalist, Godtfred said that Kjeld has fostered a new, dynamic energy within the company, but also done things he would never have done himself, and that he occasionally utterly disagreed with.

"I have to learn to stop interfering! It should be noted, though, that in my first years at the company I saw a lot of red numbers in the ledgers. Kjeld has never seen that. I think that's a very different context in which to make decisions."

Unlike his son, Godtfred never had anything against being in the spotlight, and used the attention LEGO's anniversary received as a platform to make political statements that resonated throughout the nation and emphasized that LEGO's former managing director was still going strong. On the front page of the *Jyllands-Posten*'s business supplement, Godtfred declared that LEGO may be Danish, but not at any price:

> *The Danish business climate may become so strained that, in order to ensure LEGO's survival, we will be forced to reconsider the situation. For one thing, passing LEGO on to the third generation is problematic, and for another, wealth taxes are a tremendous burden. When someone only keeps seventeen øre out of every krone earned, like I do, you can hardly claim that the Danish business climate is friendly.*

But the fact that Godtfred was left with a paltry seventeen øre per krone wasn't allowed to put a damper on the festivities. The family had put aside millions for the celebration in August. Indeed, the staff so looked forward to the eagerly anticipated anniversary gift from the owners that even before the summer break, rumors were flying, and bets were being made, as to whether the 4,000 employees would get a VHS or a Betamax player, which was the hottest consumer item of the day.

The gift turned out to be a bonus of 6,000 kroner for each employee. The money was quickly spent, giving a significant boost to local businesses; "Back in business," as the local paper wrote.

One of the two radio dealers in Billund shared that nearly everything, from color TVs to stereo sets and video players had been snapped up, and "People are paying cash!"

Their competitor on Hovedgaden, "Loudspeaker Kaj," was similarly satisfied with the money being thrown around, and the butcher, Nissen, reported that in the first days after the anniversary, you'd have thought it was the day before New Year's Eve. "People were buying steaks and expensive wine like never before!"

Kjeld's gift to himself, Camilla, and their children was a property on an island called Funen, in the middle of Denmark. Schelenborg, the property, lies north of Kerteminde and had a history going back to the

Kjeld and Camilla bought Schelenborg, north of Kerteminde, from the Juel-Brockdorff family. They turned the estate into a space where they and their three children could get some distance from everyday life in Billund, where they were constantly surrounded by LEGO. *Private collection.*

thirteenth century. The land had been owned by a notorious figure, Marsk Stig, also known as Stig Andersen Hvide, who was convicted of regicide at Finderup Lade, stripped of his estate, and declared an outlaw. By 1982, Schelenborg included stables, small outbuildings, and twelve hundred acres of land, over a thousand of which were cultivated.

The LEGO family had discovered the area, full of stunning natural beauty, on a holiday to Fyns Hoved in northeastern Funen in the summer of 1982, in Godtfred and Edith's camper van. One day after the summer vacation, Kjeld happened to see that Schelenborg, near Martofte, was for sale, and put in an offer on the family's behalf. In honor of the sensational purchase, the *Vejle Amt Folkeblad* printed a mischievous poem underneath a caricature that depicted the new landowner standing outside Schelenborg with two disappointed little boys glaring—the historic buildings weren't even built out of LEGO bricks!

LEGO Director K. K. Kristiansen
Used his power to buy a mansion.

How'd he get this great estate?
Just by raising an eyebrow, mate!
It's easy enough to snag a house
When you're not as poor as a little church mouse.
And though his money came from bricks
This manor wasn't bought on tick!

Kjeld: *We quickly started using Schelenborg as a spot to go on weekends and holidays. It was good for the family, and especially for me because I needed some physical space from LEGO and Billund.*

I was very much replicating my father's way of living. I probably made it home for dinner most evenings, but I was thinking constantly of LEGO and often worked late into the night. Many times, I had to disappoint Camilla and the kids when they thought we were going to do something together. On top of that, there were so many long business trips! In those days I felt it was crucial to travel to our major markets, to say hello and let people know who I was—and who we were, all of us in Billund.

As managing director and co-owner, I kept claiming that LEGO was a "we" company, but that wasn't always the way it came across to our foreign colleagues. So I also dispatched my managers all across the world. I went to Africa, North and South America, Australia and New Zealand, Southeast Asia, and Japan myself. Today, I sometimes regret that during those years when my children were growing up, I was just as absent as my father had been when I was their age.

In early January 1988, Kjeld and Camilla hosted the annual New Year's bash for upper-level management in Billund. Twenty or thirty male directors, deputy directors, and board members brought their wives. Godtfred and Edith, and Kjeld's sister, Gunhild, and her husband, Mogens, were also invited to the festivities, which took place at Hotel LEGOLAND.

Kjeld, as usual, had prepared a New Year's speech, but this time it was a little longer than usual. After welcoming everyone and introducing a few new faces, he talked about the year that had just ended. A sudden and unexpected dip in sales in the spring of 1987 was swiftly and efficiently reversed thanks to the strong, coordinated efforts of the management team, and Kjeld philosophized about the reason behind this extraordinary level of commitment:

> It's the fact that we at the LEGO Group work with children that makes the company something very special. We have a product idea that is based on children's limitless imagination and creativity, and this is part of what inspires managers and employees to stick to some of the qualities of children: be open to new possibilities, be ready to constantly learn new things, don't just accept the restrictions you are given. We grown-ups forget to use our imaginations and often give up too soon, because "you can't!" or "we've tried that before!" We've got to remember not to neglect our inner child.

Building on this tribute to the child in all of us, in the latter part of the speech, Kjeld looked forward to an exciting 1988. Where was LEGO going? They would discuss this at the annual international LEGO Conference, he said, a conference that would be all about vision, concepts, goals, and strategies through the year 2000.

Eight months later, in the final week of August, corporate management presented its overall strategy proposal to one hundred directors from more than twenty countries at the Hotel Hvide Hus in Ebeltoft. With an eye over the last ten years' progress and LEGO's global development, the strategy proposed for taking the company into the new millennium would be debated over the following four days.

As in his New Year's speech, Kjeld began by describing all the good things that characterized children and childhood: openness, curiosity, the ability to think differently and see the possibility in things. The proposal itself took the form of a ten-minute film entitled *The Vision*. The film's first half depicts the managing director personally, sitting at home in his living room in Skovparken, mulling over what LEGO should stand for in the coming decade. "In my vision, in my dream, the LEGO name is associated with more than just our products and with the company, and it's not restricted by a framework of specific goals and strategies. The LEGO name has become a universal term that can be described with the words *idea, exhuberance*, and *values*."

In the second half of the film there's a change of scene. Kjeld is replaced by a performer in white face paint and gloves, who mimes the various meanings associated with the three buzzwords. This wordless presentation is accompanied by selected clips from the documentary film *Moments of Play*, which the poet and filmmaker Jørgen Leth had made for LEGO some years earlier. The film is a collage of sixty-one sequences filmed at various places around the globe. It was a poetic examination of the nature of play. Why do we do it? What might be the goal of play? What drives it?

There are no explanations or interpretations offered up in the film, just images and a few words suggesting that play in itself is an exploration of reality. Play is learning.

I play, I can do anything,
Nothing is forbidden,
I make my own world,
Systematize chaos,
I keep a balance,
As long as I think it's sustainable,
I play that the world exists,
That is the game I play.

Kjeld: *I have always liked to philosophize about our values, and especially the value of preserving your inner child. Over all these years, I have always tried to shape the organization along those lines.*

I remember Dad saying, "Okay, is this necessary, Kjeld?"

My answer was that people don't just get that sort of thing by themselves, even if they may have a strong instinct for it. It's something you have to be made aware of, and something you have to want.

For me, it was absolutely central that LEGO was much more than a toy company. We had achieved a place in the hearts of parents and children that was much bigger than the company's size really justified. When we did surveys and research in our biggest markets—back then it was Germany, above all—we could see that we were miles ahead of any other toy brand. So I started preaching about how we should focus on our brand.

Many people said, "Okay, but obviously it's the bricks that are key," and they were, but from my perspective this wasn't a case—and now we're back at paradoxes—of "either/or" but of "both/and." The paradox that we had a product idea that was physically represented in the brick, but that the LEGO name also stood for something much more enduring— that wasn't so easy for people around me to understand.

There were a few other things that weren't easy for LEGO's staff to understand, not least of which was the sudden spate of layoffs in 1983 and 1985. People in Billund weren't used to this sort of thing, certainly not from such a profitable company, even if it was a little less profitable than usual. The Danish papers followed the story closely.

Land og Folk, a paper that was still published by the Danish Communist Party but was in increasingly dire financial straits, attempted to cut to the heart of the matter in the summer of 1985 with an in-depth retrospective article titled, "Uncle LEGO: a hard-as-nails multinational country boy." The journalist's premise was unmistakable: the global Danish company manipulated public opinion to make people believe that things were suddenly going badly, even though their profits were consistently growing. As *Land og Folk* wrote: "The family from the heath is trying to burnish its clog-wearing image, and for the second year in a row they have pulled off the trick of reducing their workforce, even as their profits skyrocketed at record speed."

The local mid-Jutland papers had already investigated the rumors a few years earlier, when the first 230 layoffs had been announced in Billund. On behalf of the company, Director Stig Christensen denied that they were due to developments in new technology.

In the 1980s, children became role models at LEGO, and the creative powers
of childhood became the subject of LEGO's advertising campaigns.

What it is is beautiful.

Have you ever seen any-
~~ke~~ it? Not just what she's
~~b~~ut how proud it's made
~~i~~s a look you'll see whenever
~~childre~~n build something all by
~~thems~~elves. No matter what
~~they'v~~e created.

~~Youn~~ger children build for fun.
~~The~~ Universal Building Sets for
~~childre~~n ages 3 to 7 have colorful
~~blocks,~~ wheels, and friendly LEGO
~~people~~ for lots and lots of fun.

~~Older~~ children build for realism.
~~The~~ Universal Building Sets for
~~childre~~n 7–12 have more detailed
~~pieces~~ like gears, rotors, and
~~rubbe~~d tires for more realistic
~~buildin~~g. One set even has a motor.

~~Our~~ Universal Building Sets
~~will hel~~p your children discover
~~someth~~ing very, very special:
~~themse~~lves.

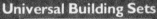

Universal Building Sets

3-7 years
old

7-12 years
old

~~LEGO is a re~~gistered trademark of Interlego A.G.
~~© 1980~~ Group

"It is certainly not the case that we have bought machinery to eliminate people from production. The reasoning behind the layoffs must be seen in light of the fact that, in 1982, we had a smaller increase in sales than the 15 percent we had expected and planned for."

The trade union representative, Tove Christensen, who also went by the name Tove Tillid, or "Tove Trade Union," didn't buy it. In her own diplomatic way, she went on the offensive, looking at the matter both from the employees' side and within a broader context. She believed that it was a cultural battle:

> As workers, we are in a very unequal competition with machines. If growth has slowed to the point that production capacity exceeds actual use, then we're the ones who lose our jobs. Technological development is only going to move forward, and every time a new machine comes into use at the company, it costs us working hours.

Tove Christensen also noted that the locals were especially hard hit by the layoffs, since many of them had been working at LEGO for less than five years and couldn't find other jobs nearby. This was particularly true for women, who made up 80 percent of the layoffs.

And what about the famous LEGO spirit? Where did that fit in all this rationalization?

That was HR boss Per Sørensen's department. After having assessed the mood at the factory, he was quoted in *Børsen* as saying that, on the whole, the employees understood that the layoffs were necessary, even though LEGO published an annual report not long afterward that painted a satisfactory financial picture. "The employees know perfectly well that it's not possible to continue producing bricks if there aren't enough people buying them. And you can't have a couple of hundred people wandering around a company without doing anything."

Employees came, employees went—and came back. LEGO weathered the cutbacks and the less profitable years, and the decade ended with the exciting launch of LEGO Pirates in 1989. The question was whether there was buried treasure to be unearthed in this new theme.

Expectations in Billund were high, but there was a little nervousness, too, visible in the employee magazine's rundown of new products. What would consumers say about the pirates, armed to the teeth, instead of the usually smiling, peaceful Minifigures? Had LEGO taken a sinister turn?

Although the LEGO Group does not produce toys related to modern warfare, and we certainly do not want to encourage violence and aggressive play, pirates—as well as cannons, rifles, and cutlasses—are perhaps a borderline case. At least for the category of "peaceful" (pious?) adults who will defend, tooth and nail, the idea that it is harmful, perhaps even dangerous, to let children play with anything related to war.

But LEGO could breathe a sigh of relief. Cuddliness was out, and the puritanical element in 1970s Scandinavian educational theory— which waged campaigns against war-themed toys through the national federation DUI-Leg og Virke and even got production of toy weapons banned in Sweden after the First World War—had gone out of fashion. The pirate-themed toys sold better than expected in Denmark, Scandinavia, and the rest of the world, and the eleven different sets became LEGO's single biggest success to date. It was yet another victory for Kjeld's old idea from 1978, that individual products should be part of overarching themes and that role-playing could breathe new life into the construction-based toy.

Within ten years, Kjeld and LEGO had managed to modernize and expand on what people could do with the bricks. More children than ever before, of different ages and from different cultures, were playing with LEGO products, now also available as teaching and educational materials in Danish, British, and American schools. Meanwhile, thanks to their fruitful partnership with Seymour Papert and the MIT Media Lab, the classic LEGO building experience had entered the computer

It sent shock waves through Billund in 1983 when LEGO laid off more than two hundred employees, most of whom lived in the town. Trade union representative Tove Christensen chose to see the issue from both sides: "I don't want to disparage the company, because it can't resist change, but it's a societal problem that there isn't enough work for everybody, and I think they should do something about that, say, through shorter working hours."

and robot age. As Kjeld remarked when he was awarded *Børsen*'s Image-pris in 1988, "I believe more in evolution than revolution, and I would like to see LEGO grow organically and naturally, based on our fundamental concept."

The following year, Seymour Papert was appointed LEGO Professor of Learning Research, and he and his team of researchers at MIT were given funding to the tune of two million dollars, which would not only cover the following year's collaboration, research, and development activities, but also allowed LEGO to appoint professors at MIT. When asked about Papert's appointment, LEGO's head of public relations observed that it was typically American for a company to endow a professorship in this way, to the benefit of both parties. He also added, "It's a shame that institutions of higher learning in Denmark don't also see the advantage here."

From LEGO's perspective, the endowment wasn't just about giving Seymour Papert and his team more funding; it was also a useful part of LEGO's new branding strategy. Kjeld was trying to bring even more focus to the brand, which is also why he launched the LEGO Prize, awarded for the first time in 1985. The reasoning behind the prize was this: "Childhood and the environment in which children live and de-

LEGO Pirates became the single biggest success to date in LEGO's history. The expressive Minifigures, which were now also allowed to look angry, marked a change in the company's attitude toward "armed" play.

velop are so important that there is an ever-present need for new ideas and new initiatives. LEGO would like to support work and initiatives that contribute to improving the lives of children all across the world."

The prize included 750,000 kroner and a LEGO model of Yggdrasil, the tree of life from Nordic mythology. Its roots reach to the core of the earth, while its top branches scrape the sky.

Kjeld: *The LEGO Chair and LEGO Prize were both my ideas and were meant to help underscore that the LEGO brand was about more than just toys. Actually, in a sense, it was the first step toward a goal I later presented and was heavily criticized for, that by 2005, LEGO should be the world's strongest brand among families with children.*

Two huge figures in Scandinavian children's culture met in 1986, when Astrid Lindgren received the LEGO Prize. During the gala dinner, Pippi Longstocking's "mother" and the "father" of the LEGO System sat next to each other. She thanked Godtfred for the prize with the words, "You Danes are very generous, giving so much money away—and to a Swede, even though we've beaten you so many times at football!" *Photo: Benny Nielsen, Vejle Stadsarkiv.*

On the cusp of the 1990s, LEGO, like everybody else in the toy industry, was peering curiously into the bedrooms of the children and teenagers of the future, where computers, keyboards, joysticks, and TVs with remote controls were increasingly part of the furniture, and computer games and films were an ever more important aspect of childhood. Not everyone was quite as enthusiastic as Seymour Papert, nicknamed the "computer hippie par excellence" by one Danish paper, about children's seemingly innate mastery of the new electronic media, but on one issue he was indisputably correct: while adults debated what this new culture would do to children and childhood, children and teens adapted the technology to their own purposes—and on their own terms.

Walls were about to come crumbling down . . .

INERTIA

THE 1990s

Mindstorms, 1998

When the Berlin Wall fell on Thursday, November 9, 1989, it was a moment of living history. The following week, *The Evening Standard* referenced a striking full-page ad printed in two other British Sunday papers. It declared that the three best reactions to the extraordinary events in Berlin had come from Chancellor Helmut Kohl, Prime Minister Margaret Thatcher—and LEGO.

The story of how a Danish toy company ended up being mentioned in this context exemplified the spontaneity and drive that LEGO's managing director had begun to feel was lacking in his organization.

On the afternoon of Friday, November 10, LEGO's UK sales office got a call from its regular advertising agency, WCRS. The creative director was on the line, having just faxed through an idea for an ad related to the event the whole world was talking about, and he asked Clive Nicholls, LEGO's British Head of Marketing, to take a look at the idea as soon as possible.

Like billions of other people across the globe, Nicholls had been watching history unfold in Berlin. Glued to his television screen that morning, he saw one clip after another of euphoric, cheering East Germans crawling over the wall with hammers and chisels, or crossing the border into West Berlin in an endless stream.

When Nicholls saw the fax with the advertising agency's sketch, he was beside himself with excitement. The idea was genius. A motley crowd of Minifigures surged across the border at the Berlin Wall, built out of bricks. On top of the wall were more Minifigures, hammering away at the hated wall, and in the background, you could make out the Brandenburg Gate, with the words "The perfect Christmas gift" hovering above the distinctive gate, which was supported by Doric columns. All of it was built out of LEGO.

It was a once-in-a-lifetime opportunity. Clive Nicholls knew that he and LEGO were unlikely to get another chance to send such a striking message with their advertising, to pay tribute to democracy and freedom, while at the same time reminding millions and millions of consumers that LEGO was ready for the upcoming Christmas season.

WCRS was able to have the ad ready to print in the Monday papers, if LEGO was on board with the idea. Clive Nicholls answered that it had to be in the Sunday papers, when the celebratory mood was still at fever pitch. Whatever the cost. It turned out that only two papers could squeeze in a full-page ad right before the deadline; it was then Saturday morning at nine-thirty. But the *Sunday Telegraph* and *Sunday Correspondent* had a combined circulation of more than one million readers, and it would still have a significant impact, the ad agency believed.

That there were only eighteen hours before the deadline was one consideration. The cost was something else. Thirty thousand pounds was a lot of money, and there was no room for it in LEGO's advertising budget. For the first time that Friday afternoon, Nicholls hesitated. Did he want to take responsibility for an ad that wasn't just expensive, but also made a political statement, breaking with the LEGO Group's guidelines? Nicholls reached for the telephone and called his boss, Gordon Carpenter. No answer. His boss had left for the weekend and was apparently unreachable.

Taking a deep breath, Nicholls set the process in motion. A lot of employees suddenly became unusually busy. The whole LEGO scene—border crossing, Berlin Wall, and Brandenburg Gate—had to be built, populated with several hundred LEGO Minifigures, then photographed. The biggest challenge was acquiring the building materials. At nearly five o'clock on a Friday, four staff members at the agency went careening off in a taxi to Hamley's on Regent Street, where they cleared the shelves of LEGO bricks, Minifigures, signs, trees, red and white railroad barriers, and everything else they'd need to re-create the jubilant crowds surging toward freedom. Over the next six hours, the model was built, photographed, and made into a print ad. Clive Nicholls slept through most of Saturday, getting up on Sunday to the first signs that LEGO's ad had attracted as much positive attention as Helmut Kohl's and Margaret Thatcher's official statements on the fall of the Wall.

LEGO was heaped with praise over the following days, and the ad was discussed and reproduced in other media. The plaudits rolled in from ordinary people and advertisers, and even their competitors in the toy industry gave them an approving nod. From Brisbane and Bangkok to Boston and, of course, Berlin, there was no doubt that LEGO would be the perfect Christmas gift.

Over the following years, as the borders opened one by one in Eastern Europe, sales of LEGO's products shot up behind the former Iron Curtain. A steady stream of tourist buses, carrying mainly Polish but also Hungarian and former East German citizens, set off for LEGOLAND every summer, putting extra pressure on the narrow access roads leading to Billund.

The Sunday Telegraph, Sunday, November 12, 1989.

Kjeld: *Even before the Wall fell, you could buy LEGO in Eastern Europe;
we were even in GUM, the massive department store on Red Square. I
was in Russia in the mid-1980s to see what we had managed to do over
there. It wasn't insignificant, but also not exactly dizzying, because we
were selling nothing at all to the general population. Our products were
much too expensive, compared to what the average Russian earned. We
had a commercial agent, like we did in Poland, the Czech Republic, and
Hungary as well. But it was all a bit on the small side, and we were only
sold in what they called the Dollar Shops.*

*When the Wall fell, the Eastern European market opened up tremen-
dously, and that was very significant for LEGO. We were quick off the
bricks on that occasion. A commercial agent who had lived in both Mos-
cow and Warsaw, and was really strong all over Eastern Europe, made
some things happen, even before the Wall fell, that I wasn't always exactly proud of. Back then, if you wanted to enter the closed Eastern European market and run any kind of decent-sized operation, you really had
to do it via "countertrades." LEGO would have to buy a big consignment
of raincoats, for example, or belts, or something like that, then try to sell
it in Denmark.*

*So we made a little company, Almo A/S, which was supposed to re-
mind you a bit of the LEGO name with the four letters, and it was an
abbreviation of "Alt i Modkøb" ("Everything Countertraded"). But, alas,
we couldn't find anyone to take most of what we traded off our hands.
That all changed in the 1990s, that's for sure. Today, Russia is our sixth
or seventh biggest market globally.*

In the USA, too, sales of LEGO exploded by no less than 38 percent in
1989 alone. Despite LEGO's defeat in several international courtrooms
in the 1980s, they eventually emerged victorious from their protracted
tug of war with Tyco, since no competitors could match LEGO's quality
in the long run. As Kjeld put it in an interview, "A while back we lost a
case against some American plagiarists, and it's deeply annoying, but as
we say to one another, our product is the best, so we'll beat the plagiarists in the stores instead of the courtrooms."

The boss made no secret of his pride and joy during the New Year's address to employees in January 1990: "During the 1980s, the LEGO Group's gross revenue more than quadrupled at current prices. In terms of volume, it almost tripled. This is a more positive development than on the toy market overall, so we have also gained a bigger market share."

The impact of the three huge copromotions with McDonald's— around thirty-seven million bricks were ultimately distributed with the classic children's Happy Meal—was now really being felt. Consumer surveys revealed that 95 percent of Americans were familiar with the brand, and in one major American brand-image survey, LEGO came in at eighth place, after giants like Mercedes-Benz, Levi's, Disney, Coca-Cola, Apple, and IBM. As the employee magazine concluded in November 1989, "Bricks and fries are a good match."

There were certainly a multitude of reasons for Kjeld to have been enthusiastic in his lengthy New Year's speech to employees, where he looked back over a fantastic decade and got a little sentimental about the state of the world at large:

We are seeing dictatorships crumble, and freedom and peace within reach. It will be a difficult process, but it gives us hope for a more peaceful world, where military might and oppression are replaced by democracies, respect for human rights, and interaction between free agents. May this recognition of mutual dependence and some much-needed collaboration make all of us realize that Earth is a small planet that we all have a responsibility not to destroy. We have been drawn closer together as citizens of the world. That, I think, promises a bright future for the 1990s.

The New Year's speech was titled "Dynamic Continuity." After so many years of constant growth and only a few, almost insignificant, bumps along the road, there was all the more reason to thank his employees for their dedication and efforts. Kjeld ended with an appeal to individual employees that surprised many of them a little: "Don't neglect your inner child!"

He announced that this appeal also lay at the heart of the "LEGO Vision" strategy, which was discussed at the conference in Ebeltoft in 1988, although no one outside the uppermost level of management had heard anything about it.

"But you will soon," Kjeld promised, because in future, children would be role models for all LEGO employees:

Children are curious; they're always asking questions. Why? Why not? Children see opportunities; we adults see problems. Children aren't afraid to try things and make mistakes because you learn from those. We grown-ups must learn from experience, of course, but we can't be afraid to do something and risk making a mistake. We've got to remember that we can keep learning throughout our entire lives. And play our entire lives. Have fun with one another, even as we're getting things done. Of course, we still need to be adults, but let's not neglect the child in all of us.

Kjeld: *As well as wanting to remind people that, as adults, we forget many of the good things about childhood, it had also long been a dream of mine that my closest colleagues would take a more playful approach*

*to their work. That they would become managers who didn't just say,
"This is my job, so I'm doing it, and I don't care what other people are
doing!" I've always liked it when people want to improve and develop
what they're working on, both alone and with colleagues. The way I see it,
that way you can always create even more dynamic energy in a company.*

In the summer of 1990, Godtfred turned seventy, and there was a nostalgic tinge to the celebrations. The country's newspapers overflowed
with superlatives like "the empire builder" and "the LEGO king" and,
as so many times before, the smiling, perpetually cheroot- or cigarette-
smoking man of the hour had a chance to clown around a little in the
spotlight. What was life without a little fun, after all?

Whereas Kjeld could come across as introverted and fairly shy, his
father was the type of extroverted leader that people instantly liked.
He'd also inherited Ole Kirk's fondness for horseplay. On his birthday
on July 8, he was given something called the Freedom of the City, an
honorary citizenship, by the Billund Council, the first time this honor
had been awarded. People waited excitedly in the town hall, when suddenly the door flew open and an elderly man with a cane and a straw
hat walked in, wearing a mask of the character Waldorf, one the elderly
hecklers from the TV show *The Muppets*.

It was Godtfred, in disguise. Through the mask, he addressed Mayor
Tychsen, twenty years his junior. "The fact that I've been given this
award implies that I'm getting old. That's why I put this mask on, so
you'll always recognize me later on."

Afterward, he was interviewed by TV Syd. The reporter had his questions ready on a notepad, the cameras were running, and GKC lowered
his cheroot.

Is it still your benevolent spirit that animates LEGO?

"No, why don't we say that my father's spirit still walks among us
instead?"

What does Christianity really mean to you?

"It means everything to me. I come from a Christian home, and I like
to say that I've got a direct line."

Why have things gone so well, do you think?

"You know what, actually. I've been trying to hold back the whole time, because I prefer small factories where you know the people. I remember here in Billund when we built on a very specific scale, and that was deliberate, because we didn't want the factory to be any bigger."

Finally, how have you managed to remain king of this empire while staying a relatively humble man?

"The same way we're standing here talking right now."

In a lengthy birthday interview, Godtfred commented on the new management culture and the use of consulting firms, which could scarcely have been imagined in the 1960s, when GKC was at the helm. Even though he'd now, as he put it, been "given the sack," his dedication was undiminished:

> *I can't think without thinking along LEGO lines. It's a difficult, difficult process to let go of the reins and hand everything over to other people. But*

GKC loved masks, dressing up, and surprising other people. When he was given the Freedom of the City by Billund Council on his seventieth birthday, he showed up to the ceremony at the town hall as Waldorf, one of the grumpy old men from The Muppets. *Photo: John Randeris.*

don't forget that although Kjeld and his fellow directors and other great
employees have done a truly marvelous job taking over the vast majority
of activities during the past ten or twelve years, I feel that I have been in-
volved from the start, so I'm still the one who has the most responsibility.
I can't shirk that. So I'm still at the office every day. Edith suggested one
day this spring that we go for a walk together in Billund, but I couldn't.
What would people say, in the middle of a workday!

Kjeld: *When Dad turned seventy, under the terms of our family agree-*
ment I took over the majority of the voting shares, so he no longer had
a say. Dad had lived and breathed the company, and he felt that he was
now finally losing touch with it. So he didn't have as good a life in those
last couple of years as he might have wanted—and that I might have
wanted, for my mother as well. She thought that now he had a bit less to
do, they could maybe go on more trips, but Dad just had such a hard time
letting go of the factory. Today, I understand him better than I did back
them. I feel something rather similar myself.

In the spring of 1993, just as GKC stepped down from his role as chairman of LEGO A/S, handing it over to Vagn Holck Andersen as agreed,
Sofie Kirk Christiansen—Ole Kirk's wife, Ulla's mother, the brothers'
stepmother, and the owner of LEGO for its first, difficult ten years—
died. Shortly afterward, Kjeld was forced to take time off due to illness,
which was why he wasn't not featured much in *Børsens Nyhedsmagasin*'s
"Golden Issue" in May, when LEGO was awarded the Imagepris for the
third time in five years. Other senior executives, including Christian
Majgaard, gave speeches instead, describing where they planned on taking the LEGO brand, though that subject had been near and dear to
their boss's heart for several years. "Kjeld says we must take a visionary approach to our brand and that there's room to further expand the
brand people know as LEGO."

One key part of Kjeld's grand plans to expand the brand was LEGO
World. A series of family parks based on the LEGOLAND concept, it

would consist of four or five locations around the world, to be constructed over the coming decades. The first concrete steps were taken when LEGO set up a special limited company in 1991 and, in order not to risk Godtfred suddenly noticing and taking issue with Kjeld's decision, it was named LEGO World A/S, to camouflage the nature of the project. Shortly after Godtfred's death, the name was changed to LEGOLAND Development A/S.

> **Kjeld:** *We only ever referred to them as "parks" and pretended we didn't quite know if they would be outdoors or indoors. We were simply talking around the word and the concept of LEGOLAND, which was Dad's domain. But for us, of course, it seemed an obvious step; since the park in Billund had been such a consistent success, making such a positive contribution to the brand for twenty-five years, why not open a range of similar parks around the world? LEGOLAND Windsor, a little outside London, was the first. It wasn't until the very last moment—in 1994, I think—when it couldn't be put off any longer and construction was well underway in England, that I dared to tell Dad we were calling it LEGO-LAND after all. He took it very well. Maybe he could see that it wasn't a completely crazy idea.*

The photograph of a calm, self-assured, and apparently poised Kjeld Kirk Kristiansen on the front page of *Børsens Nyhedsmagasin* in May 1993 was misleading. His round face and upbeat expression masked a more unpleasant reality. For a long time, Kjeld had been feeling unwell. He was strangely tired, his digestion was poor, and he couldn't stop losing weight. What was initially assumed to be a case of salmonella poisoning turned out to be ulcerative colitis—inflammation of the intestines that results in bleeding. It would require ongoing treatment, perhaps even surgery, and was considered by the medical profession to be incurable.

After several thorough examinations and conversations with specialists, Kjeld took an indefinite leave from work. To stop people in Billund from speculating too much about his condition and illness, which didn't leave him bedridden, he moved to Schelenborg. There, he found the peace and quiet he needed, and he didn't have to deal with people staring at him, or with commitments and responsibilities.

> **Kjeld:** *An excellent chief physician at Vejle Hospital examined me and said, "You should expect this to take a while!"*
>
> *Then I said something along the lines of, "So I won't feel better until after the summer holidays?"*
>
> *"No, this is a chronic illness. You should be prepared to deal with this for a really long time."*
>
> *He was amazing, the chief physician. He kept me away from the surgeons, who really wanted to get their hands on me. Slowly but surely, the powerful medication helped. Prednisolone, which is an adrenal corticosteroid hormone that can mess with your head a bit.*
>
> *I spent the whole summer and autumn of 1993 at Schelenborg. I didn't come back to Billund until Christmas, so I had plenty of time to reflect on lots of things in my life. Number one, of course, the gloomy prospect that the intestinal problem would haunt me for the rest of my life. And the question was also whether I would be able to return to my old job.*

On his Funen estate, an initially tired and depressed Kjeld was nursed by Camilla and her mother, who were very worried about his condition and his dramatic, ongoing weight loss. Godtfred was also deeply anxious, and despite his own bad heart and weak legs, he made the journey from Billund to Funen. It was painful for him to see his son so ill.

"I'm so sorry this has happened to you, Kjeld!" he told his son, who had never seen his father with tears in his eyes.

In addition to all the physical symptoms that took their toll on Kjeld's energy and mood, various issues that he had been suppressing now surfaced: the imbalance between his work and private lives, the tremendous pressure of managing a huge company, and especially his relationship with his father. He didn't fall into depression; there were no panic attacks or moments when he felt incapable of acting, but the disease triggered a personal crisis, as his brother-in-law Mogens Johansen, a doctor, later explained.

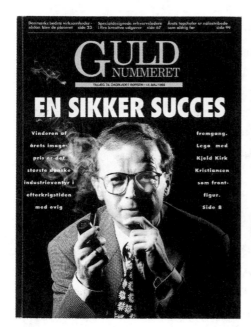

The image on the cover of *Børsens Nyhedsmagasin* in May 1993 depicted a strong, self-confident LEGO managing director with a twinkle in his eye, but, in fact, Kjeld had just been told he was suffering from an incurable illness. *Photo: Børsen.*

"Kjeld discovered that he wasn't invulnerable. The illness brought him to the point where he was considering whether he wanted to keep working in the way he had. Whether it was all worth it."

Getting some physical distance from LEGO gave Kjeld the opportunity to think and to take a clearer, dispassionate look at the organization. The company had done impressively well throughout the 1980s, but now had begun to show signs of weakness, he thought. They just kept doing what they'd always done: managing from the top down, becoming transfixed by details, and continuously hiring new people.

Kjeld: *I had already begun to see the warning signs years earlier, and it had nothing to do with my illness. There were signs of sluggishness and inertia in the company, and in a few markets overseas we had started to see a slowdown, although this was somewhat hidden by the fact that in other markets, the USA, for example, things were still going really well. It was all a bit worrying, I thought, but overall things were going swimmingly.*

From time to time, a delegation from LEGO consisting of three other senior executives—Niels Christian Jensen, Christian Majgaard, and Torsten Rasmussen—turned up at Schelenborg. The latter, Kjeld's old friend from his early years in Switzerland, was considered second-in-command, so he did most of the talking during those visits. They were there to see Kjeld and ask about his health, of course, but also to report to him and ask for his advice on a range of issues.

Kjeld: *When they sat there in front of me talking about how things were going, I used to think, "Don't go into so much detail! Can't we just stick to the broad brushstrokes?" It really dawned on me that this tremendous, very tight control we had over everything at LEGO at this point, with all the charts and tables with horizontal rows and vertical columns, was paralyzing the company. Fundamentally, it was about the law of inertia, which affects many companies that have been successful for years. You keep doing even more of the same thing instead of thinking in a new and different way. So sometimes I had enough of listening to my three directors, and I got up and asked if they wanted to go and see the horses.*

As autumn wore on, it became clear to Kjeld that his existential crisis was related to his disinclination to continue on in the role of managing director. As he said in interviews, and often repeated when he was later asked what went wrong at LEGO in the late 1990s, "It had stopped being fun."

"Fun" is a word Kjeld had used many times in the course of his life. Throughout his adulthood, the word represented a distillation of his notion of an ideal life. During the management crisis in the 1990s and early years of the twenty-first century, when Kjeld was asked to think of the most important and valuable thing about his role as managing director, he almost always used the same phrase: "It's got to be fun!"

One example among many appeared in an interview in the *Jyske Vestkysten* in February 2000, after he'd appointed a deputy managing director, relieving himself of a number of managerial tasks and obligations. "Day-to-day management isn't what I'm best at, and it's not what I think is most fun."

The word "fun" was also a recurring theme in Kjeld's vision of LEGO's future, right from the moment in 1988 when he initially presented his "LEGO Vision" to his managers. Fun was the invisible force at play in every line of the New Year's speech mentioned above. And fun was the powerful glue holding together the five central values of the LEGO Vision: creativity, imagination, enthusiasm, spontaneity, and curiosity.

At times, his stay at Schelenborg was also productive free time, offering plenty of opportunity to relax, play, and think irrationally. His suits and ties were back in the closet in Skovparken, and he grew his beard out. Kjeld listened to rock and jazz music from the years around 1968. He went on long walks, chatted with his horses, and did things just because he wanted to.

Seven months of exile at Schelenborg in 1993 were spent with nature and horses. At first, Kjeld was exhausted—the powerful medication was taking its toll—but slowly he regained his strength again. *Private collection.*

Kjeld: *I listened to a lot of music: John Lennon, Jimi Hendrix, Bob Dylan, Charles Mingus, and others from my younger days in the 1960s. I also had a rider employed at the stud farm, whose mother used to go riding in horse-drawn carriages. She took me out to a place where I bought a beautiful old carriage. In Grenå and Fredericia I found two good carriage horses with plenty of "horsepower." They were called Simon and Lada, but I quickly redubbed them Simon Skoda and Laura Lada. And then I just started driving a carriage, which was something I hadn't done since I was at a riding club in the '60s.*

At times, there was something trancelike about it. On the one hand, I was absolutely exhausted; on the other, I was high on medication, and in that limbo I was doing quite a few fun things. Among other stuff, I embarked on a major project with the basement. I set up a proper man cave full of things I had collected over the years: an old suit of armor, one of Raphael's angels on the ceiling, and an ancient workbench as a bar, and a pool table in the middle. Like the horse-drawn carriage project, it was first and foremost about doing something I really wanted to do. Something fun.

Kjeld eventually contacted Lasse Zäll, a coach he knew from previous LEGO seminars. Zäll had had great success in the 1980s applying his experience of team-building and mental coaching with everyone from top athletes to executives at companies like PFA Pension, Jyske Bank, Novo Nordisk, Novozymes, and LEGO. Kjeld liked Lasse's undemonstrative, slightly odd style and alternative way of thinking about management. His theories drew on such diverse sources as brain research, Denmark's elite special-ops Jæger Corps, Native American outlooks on life, high school pedagogy, and sports psychology. When he visited Kjeld at Schelenborg, however, he didn't bring canoeists, special-ops soldiers, textbooks, or a medicine man. He did bring his own personal crisis. A father of five, he was on the verge of his second divorce, and found himself facing as massive an existential challenge as did LEGO's ailing managing director.

As Kjeld said in *Stifinder*, a book about Lasse Zäll and the idea behind Pathfinder, the company Lasse and Kjeld were later to found together:

*When I was wondering who I could talk to on a personal level, I very
quickly thought of Lasse. The fact that he was also going through major
changes in his life certainly didn't make our conversations less reward-
ing. We had some deep chats about existence, about how to move on, and
how we wanted our lives to be. Maybe him having his own challenges to
contend with helped him understand me better.*

The two men's conversations at Schelenborg inspired in Kjeld a "proactive" boost, to use one of Lasse Zäll's coaching phrases, and helped
him think about his illness, his work-life balance, and his position and
role within the LEGO Group.

Kjeld: *Lasse was good to talk to. He helped me think more about the company and the path we should take when I returned—if I returned, that
is. Because it was also about my reluctance to be part of the bureaucracy
we had developed. That was something that would have to be changed
first, I felt, if I was ever going to return to the role. I also knew that there
was no guarantee I would regain my strength enough to carry out such a
demanding job, even when the disease got less intense.*

As the autumn months went on, unease and bewilderment became
rife in Billund. Just how unwell was Kjeld? Was it stress? Depression? And when would he come back? Head of Public Relations Peter
Ambeck-Madsen summarized these concerns in a cheery letter to Kjeld:
"We miss you and your presence, not because things have stalled, but
because the slightly hectic, dynamic atmosphere doesn't register more
than two or three on the Richter scale. And we're not used to that . . ."

But Kjeld was in no hurry. In fact, he'd just had an idea for a large-
scale managerial cure for what his former head of HR, Per Sørensen,
once called "rhino-ization." Inspired by Eugène Ionesco's play *The Rhi-
noceros*, which is about the inhabitants of a small French town who turn,
one by one, into thick-skinned rhinoceroses, Sørensen put his finger
on a relatively common phenomenon: over time, a company's management team tends to develop into stiff, slow animals that simply lumber

onward, never daring to move without the herd. Kjeld's idea, another one that had come up in conversation with Lasse Zäll and was later run by the other directors, was to set up a new, proactive management course that would release some of the pent-up energy that had gradually built up at LEGO.

> **Kjeld:** *I decided to call it "Compass Management." After I returned home from Schelenborg and very slowly got more of my strength back during the spring of 1994, the project took shape, with help from both Lasse and now also my fellow directors. We met several times and discussed it in a pleasant, relaxed setting. I told them I wanted to manage LEGO in a different way. The way we ran the business had to be simplified, and the old values—the "entrepreneurial spirit"—had to be brought back into focus. The way to do this was to give individual employees more latitude. No more waiting for everyone to agree in long meetings. In future, the whole organization had to be more agile and quick to react to whatever was important in an increasingly more rapid, changing world.*

When Kjeld returned to Billund over the Christmas break and gradually came back to work in January 1994 for a few hours a day, LEGO appeared to be a company still very much in its prime. In a speech he gave to the entire management team, at the usual New Year's party, Kjeld was eager to tell them about a film he'd just seen. The film was *Big*, featuring Tom Hanks as twelve-year-old Elliot, a boy desperate to be a grown-up. His wish is miraculously granted, and Elliot, now in the body of a young adult man, gets a job at a toy company where the grown-ups don't understand children's dreams and mindset. He, however, does. And so did Kjeld, as he confided to all the adults dressed to the nines and gathered at Hotel LEGOLAND. He asserted, "Children are unique creatures. We're the ones who should be imitating them, not the other way around."

In 1994, LEGO was Europe's largest manufacturer of toys and very much in contention to be one of the biggest in the world, standing alongside giants such as Mattel, Hasbro, Sega, and Nintendo. LEGO now had 80 percent of the market for construction-based toys in the

USA, sold its products in 60,000 shops in more than 130 countries, employed a workforce that had grown from 6,000 to 8,000 in four years, and brought in revenue of just under 9 billion kroner. Things were going pretty swimmingly, at least as seen from the outside.

In late summer, as his flare-ups got fewer and further between, Kjeld reduced his medication and, to the outside world, he started to look like his old self, full of energy and keen to run the family business. Deep down, however, there was a Kjeld who looked forward to a time when someone else could take over the day-to-day operations and he could concentrate on the stuff he thought was fun: focusing on the big picture, on values, and on developing LEGO's brand.

Kjeld: *I didn't really feel there was anyone on my team at that point in the 1990s who really, properly understood what I wanted to do with the company. One of them came to me one day and said, "I know what you want, Kjeld. You say we've got this massive tree, and we need to prune it to make it simpler. But what many of us have done, and are still doing, is to plant new trees next to it, and that's not really what it's about, is it?"*

That was true, as far as it went. But it was really difficult for me to get people to understand that the change had to come from inside.

A company doesn't make money by endlessly discussing itself, its strategies, and management principles. It also needs to manufacture goods and to constantly innovate and work on product development, especially in a toy market that, as in the 1990s, was increasingly becoming a battleground between the world's biggest players in the toy and entertainment industries.

Classic toys such as LEGO's bricks, Mattel's dolls, and Hasbro's board games had rapidly come under severe pressure and faced stiff competition not only from Sega and Nintendo's PC and CD-ROM games, whose turnover accounted for 35 to 40 percent of the entire market, but also from the film and software industry, where the major players were names like Disney, Warner Bros., and Apple.

All of these companies helped to shape and transform a market that

In August 1994, the new team met at a conference center near Horsens Fjord to discuss Kjeld's new management concept, Compass Management. Here, they enjoy a cold beer around the fire in the evening. Standing, from left: Kjeld, Christian Majgaard, Niels Christian Jensen, Kjeld Møller Pedersen, and coach Lasse Zäll. Crouching: John Bøndergaard and Torsten Rasmussen. *Private collection.*

had shifted, within a few short years, away from traditional toys to electronic entertainment for children, teenagers, and families. The battle was taking place on a massively expanded playing field, where LEGO fought for children's time, as well as the money and attention of young families. Contemporary approaches to play blurred the boundaries of what it meant to be a child, a teenager, and a young person. Children were the fastest-growing consumer group. "'Kids are getting older younger," as they said.

In the midst of this paradigm shift, with the millennium approaching and a radically changing toy market, LEGO had to cast around for new sources of revenue. Here, not only the brand, but also the digital world, offered tremendous opportunities. Kjeld had been aware of this ever since he saw Seymour Papert and his Talking Turtle show on TV.

LEGO had already invested massive sums in its attempts to digitalize the bricks, and throughout the 1990s, Kjeld, who had been interested in computer and IT systems since adolescence, was ready to take the analog LEGO System even further into cyberspace. But his year away from work and the passivity of his management team in Billund, who'd been waiting for their boss to get back on his feet, had set LEGO back at a time when things had never moved faster in the toy industry.

Kjeld: *I was out of the picture for nearly a year, and once I was properly back, I should have made a few more changes in my management team. We'd had good results together in the 1980s, but we had probably gotten a bit too insular. Things had already started going less well. We were in a period when children were spending much, much more time on electronics, and at the same time, we didn't have anything quite as attention-grabbing in terms of new products, so a feeling of stagnation was spreading. As an organization, we really needed something new to believe in.*

One day in the autumn of 1994, a short man with shoulder-length hair and a full beard, hiking boots, old-fashioned baggy breeches, and a hat suddenly appeared in the reception area of LEGO's main office. He carried a suitcase and insisted on speaking to Mr. Kjeld Kirk Kristiansen. The man, speaking fluent English, introduced himself as Mr. Dent-de-Lion du Midi, and explained to the receptionist that his French-sounding name meant "dandelion in the middle." He added that he'd brought a very special video he wanted to show the LEGO boss, one that would interest him.

Initially, the stranger had to settle for meeting the head of public relations and a software designer from LEGO Technic.

"Just call me Dandi," he said, showing them his video, which depicted some computer-generated glowing LEGO Space models whizzing around in outer space. The two men from LEGO were impressed. Nodding appreciatively, they promised to get back to him once they'd shown Kjeld the video.

Dent-de-Lion du Midi turned out to be an American living in Switzerland, and he was, by most accounts, a bit of a bohemian and jack-of-all-trades: musician, visual artist, inventor, entrepreneur, and pioneer of 3D graphics and computer animation. Six months later, he returned to Billund to meet with Kjeld. At the meeting, Dandi presented a plan to digitize and reproduce all the elements of the LEGO system in 3D, from the traditional bricks and wheels to the Minifigures and the tiniest bolts and cogs. Dandi's idea, in a nutshell, was that it would soon be possible to build with LEGO in cyberspace, offering children creative LEGO experiences on a computer screen as well as the ability to make 3D feature films, cartoons, building instructions, and ads.

> **Kjeld:** *Dandi had some pretty crazy ideas about how we should develop digitally. I could really see the potential in his presentation. That we would have our own database with all LEGO's elements in 3D, which also meant that the whole organization would be able to work with and draw on the program.*
>
> *But it required us to obtain a lot more computing power. Which is what we did. I think at one point, we had more Silicon Graphics computers in Billund, specially designed to solve advanced graphics tasks, than anywhere else in the world. We spent many hundreds of millions on the project, which was named "Darwin," and it was Dandi who spearheaded the multiyear experiment. He immediately hired ten or fifteen guys with shaggy beards, really great guys who worked with virtual reality and computer animation. I remember that at one point we did a TV broadcast in which I walked around an interactive world of LEGO buildings that Dandi and his people had created, wearing virtual reality glasses.*
>
> *Darwin was a pretty hippie-ish project at that point, and there were several people on the management team who thought it was completely crazy to spend so much money on it. But I felt confident that something good would come out of it.*

The name of the project, Darwin, was meant to evoke evolution, discovery, and development, and Kjeld didn't do things by halves. The

Dent-de-Lion du Midi (left) turned up at Billund in 1994 with a suitcase full of 3D effects. It was the start of the Darwin project, which brought LEGO into a new era. From now on, playtime would be set in cyberspace! Kjeld kept a curious eye on all his crazy experiments, both with and without VR glasses, and at one point he said to the team, "You guys are the future of the company."

department grew constantly; several foreign specialists were hired, including some of the world's most talented 3D animators and people who had worked for Apple in California.

The Darwin team rapidly became known in Billund as "The Nutters." They transformed their section of LEGO's attractive office space into a terrible mess of high-tech hardware and unshaven men in T-shirts, surrounded by empty Coke bottles and stacks of pizza boxes. Even more money was invested in raw computing power, including in an ONYX supercomputer that, according to the employee magazine, "can best be described as a purple minibar on steroids, with graphics that send most people's jaws dropping to the floor."

Kjeld: *With a little help from Darwin, we made our first LEGO building set with a CD-ROM. It was a submarine that could be programmed and steered, and the CD-ROM was nicknamed "Rubber Duck." Darwin* *sowed lots of seeds for further developments. Not least, it was a big part of why the bricks exist digitally today, and you can build with them on a PC. In a sense, Dandi and his crew—at one point, there were nearly a hundred in the department, I think—were just way ahead of their time. There weren't yet very many people who had home computers, but we achieved a lot, got plenty of great inspiration—and it was fun!*

The same year that Dandi arrived in Billund, the Canadian writer Douglas Coupland published his novel *Microserfs*. The book is about a group of friends and computer nerds who work at Microsoft but quit one day and move to Silicon Valley together to develop their own 3D computer LEGO System. Having all played with the plastic bricks as children, they operated in the same technological borderland between play and computing as Seymour Papert and his team at the MIT Media Lab and Dandi's Darwin group at Billund.

The thirty-three-year-old Coupland, who'd became world-famous in 1991 with the novel *Generation X*, had written something closer to reality than perhaps he realized. A few months before Dandi set his hiking-booted foot in Billund, Coupland visited Denmark for the first time, immediately making the pilgrimage to LEGOLAND and writing a long essay about the park in *The New Republic*. In it, Coupland described his arrival in Billund almost straight from Silicon Valley, where he'd rubbed shoulders with gifted, successful hardware and software designers. Apart from computers and high-tech gadgetry, they'd all had one thing in common: they'd been obsessed with LEGO as children. Exactly like the characters in *Microserfs*, they'd rather play with LEGO bricks than with Bill Gates.

"Now, I think it's safe to say that Lego is a potent three-dimensional modeling tool and a language in itself. And prolonged exposure to any language, either visual or verbal, doubtless alters the way a child perceives his or her universe."

In the autumn of 1994, after Kjeld returned from exile on Funen and seemed to have recovered from his illness, "Compass Management," his new management concept, was underway. It was the appealing idea that individual managers further down the ladder should be empowered to make more decisions. Some senior executives believed it to be a risky path, because in a company as large and complex as LEGO, it's easy to be unsure about chains of command and ultimately to not know who had made what decision.

Everyone turned up for the photograph, however, when Kjeld decided it would be fun to present his new and expanded senior management team as an extremely well-dressed jazz band at the international LEGO conference in October 1994. To the sound of Duke Ellington's classic "Take the 'A' Train," they struck up the company's new, in-sync rhythm.

In his favorite spot in the background was forty-seven-year-old Kjeld, conducting from the piano, which he learned to play as a child from the organist at Grindsted Church. On the trumpet was fifty-year-old Torsten Rasmussen, who as Head of Production was still considered to be Kjeld's successor. Behind the drums was fifty-year-old Niels Christian Jensen, Head of Sales and Product Development. On the clarinet was forty-six-year-old Christian Majgaard, responsible for LEGO Education and coordinating the ambitious plan to set up LEGO parks around the world. Fifty-year-old John Bøndergaard was on bass and in charge of financial management, while forty-six-year-old Kjeld Møller Pedersen, Head of Computing and HR as well as a former university professor and healthcare executive, was swinging on the saxophone.

Each of these six select individuals was following along with their conductor's jazzy line of thought: all except one, who had begun to feel out of step with Kjeld's sheet music. Torsten Rasmussen, who'd been part of the managing director's long journey right from the start of the 1970s in Lausanne, through his assumption of power in Billund, the golden age in the 1980s, and into what, in Torsten's opinion, was an unfocused 1990s. Along the way, he had worked in nearly every corner of the LEGO Group, and for much of this time he'd been Kjeld's closest and most trusted sparring partner.

But something had changed. The two had drifted apart in terms of

The management team, disguised as jazz musicians in dim lighting. From left: Kjeld, John Bøndergaard on bass, Kjeld Møller Pedersen on saxophone, Niels Christian Jensen at the drums, Torsten Rasmussen on trumpet, and Christian Majgaard on clarinet.

their fundamental view of how LEGO should be developed and led; something at the core of each of their personalities had diverged over the years. Torsten Rasmussen's military background was showing through. He believed too strongly in top-down leadership, Kjeld thought, while Torsten felt that his friend's occasionally vague, contradictory statements had become increasingly slogan-y since his long illness.

Despite participating in the development of Compass Management, Torsten Rasmussen had long harbored doubts about the course and believed that Kjeld no longer had full control over the development of LEGO. As he later commented about these years, when the new management concept was being rolled out across the company, it failed to work as intended:

> We were presented with plans and budgets and strategies that were unrealistic and would clearly create problems. There were gambles that Godtfred would never have allowed. And now the LEGO management team was supposed to do everything at once. I told Kjeld I disagreed with the strategy, and one month later we agreed to stop working together.

That moment represented not only the conclusion of a strong, collegial partnership that had lasted twenty years, but also the sudden rupture of a friendship, and in January 1997, Torsten Rasmussen left LEGO.

Kjeld: *Torsten had played a major role throughout the 1980s and early 1990s. He was very much the one who drove development by making sure we could always keep up with production. That was why he couldn't understand why it was necessary to change things, and this was probably my biggest challenge in implementing Compass Management. Whereas I wanted to make us able to respond more rapidly to changing markets—and it was moving at a furious pace in those days—Torsten thought we should act in due time, that is, when it was necessary, and not jump the gun.*

He may have been right about that, but I also felt that he was deeply at odds with me and had chosen to situate himself on the opposite side of what I stood for. It was probably a personality clash. We had had a warm and long friendship, and for many years I was really happy with Torsten's work on the management team, but now his type of management wasn't productive for the organization.

This became clear to me when the three directors came to see me in Schelenborg. Vagn Holck Andersen, who back then was chairman of the board of LEGO A/S, said, "Kjeld, if you're not able to return as managing

Kjeld and Torsten, whose friendship began to break down in the 1990s, are pictured here during a game of chess in 1983, when they still had a good relationship. Finance Director Arne Johansen is the one making sure the pieces are on the right squares.

director, Torsten is the only one who could take your place." I didn't think that was a good solution, and of course that was also one of the reasons why we had a conflict.

Godtfred's seventy-fifth birthday, in the summer of 1995, went uncelebrated. Feeble and unwell, he stayed mostly at home, coming out onto the terrace only for brief intervals during the last months of his life. His legs could no longer support him, and his heart was failing. On Thursday, July 13, 1995, the man who industrialized LEGO and transformed Billund from a rural village into a thriving hub of business, entertainment, industry, and aviation, was finally at peace.

No one, apart from Ole Kirk, had a greater impact on Billund and the surrounding area, and as GKC was carried out of the church center (the very one built on his initiative), to the mournful sound of the LEGOLAND Garden band, clusters of children from the town gathered on the pavements across from the church. They stood in front of the fence with their backs to Godtfred and Edith's house, which was still the biggest and most modern in the area.

As the hearse made its way through the town, the street corners were busy with people old and young, eager to catch a glimpse of the coffin before it vanished toward the family plot in Grene Parish Cemetery. As one local paper commented afterward, there were probably quite a few citizens who were reminded in that moment of a story about a local

One of the final times Godtfred was seen at a major gathering was at the celebration of LEGOLAND's twenty-fifth anniversary in the summer of 1993. He and Edith are joined around the cake by Camilla and Kjeld (right), Gunhild and their son-in-law, Mogens. *Private collection.*

lad explaining to a stranger how a little place like Billund could afford an open-air swimming center, an indoor pool, a stadium, a church and cultural center, a running track, family park, and airport. "It's all on Godtfred!"

The last building GKC commissioned and lived to see completed in Billund was the LEGO Idea House. This corporate museum and archive was created in the wake of the big Tyco case in Hong Kong in 1986, when LEGO's early history was on display. It was both a positive and a negative experience, and it made Godtfred realize how important it was to know the company's roots and have access to old products, patent applications, contracts, letters, and meeting minutes.

At the same time, GKC had long been eager to create a permanent place in the company where LEGO's history—past and present—could be told, and where employees could either learn, or be reminded of, the idea behind the product and the LEGO spirit. In other words, he was constructing a building dedicated to corporate storytelling long before anyone introduced that term to the Danish business community. On June 14, 1990, Edith officiated at the opening of the LEGO Idea House. Godtfred's words, "When we know the past, we can better understand the present, and when we understand the present, we're better equipped to deal with the future," were like an invisible gateway before the in-house museum and archive. Today, the exhibition itself is located in Ole Kirk's house off Hovedgaden, and it is still a ritual passage of initiation through which all new LEGO recruits must pass.

One of the many people sending up a silent, heartfelt thanks to GKC on the day his coffin was driven through town was former union representative and LEGO System A/S board member Tove "Trade Union" Christensen, who'd been given a senior role in the Danish Women Workers' Union. In Tove's eyes, Godtfred, more than anyone else in the company's history, represented the feeling of community at LEGO, which tended to come as a pleasant surprise to people who got a job at the factory. "GKC was always very responsive to his employees, which I haven't found to the same extent at my previous workplaces," she later told a local newspaper.

Tove Christensen particularly remembered Godtfred's concern for the staff during the first big round of layoffs in 1983, when 230 people were let go, and the LEGO spirit was generally much less in evidence. One day, however, Godtfred went to find Tove and made it clear how important it was to him that the families of the people laid off weren't split up. "Godtfred said, 'If there are problems, Tove, you just come to me!' As a union representative, it was great to have that support."

In 1982, Tove Christensen was the driving force behind setting up the LEGO Employees' Anniversary Grant, and on that occasion GKC invited her, on short notice, on a trip to Copenhagen with LEGO Airways. He was receiving a prize, worth a hundred thousand kroner, from the Chamber of Commerce. Tove would never forget the presentation ceremony itself, which took place at the Stock Exchange and involved all the prominent figures in Danish society:

> There I was, among all these bigwigs of the business world, with Mr. Mærsk Mc-Kinney Møller at their head. Godtfred thanked them for the award then said suddenly, very solemnly, that he had brought his union representative, Mrs. Tove Christiansen. Then he switched to his usual day-to-day tone and continued, "Tove, come up here and get the money for your fund!"
>
> Afterward, Mr. Møller came over and grabbed both my upper arms and said, "It's a pleasure to meet you!"
>
> I was so flustered I just said, "Thanks."

One of the things about GKC's style of management that older LEGO employees in the second half of the 1990s talked about, something they felt the current managing director and now third-generation owner lacked, was clear communication. During the perpetual upswing of the 1980s, it was easy to put up with Kjeld's consensus-oriented style, his interest in yin and yang, the eleven paradoxes of management, and all the idealistic talk about looking to children as role models. Now that LEGO had come under pressure on the toy market, there were people who felt that there was a little too much emphasis on group courses and discussion seminars involving games for grown-ups, as well as quotations from old children's books.

> **Kjeld:** *I've always taken the long-term view, and I have a tendency to jump further ahead in my mind than I should. It was sometimes difficult for other people to keep up with that, and to understand. It also meant that I probably never became a good day-to-day manager in the 1990s, just as Compass Management never had much success, even though we made pamphlets for all employees and arranged courses and seminars for all our managers. Two professors from the International Institute for Management Development (IMD) in Switzerland were in charge of developing them. I remember that in one of these courses you had to build your vision of LEGO's future using bricks, and in that way—through play—express your strategic ideas. I could sense many of my managers weren't on board with that, and some had started to regard me as an aging hippie who'd gotten a bit too "out there."*

In May 1996, Kjeld suddenly announced LEGO's latest objective to his favorite journalist, Eigil Evert, whose jaw immediately dropped. Right away, he asked the rhetorical question, "Wait, what's that? Loony, unrealistic delusions of grandeur?"

It was an entirely new strategic plan: by 2005, LEGO would be the strongest brand among families with children. Nothing less than that. It wasn't until 1997, however, that Kjeld and the rest of the senior management team presented the full proposal in a folder, printed with the words "Toward the Year 2005," that was distributed to all staff members. The presentation repeated the grand, overarching goals and outlines. It was a way of thinking that Kjeld would often find himself having to defend over the next five or six years, from within as well as without, because it seemed to supplant Godtfred's old doctrine entirely: "We don't want to be the biggest, but the best."

> **Kjeld:** *I think the 2005 objective has been a bit misunderstood, and interpreted as though I wanted reckless growth. First and foremost, I wanted*

us to be the world's strongest brand among families with children. It was actually a statement I'd made before, in the late 1980s, when we were on a par with brands like Raleigh, Rolex, Disney, and Coca-Cola. In every international survey, we were on top, because families in all sorts of countries said LEGO's products meant a lot to them. So I didn't feel like my ideas were completely off-base, or that that ambition was incompatible with the old LEGO doctrine of not being the biggest, but the best.

So many people said, "Phew, we've got a lot of growing to do, Kjeld, if we're going to achieve that."

And my reply was, "Of course we've got to grow, but it's even more important to build the brand around children and children's development. That must be reflected in everything we do."

That was the vision behind the objective. To many people's ears it sounded almost like delusions of grandeur. I didn't think so at all, because I was convinced we could do it. It was only a matter of time.

When the time came for Kjeld to present the goals in LEGO's employee magazine in the summer of 1997, he recommended they highlight and explain a few words from *Alice's Adventures in Wonderland*. Kjeld believed that the quotation could serve as a beacon, guiding LEGO employees toward a shared understanding and a common goal of making

Kjeld arriving at a press conference on a Segway.

LEGO the world's highest-profile brand among families with children, all across the world.

"Would you tell me, please, which way I ought to go from here?"
"That depends a good deal on where you want to get to," said the Cat.
"I don't much care where—" said Alice.
"Then it doesn't matter which way you go," said the Cat.

—Lewis Carroll, *Alice's Adventures in Wonderland*

Kjeld: *Yeah, it was probably a bit arcane, that quotation, but the thing is, what the cat says at the end is that it's about following your inner compass, and that fit with my ideas around Compass Management.*

I really like Alice in Wonderland, *just as I love* Winnie-the-Pooh. *Both books have such a lovely, simple philosophy, and there's something in them that we, as adults, can learn a lot from, in the same way that it's instructive to listen to children and learn to strive for simplicity in the things we do.*

Now that I'm reading the quotation again, of course I'm wondering, "God knows how many people actually caught my drift!" It must be said, however, that my presentation was solidly grounded in all the business-related issues, and I just added a bit of color with Alice and the Cat!

It wasn't the first time that Kjeld communicated more subtly, leaving his employees feeling uncertain and bewildered. Another striking example came in his 1990 New Year's speech mentioned above, when he appealed to the inner child in his employees, hoping to make the workplace more, as he later put it, "like when children start playing with one of our sets."

Not everyone got the message, though. What other top executive in a multinational firm would dare to praise the essence of childhood in such an open, naïve way, especially in the 1980s, the era of yuppies and cutthroat businessmen like *Wall Street*'s Gordon Gekko?

Kjeld: *When I talked about children being role models, and I stuck to that vision all the way through the 1990s, it wasn't just about our abstract way of thinking about the product and the brand, but also about the concrete, day-to-day management of the company. I clearly imagined, and desperately wanted, a more playful management philosophy that made use of all the potential we have as human beings.*

The professors from the IMD in Switzerland who helped us with Compass Management were very enthusiastic, and said to me, "Normally, visions are about how big we're going to be in ten years and how much the company is going to grow, but that's not what your vision is like, Kjeld. For you, it's also about what kind of company you are, and how you want to behave toward the outside world and your employees."

But Kjeld's management philosophy didn't go down well, and in 1996–1997, he found himself more alone than ever before. Godtfred had died. His father figure Vagn Holck Andersen had retired as chairman of the board of LEGO A/S. His friend Torsten Rasmussen had left the company that he and Kjeld once analyzed and modernized together. Finally, at home, there was no indication that any of his three children—Sofie, twenty-two, Thomas, eighteen, or Agnete, fourteen—had any desire to follow in their father's footsteps.

The three kids had had it up to their necks with LEGO and Billund. They had each had a difficult time at school in the little town. Everybody knew who they were, and many of their classmates' parents worked at LEGO, so they didn't dare show their faces at school when there'd been layoffs. Now, all they wanted to do was to get away from Billund and LEGO, and to experience the freedom of other schools, colleges, training programs, and trips. They wanted to get on a horse and vanish into the sunset, or get behind the wheel of a racing car and step on the gas. Kjeld and Camilla noticed this, of course, and they understood. It was particularly painful for Kjeld, who'd had a very different, unproblematic upbringing in a different age, when the town and factory were one big family.

In 1997, Kjeld took part in a TV show called *Denmark's Richest Man,* and toward the end, he was asked whether his children, the next generation of LEGO owners, would succeed him. Kjeld replied that it was too early to say yet, and that the most important thing was that they be happy, free people.

When Vagn Holck Andersen retired in 1996, a new man joined the team as chairman of the board of LEGO A/S. His name was Mads Øvlisen, the managing director at Novo Nordisk. He had also married into the family that owned that company, which gave him an advantage when it came to understanding the challenges of a company like LEGO. In the 1990s, Øvlisen was one of the most respected figures in the Danish business community, and now, after several years as an ordinary member of the board at LEGO A/S, he was going to help Kjeld steer the company onto a steadier upward trajectory after a few years of falling sales. This culminated in 1995, with the lowest profits of the decade.

When Øvlisen began the job in the spring of 1996, Vagn Holck gave his successor some good advice: "It's important to be able to say no when you have to! The goal is for the LEGO Group to continue as a healthy and financially independent company. Kjeld needs to be kept in check from time to time. He's very dynamic, but he still has great respect for the overriding mission of the board. He's quite different from his father in that regard."

One of the first things Øvlisen did was to bring in the consulting firm McKinsey & Company. The results of the consultancy's assessment were felt as early as September that same year, when layoffs and budget cuts of 10 to 12 percent were suddenly announced. Rounds of layoffs hadn't, at that time, been common in the last fifty years of the company history, and the local press took to the streets to gauge the general mood:

> The whole of Billund is holding its breath as LEGO's top executives announce their lists of numbers and faces, with two hundred layoffs in the first stage of this historic streamlining of the company. A few thousand of the four thousand five hundred employees in Billund live within the town limits. In many homes, both parents work for LEGO, and everybody has at least one or two LEGO employees in their family and social circle.

It was an uncertain time at the factory, where people were not only about to be laid off, but LEGO was also conducting a major reorganization. Rumors were flying, and older staff members were heard to say, "This never would have happened in GKC's day!"

Before the McKinsey consultants returned to Copenhagen, they also concluded that LEGO's management team seemed averse to change. In many companies, an assessment like that would have had immediate consequences, but it didn't at LEGO. When Kjeld was later asked whether he shouldn't perhaps fire himself after the disappointing results of recent years, he replied, "I've considered that. But I think it's because we've launched so many new projects, and now we have to be careful about our priorities. So the managing director will be staying a little while yet!"

Panic on LEGO Island is the name of the Danish edition of the action-adventure PC game known internationally as *LEGO Island*. It was developed in collaboration with Mindscape Inc., and it was a huge success in 1998. Compass Management, on the other hand, struggled, and after three years of attempted rollouts and kick-starts, it died—not with a bang, but with a whimper. The lesson of this failure seemed to be that you couldn't create change in an organization that didn't see the need for it. The inertia, sluggishness, and widespread complacency that Kjeld had tried to dismantle seemed to have become even more entrenched.

Traditional toy companies around the world found themselves struggling to simply maintain their current pace, locked in an unequal battle with the gaming and film industry, which absorbed most of children's free time in the West. Within just two generations, four years had been shaved off the age during which boys and girls played, and researchers claimed that children in the 1990s stopped playing traditional children's games at the age of ten.

This, declared Kjeld in January 1998, was precisely why LEGO's biggest challenge over the coming years would be, not its usual market competitors, but "to meet the changing way children spend their time."

It was time to get serious about bridging the gap between the old

LEGO and the digital and computer-controlled entertainment children increasingly wanted. LEGO was ready to invest ten billion kroner in the toys of the future, but the traditional bricks still need to be the foundation of the group. "The new media offer some exciting opportunities to make playing with the physical products even more exciting," Kjeld said in an interview at the time.

Nowhere was this strategy more clear and on the verge of success than in LEGO's collaboration with Seymour Papert and the Media Lab in Boston. In 1998, after thirteen years of working together, they launched LEGO Mindstorms and LEGO Technic Cybermaster. Initially, they talked to specific focus groups of information-era children and young people. LEGO Cybermaster was a computerized expansion of the LEGO Technic building range. That meant, for example, that the user could construct a robot gladiator that can be programmed to have different personalities, and which spoke to the child as he or she played.

LEGO Mindstorms became the most talked-about LEGO product of the late 1990s, by far. It was more advanced than LEGO Cybermaster, and

Kjeld in a Christmas mood in December 1997, bent over a Barcode Truck with wireless remote control, which was one of the major new products from LEGO Technic that year.

older children and young people could use it to build models with motors and electronic sensors that were controlled via infrared technology. The children who tested LEGO Mindstorms in LEGO's laboratories created all sorts of different imaginative robots. In another case, a girl built a table out of LEGO, mounting a digital camera on it to take pictures of the birds that landed there. As Kjeld said in his international presentation of the two groundbreaking LEGO sets, featuring intelligent bricks:

> *The products have been developed for a new generation of children who are accustomed to using computers. Our goal is, and has always been, to create up-to-date products for children. Products that are fun and stimulate children's imagination and creativity. Now, children are able to use computers for creative play, not in an isolated PC world, but in the real, human world outside the computer.*

And most important of all, Kjeld pointed out, was that Mindstorms encapsulated the company's universal values, those of stimulating creativity and imagination. "Often, children will find that the robots don't do exactly what they expected, and then they'll have to figure out whether it's the programming or the robot that needs to be changed. That's an incredibly creative process."

Despite its high retail price, LEGO Mindstorms was an instant success. It turned out, however, that 40 percent of the buyers and users were fathers and other adult men who played with LEGO in their childhood, when there wasn't much to do with LEGO, construction-wise, except put the bricks together and separate them again.

Wasn't the old product good enough? asked a journalist at the launch of LEGO Mindstorms in London. Why did the good old-fashioned LEGO brick need to be digitized?

Kjeld's response was that digitization was a natural development of the LEGO System:

> *This is the fourth phase of our product development. We've gone from just the bricks in the 1950s, to the wheel and motor in the 1960s, which*

*brought movement to the LEGO product, and the Minifigures in the
1970s, which brought life and context to the buildings, and now we see
the bricks interacting with computers. For nearly fifty years, we've added
a completely new dimension each time.*

By 1998, in addition to Mindstorms and Cybermaster, LEGO had
launched so many other forward-thinking initiatives—software, parks,
PC games, children's clothes, shoes, watches, and so on—that even
Kjeld started to lose track, confessing in the employee magazine that
there were so many projects underway that "we're wondering whether
we can prioritize a bit better."

On the other hand, Kjeld also knew that this range of offerings
strengthened the LEGO brand and offered the company plenty of new
and exciting opportunities, at a time when everyone in the industry had
to take a scattershot approach.

The launch of LEGO Mindstorms in 1998 was an international event, with
journalists from all over the world flown in for the press conference in London.
Kjeld posed with the landmark invention, which turned out to be a toy for
adults as well as kids.

"It's difficult to imagine where it will end," he commented in a news-paper, emphasizing that LEGO was happy to pay a high cost now in order to secure future earnings. In other words, the coffers were open. Kjeld added that LEGO would put serious financial resources into staying competitive in the world of "edutainment," a rapidly expand-ing market for products that combined learning and play. Last but not least, LEGO was increasingly on the lookout for new digital partners, and would certainly not rule out a licensing deal with one or more film companies in Hollywood.

> **Kjeld:** *With many of the things I started, I was just too early, and that created uncertainty, partly because during those years our core products weren't selling very well. And then at the same time, we had to spend time on media products and licensing products and clothes for children and watches and all sorts of things. We do the same thing today, but now we just have other people doing it for us. The mistakes made in the late 1990s were my responsibility. I got my organization involved in way too many things. It was never my intention to create independent areas of the business, or to enter the fashion industry, but that's how it was perceived, even internally. When we held our seminars, people were confused about what I wanted.*
>
> *"Are the bricks still the essential thing, Kjeld?"*
>
> *"Yes, of course," I answered, and I tried to explain that there were tons of children, young people, and parents who wanted to express their affection for our brand, so we should think about these other things as fan merchandise.*

At no point during these years did Kjeld doubt the power of the brick. When the *Jyllands-Posten* asked him whether the revenue from the new PC-based toys, licensing deals, and other nontraditional LEGO prod-ucts would eventually far outstrip the revenue from the bricks, he an-swered, "No, even in ten years' time; the LEGO bricks will be our core product. We still firmly believe that our concept, a family product, can help children develop their own imaginations rather than having a fan-tasy world imposed on them from the outside."

Yet all these new initiatives, as well as the struggle to please various major media and entertainment companies, and the various new LEGO sets with countless new, special elements, were expensive. LEGO was at risk of overexpansion and hemorrhaging money.

Not until early 1998 did Kjeld and Board Chairman Mads Øvlisen react. With concerns justifiably growing over LEGO's financial health, the two men began to search for a CFO, a chief financial officer who could help drag the company out of its slump and steer LEGO toward its ambitious goal of being a more popular brand than Disney by 2005.

Once the headhunters narrowed the field of candidates to two, the final choice was forty-nine-year-old Poul Plougmann. Known as "the business doctor," he specialized in saving companies in crisis. Ploug-mann was especially renowned for his involvement in turning around Bang & Olufsen in the early years of the 1990s.

When Poul Plougmann was offered the top job at LEGO, he was living in Paris and considering retirement. But he couldn't say no to LEGO.

Kjeld: *It was clear to me that we had to bring in new blood as soon as possible. We couldn't handle the situation ourselves, so we were looking for a strong, energetic, action-oriented manager, and both the board and Øvlisen were with me when we chose Poul Plougmann. He had a good reputation from his time at B&O, but on the other hand he was also known as "The Smiling Killer," so it wasn't without a certain trepidation on my part that we hired him.*

Nor was it exactly reassuring when, shortly before Plougmann was due to join the company, Kjeld read an interview in the *Jyllands-Posten* in which his new CFO described himself and his methods as, "once a decision has been made and a strategy adopted, it's full steam ahead! I never look back."

Humility had always been prized at LEGO, but the new executive joining them in 1998 had confidence in spades. Even so, Plougmann had accepted the job only because it was at LEGO. He was very fond of the brand and family-owned companies, and later said that he was eager to help prove that this type of ownership was a hundred times better than a listed company. Yet many people in the business community were very interested to see how Plougmann's anything-but-conflict-averse approach would jibe with Kjeld's low-profile style of management.

The skeptics miscalculated. At the core of the Eastern philosophy Kjeld always loved was a respect for polar opposites and the inherent duality of all things, and it turned out that the new duo—hard-hitting Poul and gentle, consensus-oriented Kjeld—actually seemed to work, even six months after Plougmann's appointment, when LEGO was confronted with extremely poor financial results for 1998.

For the first time in LEGO's sixty-six-year history, the company was in the red, and not in a small way! There was a 282 million kroner shortfall. In the annual report, Kjeld stated that this was "unsatisfactory and unacceptable." They were in dire need of emergency attention, and the business doctor sprang into action. Drawing on the observations and studies of LEGO he'd made since his arrival, Plougmann decided that they had to save no less than one billion kroner over the coming year.

Putting their heads together, he and Kjeld came up with a plan to trim and tighten the entire company. As with other great battles in the history of war, this plan had its own name, "Fitness." A somewhat flippant term, perhaps, which Kjeld defended on local radio: "Look, when we use the term 'fitness program,' it's because we're really saying that as a company we don't just need to lose a few extra kilograms; we also need to get into better shape to achieve our long-term goals. And I think it's actually a very good metaphor for that."

As it turned out, "bloodletting" might have been more apt. A thousand employees, about one in ten at the LEGO Group, soon found themselves out of a job. To begin with, Plougmann focused on the well-padded layers of upper management. It was time to do away with the "overadministration" and decades of "inbreeding" caused by internal management recruitment, Plougmann determined, believing that this would send a healthy signal: the good old days at LEGO were finally over.

One of the first things he said to the staff at the large-scale meetings was that hearing all this talk in the press about poor results, lethargic management, and extensive cuts had created an atmosphere of pessimism. "We need to regain self-confidence," Plougmann announced.

He also found another symbolically important area in which to conserve funds.

"Last year, we spent 225 million kroner on external consultants. It's as though we passed all problems of any significant size on to consultants. This is an utterly absurd sign of a lack of confidence. We have no problems that we cannot solve ourselves."

Plougmann's energetic and optimistic approach to LEGO's worst books in living memory were the start of a dramatic, turbulent five-year period in the company's history, full of ups and downs—but mostly downs.

Kjeld: *What Poul did was necessary, but I could see it was a tough pill for the organization to swallow. As Poul said about all the layoffs on the management team, "Steps are best washed from above." True, he was a*

good speaker and a fantastically lively and dynamic manager, but he was
also brutal, and that didn't really fit with our culture.

Afterward, I was sorry we had fired so many great employees who had
been with us throughout the 1980s and '90s. It also drained the company
of management resources. To replace them, we brought in new managers
who had their own ideas and wanted to take product development, mar-
keting, and so on in completely different directions.

At first, Kjeld supported his CFO's proposals, but at the same time, he
repeatedly rejected the notion that the Fitness plan was an intervention
born of crisis. The two executives took turns at the podium on Friday,
April 16, 1999, presenting the company's new structure and strategy to
sixteen hundred employees across six orientation meetings taking place
that day.

The upbeat duo and the rest of the senior management team emphasized that the cuts were neither "nervous" nor panic-driven. According
to Kjeld, they were "a carefully worked-out and ambitious plan that will
serve as a springboard for us to reach our goal: to become the highest-
profile brand among families with children. We need to get 'fit for the
future.'"

Message received. Ditto for the information that no date could yet
be announced for the upcoming round of layoffs. All employees would
have to sit tight and wait another couple of months before they knew
where they stood. "It's obviously not a nice situation. It creates uncertainty, because everybody is wondering whether they or some of their
close colleagues are in the firing line," remarked the spokesperson for
unionized workers.

But it turned out, as so many times before in LEGO's history, that
many employees felt a sense of solidarity with their workplace, and
with the family that had owned and run the company for almost seventy
years. Nobody refused to work, and the general feeling at the Billund
factory was summarized by one young man who, after the informational
meeting, told the employee magazine, "The whole process becomes
much more human when you hear it from Kjeld in person."

Poul Plougmann did the impossible. In the midst of a prolonged up-heaval caused by layoffs, restructuring, and massive cuts, he managed to turn the record shortfall into a profit of half a billion kroner. All observers agreed that the credit for yet another successful, lightning-fast cure should go to the business doctor. As one unnamed source remarked to the *Økonomisk Ugebrev,* "Plougmann has a resoluteness, an analytical ability, and a forcefulness that nobody else has had at LEGO before."

There was another significant factor in this extraordinary about-face, a highly lucrative deal inked in the spring of 1998, several months before Poul Plougmann had even set foot in Billund: a contract between LEGO and Lucasfilm Ltd. A multiyear, exclusive license to develop, produce, and market LEGO products related to the *Star Wars* universe was to prove immensely profitable for LEGO.

The fourth installment in the science-fiction and adventure saga hit American screens in May 1999, at a time when everyone in Billund was more preoccupied with Fitness. But the two new LEGO Star Wars prod-

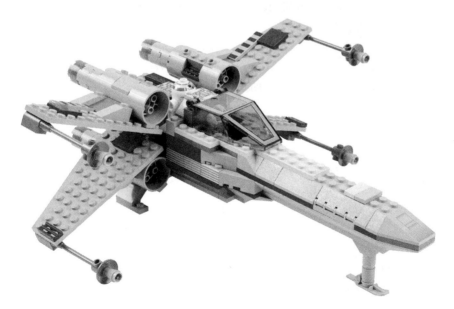

LEGO Star Wars was launched in 1999, and the biggest hit during the first wave of Star Wars sets was Luke Skywalker's legendary X-wing Fighter.

uct series were already in American stores, and the sets, including the legendary X-wing Fighter, flew off the shelves. On the day *The Phantom Menace* premiered, fifty thousand LEGO Star Wars sets were to be sold in Toys "R" Us alone, and the sum total of LEGO Star Wars products sold on American soil that year would reach 130 million dollars. Later that year, sales exploded elsewhere in the world, as the film premiered abroad.

One of the advantageous things about the film licensing deals, the kind that LEGO was also negotiating with Disney and Warner Bros., was that the sets could now be sold at any time of year, not just in the run-up to Christmas. The succcss of the *Star Wars* collaboration was also especially important to Kjeld because it proved to the traditionalists on the management team, who'd been opposed to licensing deals for many years, that the time has come to evolve the old LEGO philosophy. Previously, LEGO had been reluctant to get involved with other players on the toy market, preferring to manufacture their products independently so that they could maintain full quality control from beginning to end.

Kjeld: *Initially, it was our American branch that had the idea to collaborate with Lucasfilm, but in Denmark there certainly wasn't broad agreement in the beginning. The film had a lot of war stuff in it, some people thought.*

Then I said, "Okay, stop, just go home and see the films!"

Star Wars *is a modern adventure story that takes place in a fantasy world, and it's about the eternal battle between good and evil. It's not remotely unhealthy for children to be thinking about that and playing games about it. We could easily accommodate it within the LEGO brand, I thought, so I gave the green light for the deal with Lucasfilm.*

Star Wars turned out to mint money, and although children weren't allowed to see the films in cinemas, younger fans discovered the tale of Luke Skywalker and Darth Vader through gaming consoles, TV screens, and DVDs in the darkness of home theaters. As Kjeld remarked in a newspaper:

In the autumn of 2000, the LEGO strategy called Desert Storm was announced. LEGO wanted to focus on fewer, but bigger, global launches every year. "If we were spending 40 million kroner per launch before, we will now spend typically 120 million kroner," said Plougmann. Business journalists shook their heads, and wrote that the strategy sounded like a castle in the air. *Photo: Per Morten Abrahamsen.*

Children today are incredibly influenced by mass media. In the old days, when I was a child, we had to create our imaginary worlds almost from scratch. We only knew about cowboys and Indians, so that's what we played. But today, children are bombarded with input at a very early age. For better and for worse, and I think mostly for better. Even at the age of five or six, they're incredibly aware of trends and what people are talking about. And that includes stuff like Star Wars.

And so the decade, and the century, came to an end. Obituaries were written about the childhoods of the olden days, the children's books, and all the forgotten games of the past. In December 1999, LEGO's bricks were named "Toy of the Century" by *Fortune* magazine and the British Association of Toy Retailers, placing it alongside such international icons as Barbie, Action Man, and the classic teddy bear.

In Billund, the company was delighted, and strong financial results were predicted. On the board, a relieved and extremely pleased Mads Øvlisen felt that the partnership between Plougmann and Kjeld seemed to run deeper than fact that they both smoked pipes, spending meetings and long flights enveloped in a thick fog of smoke. Plougmann had, by this time, completed the most bruising part of the Fitness strategy, which ensured significantly tighter control over day-to-day operations and allowed Kjeld to focus more on the big picture.

Confident in the knowledge that he could expect good annual results after several years of disappointment, Kjeld officially handed over responsibility for day-to-day management to Poul Plougmann, who that November was promoted to COO, Chief Operating Officer. A happy, smiling LEGO owner commented a few months into the new millennium, "Now I'm doing what I've been wanting to do for many years. I deal with the forward-looking stuff, the values, the development—all the fun things. And I have other people to run the business."

TURNING POINT

THE EARLY 2000s

Star Wars Millennium Falcon, 2008

Everything was in place when, on the morning of January 8, 2004, LEGO sent out invitations for a press conference in Billund. It was due to take place at one o'clock that day, and a plane would be waiting at Copenhagen Airport to transport business journalists and photographers. For several days, the senior management team and the board members had been trying to agree on what to tell the journalists and include in the press release, which was to announce three things: a record loss, Poul Plougmann's immediate resignation, and Kjeld Kirk Kristiansen's decision to take full managerial responsibility once more.

Kjeld: *It was really Poul who had run the company for several years, and it wasn't working out anymore. I had already spotted Jørgen Vig Knud- storp in 2002, and the following year we got Jesper Ovesen on board on the financial front. The two of them were the future, I could see, and over Christmas 2003 we came up with a final plan for how the new manage- ment team should be put together and how it should act. The agreement was that I would stay on as managing director for a while, but otherwise it would be the two of them who would run the place and be in charge of putting things back to rights. On the first day of work after the New Year, I had the conversation with Poul, and it did not go down well. He imme- diately cleared out his office, I let our executives know about the situation, and the next day we called a press conference.*

Forty-six-year-old Jesper Ovesen was highly qualified, having held positions as CFO at Novo Nordisk and Danske Bank. In the autumn of

Kjeld had been drawing on the whiteboard and announced that he was now taking over day-to-day management from Plougmann. "We need to get back to our good old values and to good business savvy, where you ask if something will pay off."

2003, Ovesen had been asked to take stock of LEGO's financial situation, and the veteran number cruncher was shaken by how badly things looked. As the new man at the company, he didn't want to be blamed for other people's mistakes, and he strongly believed that everything, including LEGO's dirty laundry, should be aired at the press conference.

Mads Øvlisen, chairman of the board, didn't agree. As a popular and respected leader in the Danish business community at both board and management level, sixty-four-year-old Øvlisen had his own reputation to consider. He had been on LEGO's board for fourteen years, most of them as chairman, and he didn't want to be castigated or implicated in front of a bevy of Danish business journalists.

Caught between these two very determined men were two slightly smaller egos: fifty-six-year-old Kjeld Kirk Kristiansen and thirty-four-year-old Jørgen Vig Knudstorp, who'd worked at LEGO since 2001. He'd started as a business developer under Plougmann, steadily working his way up the ranks. It was Knudstorp, analytical and quick-thinking, who made Plougmann, Øvlisen, and Kjeld aware in the summer of 2003 that the company's core financial assets were so eroded that LEGO might soon be unable to pay its debts.

To solve the problem of the disagreement over the press release, and to get a handle more generally on the whole setup around the conference, LEGO hired experienced communications consultant Jess Myrthu. Myrthu, more than almost anyone else in the country, had the skills to orchestrate this kind of event and transform an extremely unfortunate narrative into a less dramatic story.

He proposed a compromise between Ovesen and Øvlisen, suggesting, for example, that in the press release they use phrases like "when there is a discrepancy between the map and the terrain, one ought to follow the terrain." During the press conference itself, he recommended sticking to phrases like "we're turning the rudder" and "tapping the brakes" and so on. He also had some ideas for visual aids, including an illustration that Kjeld might "spontaneously" draw on the flip chart, to make the record loss sound a little less doomsday-ish.

Despite fog and a delay in Copenhagen, all the journalists made it on time. When Kjeld Kirk Kristiansen entered the room, followed by a solemn-faced Øvlisen, Ovesen, and Knudstorp, everyone in the audience realized that the rumor was true. Poul Plougmann, the business doctor, was no longer with LEGO. Kjeld, meanwhile, was seen without his usual smile. He was also discreetly dressed, having left his customary bold LEGO tie at home. He welcomed the audience, which included not just journalists and photographers, but also several hundred LEGO managers and trade union representatives, who were following along on the big screen in a nearby auditorium.

Kjeld began by saying that the management team had made no secret of the fact that they were expecting a poor performance for 2003, which is why there'd been such interest in the results of LEGO's Christmas sales. Unfortunately, the numbers hadn't been as mitigating as they'd hoped.

I must admit that our losses haven't just been big; they've been record-breaking. Our pretax shortfall will be around 1.4 billion kroner, and turnover has decreased by approximately 25 percent. This, of course, is entirely unacceptable, and shows that we haven't just had an unlucky year, with a series of external events that impacted us negatively. We've also got to admit that we've been pursuing the wrong strategy. As a consequence, I have agreed with Chief Operating Officer Poul Plougmann that we should go our separate ways. My task now is, therefore, to make the necessary adjustments to the company and changes to the strategy.

Suddenly, cheers and bursts of applause could be heard in the distance, coming from the auditorium, where people were overjoyed to hear the news. Kjeld heard the noise and smiled inwardly, but he concentrated on his speech and the key question of why things had gone so wrong. Here he reached the rehearsed break in the presentation, when he was supposed to go up to the flip chart and illustrate LEGO's series of crises over the past five years.

Getting to his feet, Kjeld picked up the blue pen and started drawing on the flip chart. He then took a step back so that everyone could see: the drawing rather resembled the profile of the lethal-looking mountain stage during the Tour de France. "We've been zigzagging," he said, pointing to the peaks and troughs. The shortfall in 1998 preceded a comfortable profit in 1999, which was then followed by two modest profits in 2000 and 2001, a significant loss in 2002, and now the record-breaking loss in 2003.

The reason for this instability, Kjeld explained, was the toy market, which for the past five years had been strongly affected by trend-led individual products, alternatively benefiting and damaging LEGO. Hitching their wagon to the new *Star Wars* and *Harry Potter* films worked out as planned and created colossal growth for the past few years, but what it hadn't done, unfortunately, was generate interest and increased sales in the other, more basic, LEGO products:

Our strategy for growth has simply failed. Therefore, we have now begun to design a strategy that concentrates on the company's core product idea, represented by the LEGO bricks and the values that have been built up around the LEGO brand, which is of timeless and universal value. Our objective for 2004 is to break even. It will be difficult, but it is realistic, given the measures already underway. We've got to get out there and recapture our share of the market!

"All right, but can you?" most of the journalists in the room thought.

Several of them were already preparing a story with a critical slant, describing how the third generation of the LEGO family had failed and asking one huge, forward-looking question that every reader would be wondering: "Is Kjeld Kirk Kristiansen the right person to save the company?"

Despite the fantastic results he'd achieved leading LEGO, especially in 1978–1993, wasn't Kjeld the one ultimately responsible for LEGO's erratically changing fortunes and the problems simmering over the past ten years? Hadn't there been too many organizational changes, too many senior executives replaced, and too much know-how lost, too many costly investments in digital fads, and, most crucially of all, too many overly ambitious growth targets?

On top of that, some blatantly poor decisions had been made, most recently the decision to drop the LEGO DUPLO name. A well-recognized and successful brand, DUPLO had abruptly been renamed LEGO Explore to try to please the American market. There were immediate consequences, slashing more than 10 percent off revenue.

At one point, a journalist asked how Godtfred would have reacted on a day like today.

Kjeld replied frankly, "Dad would have been disappointed today." End of story.

Another inquired whether Mads Øvlisen should have fired the managing director.

The chairman of the board didn't have time to answer before Kjeld cut in, "Let's just bear in mind that this is my company!"

Øvlisen diplomatically remarked later that he didn't feel ignored or humiliated by Kjeld's interruption. Far from it. It had been only natural, seeing as Kjeld was born with LEGO in his blood. Also natural and most appropriate was that Kjeld should take charge of operations, because he was the only one who could strip LEGO back to its roots with any credibility. "He is the one responsible for LEGO. He enjoys tremendous respect within the company. People simply need a clear path to work toward, and Kjeld will give them that."

A couple of days after the press conference, Mads Øvlisen gave a long interview in the *Jyllands-Posten* in which he promised that there would be no layoffs or factory closures, although this didn't prove to be true. And he emphasized that the board would give its full support and backup to the new managerial troika, which consisted of Kjeld, Knudstorp, and Ovesen, who now intended to bring LEGO back to its core business: brick-based products.

When asked by the newspaper whether Jesper Ovesen—LEGO's new keeper of the purse strings and a man who, like Plougmann, had experience reconstructing and tidying up companies in crisis—had essentially been appointed deputy CEO, Øvlisen's answer was brief and definite.

"We have no crown princes at LEGO."

This wasn't true. Kjeld had long since had his sights set on Jørgen Vig Knudstorp. At a board meeting in June 2002, held in the newly opened LEGOLAND in Günzburg, in southern Germany, Kjeld realized for the first time that the young man was an extraordinary analyst and communicator. At this point, Knudstorp had only been at LEGO for twelve months. He still reported to Plougmann, and his job was to solve strategic problems around the company. Like the problem, for instance, that was at the top of the agenda at the board meeting in Bavaria: how to expand the chain of LEGO brand retail stores?

LEGO already had a handful of branded stores, but the plan was to expand swiftly over the coming years. It was an ambitious objective, and Knudstorp had been asked to make a financial and strategic assessment. Brand retail stores were a hobbyhorse that Plougmann had brought with him from his time at B&O, and the LEGO stores were one of the linchpins of Kjeld's plan to make LEGO the strongest brand among families with children.

As it turned out, the analysis threw a monkey wrench in the two senior bosses' plans. In Knudstorp's opinion, the idea didn't make sense financially, and it might cost LEGO dearly, particularly now. Instead of the expected PowerPoint, with running commentary, abbreviations, and foreign terms, Knudstorp got down to brass tacks, putting his assessment in terms anyone could understand. What is this really about, how risky is it, and how much money does LEGO stand to lose?

For a fleeting moment, the presentation became an emperor's-new-clothes situation, with Knudstorp in the role of the child unmasking the adults' perceptions of themselves. The silence around the table was deafening. Plougmann was furious, with Kjeld even more astonished. He eyed Knudstorp, who was thinking that he'd just sabotaged everything LEGO's top executives wanted to implement, everything for which they were expecting him, the young upstart, to do the groundwork, so that they could get on with their bid for global brand dominance.

On the plane on the way home, while Kjeld was in the restroom, Plougmann stared intently at his young colleague. "You must have some gigantic balls!"

In October 2004, thirty-five-year-old Jørgen Vig Knudstorp was appointed CEO of LEGO.

Later on that same trip, while the two bosses were preoccupied with their pipes and paperwork, Kjeld suddenly looked up and said, "You did a fantastic job of explaining that, Jørgen! I've never heard such a clear presentation before."

Kjeld: *I already admired him at that point. The calculations he presented were razor-sharp, and then there was the fact that he dared to speak his mind in his own simple, quiet fashion. It made a strong impression. I was already having sleepless nights, wondering about who should be my successor. It wasn't going to be Poul, I knew, because he and I were about the same age, and also, by that point, it was already becoming clear to me that he wasn't really a good fit for our culture and way of doing things.*

Two years later, in October 2004, Jørgen Vig Knudstorp was announced as the new managing director of LEGO, and Kjeld moved out of his office and away from LEGO headquarters on the same day. He wanted to make sure that nobody, especially not the new CEO, worried that he intended to meddle in the day-to-day running of the business, the way he'd felt for fifteen years under his father.

The announcement took many people in the Danish business community by surprise, and several figures in the industry came straight out and said that Knudstorp was far too green to turn LEGO around. One partner at Russell Reynolds Associates, an American headhunting firm, declared that if they'd presented a candidate with Jørgen Vig Knudstorp's qualifications to LEGO's board themselves, the suggestion would have been rejected out of hand.

Kjeld: *I was well aware that many people would shake their heads when we promoted Jørgen. That was also why I waited for the better part of a year. I wanted him and Jesper Ovesen to get a chance to make their mark, which they certainly did, but it was always my intention that Jørgen would be my successor, and I made sure he knew that, too. It was the board that formally appointed him, and some of the members did have their doubts beforehand. Was he too young and untested? Wouldn't it be better to wait?*

But I pushed for it to be now, and I felt Jørgen was absolutely the right person. Not just because of his talents, but also because his heart was really in it and he really understood what LEGO was all about.

But just who *was* this guy? Tall, with a kindly smile, a well-groomed beard, and thick-framed glasses, Knudstorp had an intellectual air about him. His résumé paints a picture of a hardworking and curious person who graduated with flying colors and completed a PhD in Business Economics at Aarhus University, where he also taught and conducted research. He was awarded Den Gyldne Pegepind (The Golden Pointer), a prize given to particularly inspiring lecturers. In 1998 he was hired at McKinsey & Co., then assigned to Paris for three years as a consultant to French companies. He returned to Denmark in the autumn of 2001, where he joined LEGO and was promoted five times in two years. He was husband to a woman named Vanessa and the father of four children.

When the announcement was made, Knudstorp told journalists that one of his main challenges would be to devote his energy across the

One of the first things the new boss did was to take a tour of the company, getting to know the business practices and employee groups and putting into action Kjeld's words from an interview a few years earlier: "The LEGO spirit will live on with the help of an open and very close dialogue with employees, who must feel that they are taken seriously, and that the management will act when good ideas and initiatives are fed through from employees."

eight thousand employees. "I will do this by being ruthlessly honest and responding to everyone who approaches me. At the moment, I'm starting to realize that there are a lot of people I'll need to take into consideration."

For this reason, Knudstorp set up an internal online chat immediately after his appointment, inviting any LEGO employee across the world to ask questions and send comments or suggestions to the new CEO. It was Knudstorp's New Year's resolution to maintain this ongoing global conversation with his staff, so that everyone felt that the new management was visible during the tremendous challenges facing LEGO.

"I get three or four emails a day, and I prioritize that dialogue very highly. It's always crucial for me to set a course for LEGO, and we're heading toward a cultural and managerial shift. I can't just sit in my office and see what happens."

Several journalists, who were now also finding it easier to get in touch with the head honcho at LEGO, noticed that in the corner of Knudstorp's office in Billund was a neon life jacket, not exactly in high demand when you're in the middle of the landlocked heath. It was a gift from some employees after a big meeting at which Knudstorp tried to illustrate the task ahead of him with a story about a ship hitting a huge iceberg. He said it was the captain's job to back the ship away from the iceberg, and if he didn't succeed, it was his duty to get as many people into the lifeboats as possible.

Knudstorp's first year as managing director was a veritable obstacle course of icebergs. As expected, 2004 saw yet more huge losses, while Knudstorp and Ovesen wrote down assets, scrapped things, made cuts, set limits, reorganized, dismissed employees, and sold things off. Nothing was sacred, and no one got a free pass.

This was the part of what the journalists later dubbed "the Knudstorp cure." They had to get their hands dirty. Strictly speaking, "the Knudstorp and Ovesen cure" would have been more accurate, because Jesper Ovesen was the primary force behind the concrete part of this struggle for survival. The method, explained Knudstorp, was inspired by the legendary boss of General Electric, Jack Welch, who advised good managers to "face reality as it is, not as it was, or as you wish it were." Welch added that when things start to go awry, managers shouldn't hesitate to be "brutally honest" about the company's situation.

Knudstorp and Ovesen went so far in their "brutally honest" divestment of everything from planes to factories and land that Kjeld's elderly mother, the usually calm and gentle Edith, slammed her fist onto the table when she heard that they wanted to put the Lion House up for sale as well.

"Over my dead body!" she declared, and threatened to buy the legendary building herself. It wasn't just her late husband's childhood home; it was also the pure, unadulterated foundation of LEGO's history.

Edith got her way, but the many workers at Billund whose jobs were at risk didn't. On April 7, 2005, the board and senior management were forced to announce yet another massive loss, this time amounting to nearly two billion kroner. Knudstorp and Ovesen warned of "outsourcing," intending to move production to lower-wage areas close to their biggest markets in the USA and Germany, making up to a thousand workers at Billund expendable.

Knudstorp, who was unsentimental but fully aware of LEGO's social responsibilities to the city and the region, knew that he could no longer afford to beat around the bush. He answered a few short questions with brutal honesty, and his comments were front page news in West Jutland's biggest paper the following day.

Can you make any promises to Billund?

"No."

Will there always be LEGO jobs in Billund?

"The way things look now, yes. But it's possible to imagine a Billund without LEGO. We'll be in Billund for as long as it makes sense. There are no guarantees."

To many observers, it looked as though it was already too late. Time had run out for the LEGO brick, both as a toy and as an export. In the wake of the various unflattering news stories about LEGO, there was a funereal mood in the Danish press when discussing the country's once proud flagship toy company. As one executive at a large advertising agency wrote in the *Berlingske*, "I love the LEGO brand, but I love it a bit more than my children do. A product can always die, and the question is whether the LEGO toy is simply dead, although, as a Dane, it hurts me to say that."

A couple of days earlier, Mads Øvlisen, who had begun commuting more frequently, and could now be found in Billund more than ever, also issued a serious statement in the press: "We've only got one more shot." By this, he meant that if Knudstorp and Ovesen's plan to save the company failed, and they didn't manage to turn a small profit followed by a more significant one in 2006, then the owners should consider selling LEGO. Øvlisen concluded his statement with a few words that were to be quoted many times over the following months: "There will always be a LEGO brand. The question is who owns it."

Some of the biggest companies on the American market had already started putting out feelers, and even at this early stage, a meeting had been held with the international investment bank Morgan Stanley, whose senior executives visited Billund in late 2004 to negotiate a possible sale with Kjeld.

The meeting took place in the hunting lodge at Utoft, and Kjeld attended mostly out of politeness and curiosity. He'd long since taken stock of his, and his family's, situation. The American investment consultants, meanwhile, had spent weeks preparing. They knew everything about the key figures and the challenges of the industry and had come up with a ballpark valuation: roughly two billion dollars.

Kjeld: *I never considered it for a second—never!—and I want to emphasize that. I was ready to put everything I owned into saving LEGO. We also had KIRKBI, of course, the family's investment company, but the possibility of getting an injection of capital from them was never on the table, out of consideration for my sister, Gunhild, and her branch of the family, which at that time owned half of KIRKBI. In an emergency, it might have been smart to borrow from there, instead of an ordinary bank, but this was something my family and I had to deal with on our own. The meeting with the people from Morgan Stanley lasted a couple of hours, while they tried to convince me, "Just sell the company while it's still worth a few billion!" In the long run, I didn't have the patience to listen to them, and then we parted ways.*

The LEGOLAND family parks, sadly, were past recovery. Knudstorp and Ovesen made it clear to Kjeld that if the company is going to get back on its feet, financially speaking, they have to get rid of all four parks: in Denmark, Germany, the USA, and England. The sale closed in July 2005, when the American investment fund Blackstone and Merlin Entertainments Group bought the parks for the net sum of 2.8 billion kroner.

The agreement included the proviso that LEGO retained some ownership. Through KIRKBI A/S, Kjeld still held just under a third of the shares, and he promised that LEGO would one day regain control over the popular parks, which had meant so much to the company, the fam-

ily, and the brand. Had it been up to Knudstorp and Ovesen, the LEGO-
LAND parks would have been sold off, lock, stock, and barrel.

> **Kjeld:** *Their attitude was that we should get out of the parks, once and
> for all.*
> *"There's no way we're pulling out completely; I want to keep a third!"*
> *I said.*
> *"All right, Kjeld, but then we won't get as much money for them!"*
> *No, but I've certainly been glad I insisted. The parks have always been
> our life's blood, and LEGOLAND meant a lot to my dad. The fact that we
> even managed to build the first park in Billund in 1968, which became a
> fantastic showcase for the LEGO product and the ultimate brand expe-
> rience for visitors . . . that's what I was so eager to expand on by adding
> more parks in the 1990s. Dad didn't like it, but I did it on the sly anyway.*

Anyone who thought LEGO would be going back to basics with
Knudstorp and Ovesen at the helm (as one might have been led to believe, given the messaging coming out of head office in Billund between
2004 and 2005) was going to have to think again.

The reality was that there was no alternative to LEGO's continued
involvement with contemporary media, film, and gaming culture, which
had become increasingly a focus during Kjeld's and Plougmann's tenure. As several Danish researchers on children's toys, games, and cultural consumption, including Professor Stig Hjarvard, pointed out,
everything that was then considered a traditional toy was enormously
influenced by modern media culture.

"Many of LEGO's products are based on licensed characters from
Harry Potter and *Star Wars*, and this has clearly helped to promote the
products. LEGO has ambitions to be the best-known brand among children. I have a hard time seeing how they can realize such an expansive
strategy if they want to concentrate on the traditional bricks."

So it was good news for LEGO that *Star Wars: Revenge of the Sith* was
premiering in the spring of 2005. It was another new film that would
boost sales of LEGO, not just the range of new building sets like the

During LEGO's struggle for survival in 2004–2005, Kjeld's childhood faith became an important pillar of support. As he says today, "At home I learned to say grace before every meal, and I still say evening prayers and just generally pray to the Lord in situations where I feel I really need help from above. My religious, spiritual heritage isn't just about faith, but also about attitudes and values." *Photo: Casper Dalhoff/Ritzau Scanpix.*

Clone Turbo Tank and the Arc-170 Starfighter spaceship. There was also *LEGO Star Wars: The Video Game,* in which the characters, from Anakin Skywalker and Boba Fett to Obi-Wan Kenobi and Princess Leia, were represented by LEGO Minifigures. The game was designed for all ages, including children who weren't allowed to see the films in theaters yet, and it could be played on PlayStation 2, Xbox, PC, and Game Boy Advance. If it proved a success, the LEGO Group and coproducers TT Games were ready to make a sequel.

The average age of LEGO's eight-strong team of senior executives, appointed in 2004, was forty. They were young but experienced businesspeople who understood that, although the message from on high was, consistently, that they wanted to focus on "good old values and good business savvy," there was no getting away from licensing deals with the American film and media industry. Saving LEGO didn't mean retreating entirely to the core product. As one Danish paper put it in the headline of an article about the financial boost LEGO expected from the upcoming *Star Wars* film: "May the billions be with you!"

It's important to remember, however, that one of LEGO's own inventions, the Toas and the various other warrior characters in the BIONICLE universe, actually topped the sales chart in 2004. In 2005, the series was still the most important product line, Mads Nipper, a member of the senior management team, noted. The new range also included *Harry Potter*–themed products, which many in LEGO had dismissed; yet the heroes and villains of Hogwarts started flying off the shelves, becoming LEGO's sixth best-selling item in 2004.

In anticipation of the premiere of *Harry Potter and the Goblet of Fire* in November, LEGO launched a new series based on the film's dramatic wizarding tournament, in which Harry and the other participants undertook a series of tasks. One involved snatching a golden egg guarded by a fearsome dragon, which in LEGO's version was magnetic, so that it could "float" up to Harry Potter when he flew over it. You could also build the forbidding-looking Durmstrang Ship, which transported one of the wizarding schools to Hogwarts. And, for the first time in company history, LEGO created a "creepy" churchyard, filled with eerie little surprises, representing the backdrop to the film's climactic battle between good and evil.

To an older consumer glancing over the product range in the mid-2000s, it must have seemed odd that the new management team's stated aim of "concentrating on the group's classic core products and the values that have accrued to the LEGO brand over time" didn't produce products more in keeping with LEGO's nonviolent roots.

What with the muscle-bound, warlike LEGO BIONICLE, the heavily armed LEGO Star Wars aircraft, and, especially, the new macho fighting machines LEGO Exo-Force, which were inspired by the violent classic *The Terminator,* the fascination with war and combat had never been a more visible or prominent element of LEGO's toys. As already mentioned, however, it also reflected the reality of the toy market in a new millennium, in which children no longer played the way they did in the old days. Unless they wanted to risk ending up as a niche, retro product, they had to accept that the landscape of childhood had become an eerily adult place.

This was noted by the American professor David Elkind, among others, who researched children's development and environmental context. In a lecture at a conference in Denmark that LEGO co-organized, he argued that we should allow modern-day children to be children, instead of making them little grown-ups, as was common across the Western world. And Elkind made no secret of the fact that he preferred LEGO's classic concept, for exactly this reason:

> *The early LEGO bricks were great. You provided toys that stimulated children's development, but that has changed. Now, you are telling kids how to build. On my way here, I read that you have launched LEGO Basketball with Minifigures of Shaquille O'Neal and the other NBA stars. That kind of toy is giving directions on how to play, and that's a shame.*

Amid all the attention focused on LEGO during these years of crisis in the first decade of the new millennium, a discussion was brewing in

Denmark about children and culture, play, and toys. Numerous opinion pieces, often written by adult men and fathers who had played industriously and built abstractly with LEGO bricks in their boyhoods, were criticizing, like Professor Elkind, the modern LEGO toy, which was no longer an exercise in creativity, but rather an exercise in following instructions. As one of the writers put it, the jumble of old bricks created a generation of designers and engineers, while the appealing modern-day sets with their thick manuals and bricks in numbered bags created assembly-line workers.

Under the headline "Whatever happened to the good old bricks?" a journalist in *Politiken* remarked, "If you want, you can see the story of LEGO as a kind of creative fall from grace." The question was whether LEGO was still really LEGO, the author continued, given that the brand once stood for cultural and social values that emphasized unrestricted creative play and rejected warlike weaponry entirely.

Kjeld: *I have always been able to understand that discussion about creativity and, to some extent, the criticism as well. Our tendency to produce everything in sets with instructions got more and more pronounced over the 1990s. Suddenly, it just took over because now we had to make even more themed toys that were also increasingly similar. Of course, it's necessary to include instructions with LEGO Technic, because otherwise it would simply be impossible to build the complex models. And yet, there are still many young and older fans who construct the most fantastic things from their imagination, using LEGO Technic elements.*

You can argue that instructions don't stimulate this kind of creativity to a sufficient extent. On the other hand, it's also a way we can give children a lot of great learning opportunities. I think our developers have become incredibly sharp at creating manuals in a way that makes children think, "Aha, so you can use the elements that way too!" There's been a positive development in that regard.

The instructions are an important part of the LEGO System, but they must never replace the free, creative building experience and the kind of play in which people create whatever they want. Deep down, I hope that there are many children and adults who don't just keep what they've built as decoration but constantly remake it and rebuild the world in new ways. That's what we've always wanted with LEGO.

It came as no great surprise when, in March 2005, LEGO's new top executive denied that children were playing less in general, and showing less interest in LEGO bricks in particular. Knudstorp told one newspa-

With BIONICLE, LEGO entered the world of action figures in the first years of the twenty-first century. It was a "biological chronicle" that blended technology with mythology. On the fantasy island of Mata Nui, LEGO created a world full of heroes and villains that could be told through LEGO bricks as well as comics, books, films, and online games. This image depicts Tahu Nuva with his Magma swords, which can be transformed into a lava surfboard.

per that he didn't believe for a moment that children stopped playing at the age of nine, as some people suggested. "Just look at how many thirty-five-year-old men love playing PlayStation!"

Knudstorp knew what he was talking about. He'd already had several encounters with what was the fastest-growing group of LEGO consumers. They were known as the Adult Fans of LEGO (AFOLs), and they were a large group consisting primarily of adult men scattered across the globe. They began in the mid-1990s to seek one another out and create various communities on the internet. Around the same time, LEGO launched its official website, LEGO.com. Its stated aim was to create a

Graveyard Duel launched globally in the autumn of 2006. On the outside of the box, parents were warned that the contents were not suitable for children under the age of three—not because it was too frightening, but because it included lots of small parts.

virtual world where children, parents, and fans of LEGO could meet to play, have fun, and share activities. But the new "adult" LEGO communities preferred to meet in their own circles, or as part of fan events in the USA and Europe, where they gathered face-to-face and swapped tips and experiences.

Kjeld: *During the 1990s, we kept thinking that much more should be done for the adult "hobbyist builders," as we called them at the time. Most people on the management team thought we should concentrate on children instead, but I felt that a person could have an inner child at any age. We couldn't really make a special LEGO range for them, however, and at that point we didn't know how to get hold of them, because they were sitting in their little basement rooms, each thinking they were one of the only adults in the world who still loved playing with LEGO. But then, in the mid-1990s, the internet started gaining momentum. Soon, small websites sprang up, and little by little, larger communities too, where the*

Kjeld took his young successor to LEGO festivals abroad so that he could meet all the dedicated, deeply committed, adult fans. Here the two are at 1000steine-Land in Berlin in 2006. *Photo: Anja Sander.*

adult fans met and discussed their LEGO plans and projects. It became a community that just grew and grew, passing on a lot of useful knowledge and great inspiration, and in the early years of the twenty-first century, it developed into festivals around the world, even though the LEGO Group wasn't directly involved. One summer I took Jørgen to BrickFest in Washington, where hard-core fans met up to show off their creations, geek out with LEGO, and give lectures on construction techniques, old, rare sets, and that sort of thing. Meeting these dedicated fans was really eye-opening for Jørgen. It got him thinking about an adult market segment that could be nurtured and much more involved than had previously been the case.

"Kel and Jorgen" were by far the top attraction at BrickFest 2005. While the young CEO attended various miniseminars and discussions, the old CEO wandered among the exhibitors and hung out with the crowds of fans, who, as always, were brimming with good suggestions for improvements and future products. Kjeld admired and commented on their builds, signed autographs, and posed for selfies like a rock star.

Coming amid the mentally draining task of getting LEGO back on track, BrickFest 2005 was an invigorating break for Knudstorp, whose encounter with the eager fans rekindled his own enthusiasm for the timeless product. *Star Wars* fever still raged, and both during and after the big Q&A session, where Kjeld and Jørgen were brought onstage to answer questions from an insatiably curious audience, photos of the two LEGO stars were shared on social media. One of them was accompanied by the following caption: "The Young Padawan and his Master." In *Star Wars* terms, this meant "the apprentice and his master."

After returning from BrickFest, a profoundly inspired Knudstorp sat down to formulate a few thoughts about LEGO's sense of self and the way the company had previously innovated and created value. In the future, it would still be LEGO that brought the products to market, noted Knudstorp, but unlike before, it was easy to imagine that many more LEGO products would be developed in direct collaboration with consumers of all ages and genders.

IS THE NEW TECH BOOM FOR REAL? (PAGE 113)

WIRED

THE LEGO ARMY WANTS YOU
How obsessed fans are helping Lego reinvent the world's coolest toy

LIFE ON OTHER WORLDS! (We've Got Pictures)
THE PRIUS KILLERS: Inside GM's Chop Shop
One of Our SPY SATELLITES Is Missing

In the first years of the new century, LEGO deepened its relationship with consumers, and in 2006 the American computing magazine *Wired* wrote about "obsessed fans" who would go through fire and water for LEGO, explaining how they'd recently helped the company develop the new LEGO Mindstorms NXT.

Knudstorp unveiled his ideas to the *Jyllands-Posten* in early 2006. Under the headline "All Power to the Nerds!" he explained that in the future, older children and adult fans would help LEGO pick out best-sellers, going by the logic that if "LEGO nerds" loved something, other LEGO customers would probably like it, too. Knudstorp was careful to emphasize that he would never use the journalist's term himself ("nerds") because it implied that they were a bit weird.

"In fact, they're our best customers. I'd prefer to call them 'enthusiasts.' They're older children, and they're adults. They just think it's still fun and cool to play with LEGO."

He went on to explain that these young and older fans never bought LEGO at toy stores or department stores, because the selection there wasn't good enough. Instead, they went to LEGO's own stores, or bought online, or through mail order. They also held meetings and conferences, formed clubs, chatted on the web, and wrote books and, most of all, emails.

In a sense, Knudstorp and LEGO had already begun to engage with consumers in this new way. Knudstorp had been writing weekly blogs and keeping his mailbox open to anyone, even those outside LEGO, who had something on their mind when it came to the company and its products. LEGO opened a dialogue with adult fans around the turn of the millennium, when they decided to embrace the burning interest in LEGO Mindstorms and think of adult users' dedication as an innovation that would ultimately benefit the company.

As Don Tapscott wrote in his book *Wikinomics,* in the late 1990s a new form of global economy was emerging, created through "mass collaboration" between producers and consumers. And LEGO, according to Tapscott, was a flagship company in this regard, allowing Mindstorms fans to have their say, turning them almost into coproducers. When LEGO harnessed its users' collective intelligence, although users weren't paid directly, they did get a better product, added Tapscott.

For Knudstorp, the repeated encounters with AFOLs around the world signaled a cultural landslide, one which would have consequences for LEGO's perception of itself as a company. Innovation was no longer something that only existed within LEGO's four walls. This epiphany was one of several criteria for success that Knudstop drew up, criteria that he felt must be met in order for LEGO to say that it had truly emerged from crisis and was headed for renewed growth and strength. As he remarked to a newspaper in January 2007: "Products can be developed in collaboration with customers. We must have faith that collective wisdom is stronger than what the company can ever become alone. For a company that's used to vigorously defending its intellectual property, it's a big leap."

The collaboration with end users was put to the test at the launch of the next-generation "LEGO Mindstorms NXT" in 2006. A crucial part of the story of how this new product was created was LEGO's multiyear collaboration with certain select consumers. Initially there were four superusers, and later the user group was expanded to include another hundred people from seventy-nine different countries. Not only did they find numerous bugs in the product, but they also came up with suggestions for new modes of playing and building that LEGO's own people hadn't thought of. Over a two-year period, project manager

In the wake of LEGO Mindstorms, a huge community of younger and older users was emerging, including eighty-five thousand children between the ages of ten and sixteen from thirty-five countries, who participated in the FIRST LEGO League in 2008. The finals took place in Atlanta, and an enthusiastic Kjeld was, of course, present. *Photo: Joe Meno/Brick Journal.*

Flemming Bundgaard received around 7,500 emails from the 104 fans involved. At the launch, he concluded, "We have got a better product. Both for us and for consumers."

The annual results for 2005 were expected to be poor, but by the start of 2006 the company had turned a profit of half a billion kroner, the best results in five years. The newspapers wrote that LEGO was now finally getting its freedom back, which in this context meant that the company had technically been placed under administration by its bankers, despite an injection of eight hundred million kroner from Kjeld's private fortune. The sale of the LEGOLAND parks and a number of properties and areas of land had relieved much of the debt, but they needed revenue to be strong over the coming years, as Knudstorp noted.

With a rejuvenated, dynamic team of executives at the helm, product development was soon given a clearer sense of direction and realism. For a long time, they'd been focusing on trying to make girls want to play with LEGO, something that had been the company's ongoing challenge since 1955. Time after time over the decades, LEGO had attempted to interest girls in the bricks, but they'd never really succeeded, and Knudstorp now believed it was best to abandon this old ambition and accept that LEGO was, and would remain, primarily for boys between four and nine years old.

"If I'm a little reluctant to pour resources into the girls' market, it's because it's a market on which other very big global players have a monopoly, and the competition is extremely intense. If we shouted, 'Hey, look! A new LEGO princess!' . . . it just wouldn't be sustainable."

If things looked a little bleak for LEGO fans who missed the warmhearted product ideas aimed at girls, then at least there were finally some positive changes when it came to real-life equality in the boardrooms at Billund, where historically women had only been hired as secretaries or clerks. In 2006, for the first time in LEGO's seventy-year history, a woman was appointed executive vice president. Thirty-nine-year-old Lisbeth Valther Pallesen was put in charge of a new division, Community, Education & Direct Sales. Her role was to develop new areas of the digital business, including the online "LEGO Universe" game, which was the next major upcoming venture. Pallesen had seven hundred employees working for her in Denmark, the USA, and England. They developed new internet-based games, took care of the 2.3 million members of LEGO's clubs at LEGO.com, and served more than forty thousand fans worldwide.

As the first senior female executive at a company where succession and leadership had always been overwhelmingly patriarchal, Pallesen naturally felt a certain responsibility to her gender. Speaking about her historic promotion, she remarked, "I hope, as a woman, I can contribute to a different kind of discussion at management level than those they are used to."

The year 2006 was also when the media turned its attention to the conspicuous and ongoing inequality at the highest levels of Danish industry. Over the preceding decade, the proportion of women in senior executive positions at private companies had been extremely low, sitting at 4 percent, so LEGO was far from the only illustrious company in Denmark where time seemed to have stood still for fifty years. The topic was discussed during Plougmann's tenure earlier in the decade, when internal surveys conducted among female managers at lower positions revealed that their career options at LEGO were limited by three factors: family life, the women's own reticence, and men's perceptions of women at the LEGO Group. As in so many other areas of the business community, gender stereotypes held women back as they climbed the management ladder.

Kjeld promised at the time that they would take action to address the inadequacies in their recruitment and talent-scouting among female

In August 2006, a woman appeared for the first time on LEGO's management team, but the toys on the table were still mostly for boys. Knudstorp remarked, "I'm glad we have a woman on the team, but I'm even more happy that we've got a non-Dane." From left: Briton Bali Padda and the four Danes, Mads Nipper, Jørgen Vig Knudstorp, Christian Iversen, and Lisbeth Valther Pallesen.

employees, and the male HR boss declared that "LEGO is a company with broad appeal and a brand with universally relevant values, but there's a need for more diversity. The more diversity, the more inspiration and creativity." Lisbeth Valther Pallesen took part in those original debates, and put her finger on the core problem.

"We need to reassess how we measure skills. Women are more aware of the process: is it good enough, and are people enthusiastic about what they're promising? Men think about results: did we achieve our goal and stick to deadlines? These masculine values are most conspicuous because it's easiest to measure hard facts, but we need to measure both at the company."

It would be over ten years, however, before the LEGO Group really shook up the company's patriarchal foundation. Things took an unintentionally comical turn in 2011, when Knudstorp, after serving for several years as one of the Minister of Gender Equality's handpicked "ambassadors for women in management," appointed a new team of executives and ended up choosing . . . twenty-two men! As a ministerial ambassador, however, he had initially got off to a more promising start, making comments in 2008 such as, "We can't keep following the gray-haired old gorilla tramping through the grass and saying, 'This is where we'll find berries!'"

The decision to appoint twenty-two men kicked off a minor revolution, and after a prolonged effort, by 2017 there were three women on the list of LEGO's twenty-five most senior executives: Chinese-Filipina Marjorie Lao (CFO), Russian-American Julia Goldin (CMO, Chief Marketing Officer), and Italian Lucia Cioffi (Senior VP). These three names reflected the fact that LEGO's international "hubs" were also now recruiting female executives. All three departments were originally located in Billund but had since moved to Shanghai, Singapore, London, and Enfield, Connecticut, and were helping to create more diversity at LEGO. Despite the fact that women were still nowhere near as well-represented as men in the company, some male employees wondered, as one man wrote on Knudstorp's blog, "Do I have to have a sex change to get a management job now?"

Avivah Wittenberg-Cox, author of several books on gender equality in business, pointed out in the *Harvard Business Review* in 2014 that fifty years of inequality at senior management levels might be partly why LEGO had always struggled to attract and retain girls' interest. When the team of senior executives isn't gender-balanced, it's hard to maintain a balanced group of consumers, Wittenberg-Cox wrote, expressing frustration that even in a new millennium, the "male-dominated" LEGO Group still saw the female gender as a single market of "girls," bringing out products like the pastel-colored LEGO Friends line in 2012, instead of as a huge market containing a multiplicity of profitable niches:

> *This is what the phone companies like Siemens and Nokia used to do with their range of pink ladies' phones before Apple blew them out of the water with a gender "bilingual" iPhone that integrated the preferences of both genders to make their market fifty-fifty gender balanced. That's where the gold mine lies. So let the immediate, sold-out market response to the timid introduction of the three new figurines be a message to the gentlemen at the table. Be bold! Innovate! Think outside last century's box. Invite some of these innovative female LEGO-lovers onto your board or into your top team.*

It was good advice, and neither absurd nor incomprehensible to Knudstorp, but in those years it was at the bottom of his to-do list. He was still focusing on LEGO's recovery, and investing in toys for boys aged five to nine was top priority. Most important of all in 2006, however, was a new strategy for LEGO's eight thousand employees, Shared Vision, which was the company's third big management initiative in ten years. First had been Compass Management from 1996 to 1998, then Fitness in 1999, and now Shared Vision, a seven-year plan in three phases. Phase one was already underway, and employees were having to learn the ropes and make it a part of their daily working lives.

Knudstorp had written so extensively about it that an entire special issue of the employee magazine *LEGO Life* was devoted to communicating his thoughts. On the cover was a picture of a boy in the primary target group building a tower of LEGO bricks and underneath that image was a list of the three stages of the new strategy:

- To lead the industry in creating value for our customers and sales channels.
- To refocus on the value we offer our consumers.
- To increase operational excellence.

Some employees might have thought that this smacked of pouring new wine into old bottles, but most were glad to have a plan that seemed realistic. Now that these three phases, which, taken together, focused on a shift from survival and turnarounds to forward-looking growth, had been sketched out, there suddenly seemed to be light at the end of the tunnel.

Instead of cloaking Shared Vision in management platitudes, Knudstorp anchored his plan in LEGO's history and values, going by Ole Kirk's old motto: "Only the best is good enough." What LEGO's founder meant by these words and their origin is unclear. Ole Kirk wasn't usually one for slogans, and there's some suggestion that he got the inspiration for the words on a trip to Germany in the spring of 1937, when he visited the Mustermesse, a big trade fair in Leipzig. There, he seems to have paused by the Steiff stand, displaying the stuffed animals popular with children at the time, and he noticed the German company's slogan: "*Für Kinder ist nur das Beste gut genug!*" ("For children, only the best is good enough!")

In 2006, through the liberal use of this motto, Knudstorp managed to signal that LEGO had a new strategy, and that the company's fundamental position on key points was exactly the same as in Ole Kirk's day:

Only the best is good enough for consumers, by which I mean children. We've got to give children a proper experience with our products. But only the best is good enough for our retailers, too, and, of course, for our employees. For me, the motto also means that we need to run an absolutely outstanding operation. We need to maintain high levels of quality, excellent logistics, and good customer and consumer service. We need to be constantly looking at how to improve our work. But perhaps most important of all, as Ole Kirk understood, is that repeat purchases are important, and that positive recommendations from one consumer to another create sales. Ole Kirk added three whole coats of varnish to the wooden ducks that would be pulled along by the child, because they would often be bumped into furniture and get scratches. He knew that the varnish would mean consumers would have a good experience with their LEGO toy, and then they'd buy it again or recommend it to someone else.

The founder's old motto had hung on the walls of LEGO for decades. It is pictured here in the early 1950s, behind Dina Thomsen, Lilly Munk, and Valborg Madsen, who sand and paint trucks.

Kjeld: *My grandfather's motto has always caused us problems when we have to translate it into English. We simply haven't found the right way of putting it, maybe because "too good" is very Jutish (the Danish phrase is "Det bedste er ikke for godt," literally, "The best is not too good." Since this implies something much more negative in English, it is usually translated as "Only the best is good enough"). For me personally, the words have always been a reminder that no matter what you have done and what you have achieved, you must never stop innovating. That, to me, is the truest interpretation of Granddad's motto. Never forget to be creative and innovative! But I also know that there are many people who have interpreted it as a demand for an almost obsessive perfectionism, which I think is awful.*

Knudstorp's presentation of Shared Vision coincided with another important company announcement in the spring of 2006, which was that production and packaging would be relocated to low-wage areas like the Czech Republic, Hungary, and Mexico. For more than a year, the possibility had been a dark, threatening storm cloud looming ominously over Billund. It was now about to be made very real.

Closing the molding plants in Switzerland, the USA, and South Korea and, to a certain extent, in Billund as well, would mean not only massive job losses, but also that most of the future production would be handed over to a company called Flextronics International. That constituted a massive shift, and one that was a crucial part of Knudstorp and Ovesen's plan for recovery. On paper, it meant that the total number of LEGO employees would be reduced from eight thousand to three thousand worldwide by 2010. It would have been a bloodbath, but Knudstorp's open, honest style of management and his peaceable tone let him present this grim announcement in a more palatable way.

Knudstorp, Ovesen, and Øvlisen, however, were not willing to make any promises to the residents of Billund. They all felt that the family had given plenty to the region already over the past fifty years. The inhabitants took the news surprisingly calmly, perhaps because no one could seriously imagine that LEGO's owner, Kjeld, the son of Godtfred and Edith, would ever agree to move LEGO away from Billund.

Kjeld: *Nothing was sacred once Jørgen and Jesper got their cost-cutting measures underway. I was against outsourcing on principle, but I could also see the sense of moving packaging, for example, to lower-wage areas. Relocating the whole of production, on the other hand . . . I was worried would mean a huge loss of know-how at the molding plant. I agreed to move 80 percent to the Czech Republic and Mexico, and that we would close the factories in Switzerland, but I insisted on keeping the most important part of the molding here in Billund. That was sacred for me. As the owner and as a resident of Billund, I felt like a sort of guarantee that there was method to the madness, now that we were making such drastic cuts and layoffs. And in the long run, putting such a large part of the production into other people's hands turned out not to be much use.*

The final balance sheet showed an astonishing profit of 1.5 billion kroner, and 2007 was a jubilee year in Billund for more than one reason. The looming job losses due to the relocation of production were postponed, only to later be canceled entirely. It turned out that Flextronics couldn't live up to its obligations, and Knudstorp was forced to abandon the idea of letting other companies mold LEGO's bricks once and for all. There was good reason, then, to celebrate the company's seventy-fifth anniversary in August 2007, followed by Kjeld's sixtieth birthday at the end of December. It was clear at the anniversary party on August 10, which was held in the large carpark at LEGOLAND, that his good mood and zest for life had returned after the worst years of the crisis. The sun beamed down on the three thousand employees. On one side of the festivities, there was a play area for the adults' inner children, and at the other end there was a circus tent, where lunch was served and where Kjeld and Knudstorp stood outside, shaking hands with everybody.

The apprentice and his master were enthusiastic participants in the activities. Over lunch, Kjeld challenged Jørgen to a race where they were both tethered to the ground by an elastic band around their waist. The stands around the track were packed. Even the local press was in attendance. The combatants emptied their pockets, took off their glasses and threw their shoes and socks aside before putting the strong elastic band around their waists. There was a loud cheer, and then a gasp ran through the audience as Kjeld was jerked back in a half-somersault by the band. With a big grin, he acknowledged his defeat. "Jørgen is a fantastic competitor, I must admit. But it helps to be carrying a bit of extra weight!"

The year 2007 also saw KIRKBI, the investment company, split between the two branches of the family. On the one side were Gunhild and her husband, Mogens Johansen, and their three sons. On the other were Kjeld and Camilla, and Sofie, Thomas, and Agnete.

Kjeld took over his father's LEGO shares in the changeover after Godtfred's death, while Gunhild remained a co-owner of KIRKBI A/S. She remained in that role until 2007, when the Kirk-Johansen family decided to remove itself from direct ownership of LEGO in the wake of the crisis. Jesper Ovesen, who after the financial cleanup at LEGO became CEO at KIRKBI, oversaw the handover, which involved merging the ownership of LEGO into one company under Kjeld's family's control.

The money, which was split into two portions, was officially valued at twenty billion kroner, but it was estimated by observers to be more than twice that. It consisted of securities, equity interests in various investment companies, properties at home and abroad, and, crucially, the rights to the LEGO brand. Roughly speaking, Gunhild Kirk Johansen's family got the portion of KIRKBI's investments that have no direct contact with LEGO, while Kjeld's family received everything LEGO-related. As he remarked to *Berlingske,* "You could say that the current breakup of KIRKBI is a final resolution of the division of the company that my father prepared many years before he died. It's important to do this sort of thing while everybody in the family gets on well, as we do today."

In the run-up to his sixtieth birthday in December 2007, Kjeld gave several major interviews for the first time in three years, explaining in several national newspapers about the relief he felt in letting go of the day-to-day running of the company. Readers were presented with a relaxed, mellow Kjeld, who accepted much of the blame for LEGO's crisis in the early 2000s and confessed that much of what went wrong was due to hesitation on his part.

"I can see now that we started taking radical measures too late. I should have seen earlier that we needed new people at senior management level. Evidently we had to have some really poor results before we could do what it took to turn the tide."

Kjeld also revealed insight into his personal life in a way he never had before. He said that out of consideration for his family, he should have bowed out sooner from day-to-day management.

"As I said to my son, Thomas, 'Even though I constantly emphasize that family is the most important thing, that's no use if I'm signaling at the same time that that's not the case.' It's a bit tough to admit, but it's true. You can't say that family comes first if you don't consistently practice what you preach."

At the end of that year, his closest family included his wife, Camilla; Sofia, aged thirty-one; son Thomas, aged twenty-eight; and daughter Agnete, twenty-four; plus two small grandchildren and their great-grandmother, Edith. She had turned eighty-three but still played a key social role in the family. She was the one, for example, who continued to put on the annual Whitsun lunch at the family's hunting lodge in Utoft, where she, Kjeld, Gunhild, and their families gathered with her six aging siblings and their children, grandchildren, and great-grandchildren.

In 2005, just under a hundred family members took part in Edith's Whitsun event, which began with a church service in Grene Parish Church and continued with lunch and a get-together in the woods for the rest of the day. The year before, when Edith turned eighty, the occasion had been celebrated in the employee magazine, and she opened up about herself and her marriage to Godtfred: "I had to make plans for the weekends, because if I hadn't planned anything, he worked on both Saturday and Sunday. I wish he had spent more time at home. The children missed him a lot at times, but Godtfred struggled to take time off."

Sixty-year-old Kjeld didn't seem to be keen on a sedentary retirement either and had found himself a role as a behind-the-scenes operator, with an office in the KIRKBI building on the corner of Vejlevej and Koldingvej. From this somewhat unobtrusive spot, using his position as owner and as a member of the board of LEGO A/S and KIRKBI

A/S, the former managing director continued to shape the spirit and overall framework of the company's development. Kjeld was also part of the LEGO Foundation and the LEGO Brand & Innovation Board, which sets the overall direction of the brand and the development of new products.

Since 2004, Kjeld has also acted as a mentor for Jørgen Vig Knudstorp, a relationship that deepened on the many flights they took together during the years of about 2005 to 2009. This is where Knudstorp got to know more about Kjeld's mindset based on Eastern concepts, becoming so familiar with it that he used the word "irrational" about his mentor during a birthday speech, explaining that with Kjeld there was never a clear beginning or ending. Ideally, things should always be playful and intuitive. As with *Winnie-the-Pooh*.

> **Kjeld:** *When you're traveling with two men in a private plane like that, you're in your own bubble and you're free to chat about whatever's most on your mind. Jørgen and I went on lots of long, great trips, because I felt it was important that he also got out there and got to know our organization closeup. We went to the USA, Australia, Singapore, Japan, and China. And when we sat there on the plane or lay down to sleep, I could tell him a bit about LEGO's history, which Jørgen asked a lot of questions about.*

Financially speaking, the years 2008–2010 continued the three previous years' positive trend. The LEGO Group was back; once again, it was one of the world's leading toy manufacturers, and not even the global financial crisis, which gouged a deep mark in the world's economy, had much impact on the bottom line.

In 2006, the final fiscal results for the year were 1.3 billion kroner, rising steadily year after year to 4.9 billion kroner in 2010, the year that had been set as the finish line for the Shared Vision strategy. The LEGO Group experienced strong growth in terms of turnover, earnings, and, not least, the number of employees, which Knudstorp and Ovesen's original recovery strategy forecast would be cut down to three thou-

With Knudstorp at the helm, the company seemed to be regaining its former strength. Kjeld could give up some of the responsibilities of ownership and go on trips with Camilla, including to Greenland, which the couple visited several times, seeing the inland ice from a dogsled. *Private collection.*

sand. Reality overtook their gloomy predictions, however, and by 2010 LEGO employed more than nine thousand staff, all of whom were invited to a global party at the end of the year. It was to be held at various LEGO locations all over the world, to mark the success of Shared Vision.

In Denmark, the party was held on Friday, November 19, 2010. All LEGO employees from across the country were picked up early in the afternoon and bussed to the Vingsted Center between Vejle and Billund, where there were various activities on offer, everything from foosball and playing dress-up to temporary tattoos and a game involving hammering nails into a log. As entertainment, and to coax the three thousand employees into dancing led by Kjeld and Camilla, they hired a who's who of contemporary Danish pop music, from Medina and Rasmus Seebach to Hej Mathematik, Ida Corr, and Infernal.

A huge thanks expressed to LEGO employees across the globe (which in Denmark was displayed on a big screen) got a massive cheer. They aired a music video featuring senior executives, including Knudstorp, Mads Nipper, Lisbeth Pallesen, Bali Padda, Sten Daugaard, and Christian Iversen.

The video starts with a sneak peek into the boardroom at the main office, where the senior management team has gathered to discuss the strategy for their thank-you speech to employees at the global party. Everyone around the table agrees, of course, that the speech should be presented with PowerPoints, "lots of PowerPoints," as one of them says. But then a mobile phone rings in the middle of the table. It's Kjeld!

Knudstorp listens, nodding earnestly, then passes on the message to the rest of the table: "Kjeld says no PowerPoints!"

The LEGO executives exchange incredulous glances. No Power-Points? Then what?!

Knudstorp steps up. "Guys, let's turn the clock back to 2004, when we were in the middle of a terrible crisis, and everything looked bleak. How did we feel then?"

At these words, the dam breaks. Something gets into the supposedly prim and proper executives, who cast off all their inhibitions and transforms the dull boardroom into a sweaty 1970s dance floor, complete with subdued lighting, a rotating disco ball, a stirring beat, and the sound of Gloria Gaynor.

They join in with "I Will Survive," adapting the lyrics into a song about the company everyone thought would be sold but which survived due to its employees' "strength and creativity."

We grew strong
The Shared Vision spurred us on
And now we're back
Because of you, we have survived.

A wave of excitement washed through the Vingsted Center. When was the last time executives were seen singing and dancing like a seventeen-year-olds in front of ten thousand employees across the planet? The CFO was bopping around with the head of digital ventures, while the head of marketing launched into the chorus, "The LEGO Group is strong / It's the greatest place to be, hey hey!" with as much verve as though he were on the main stage at Wembley. Knudstorp put his arms affectionately around Bali Padda and looked to the future.

We're on a mission to invent
The future of play
Let's share
A bit of magic every day
Then you and I,
We'll reach the sky.

And then—poof!—the disco ball switched off, and the executives sat around the meeting table once more, staring at one another. They exchanged wry smiles, until the CFO brushed a bit of silver glitter off the sleeve of his jacket and said, "That won't work, my friends. Nobody would ever be able to take us seriously again!"

"Yeah, let's stick to PowerPoint," replied Mads Nipper.

"I like that," Bali Padda said. "PowerPoint rules!"

And so the decade was brought to a close at the LEGO Group with a tribute to the playfulness within all human beings, broadcast across the world. Or as the singing and dancing CEO put it a few years earlier, "What toys do for children . . . why shouldn't they do the same thing for us? We need to be a workplace that embodies that spirit."

INHERITANCE

THE 2010s

Friends, 2012

The year was 1964. It was the height of summer in Denmark, and sixteen-year-old Kjeld was at a riding school with a lot of other horse lovers. A popular riding instructor from Vejle, Gustav Martens, had put together the annual Ox Road Camp, featuring a stagecoach and a covered wagon drawn by a workhorse called the Elephant. The merry procession of children and adults on horseback, at the reins, or lying on the roof of the stagecoach always followed the *Hærvejen* (literally "the army road," but often known in English as the Ox Road), an ancient thoroughfare that runs through Jutland. In the Middle Ages, it connected Denmark with Germany and the rest of Europe. The path was famous for its motley throng of people, everyone from pilgrims, wanderers, and soldiers to junk dealers, ox drivers, and horse dealers leading herds of animals.

The Wild West in Central Jutland. The wagon goes off-road on the Ox Road in the summer of 1964. *Private collection.*

In July 1964, the landscape around the old road was disturbed only by Martens's menagerie. One afternoon, they set up camp near Korshøjgård, a property in Randbøldal, one of the most beautiful areas on the trip through the valley of Vejle Ådal. The place made an indelible impression on Kjeld.

This was also the summer that he became good friends with Poul Erik, who, like Kjeld, loved horses. But Poul Erik wasn't going to inherit a toy factory, so he had already started to picture a life for himself that included horses and riding.

Ten years later, in the mid-1970s, Kjeld no longer spent much time on horseback. He was a young guy in a tight shirt with big lapels and flowing gabardine trousers, newly married, and the managing director of LEGO AG in Switzerland.

Kjeld and Camilla lived in Alpine country, but they would soon be moving home to Denmark, where Kjeld's father had reserved a large, detached home for his son and daughter-in-law. On one of their short

trips home, they briefly discussed maybe finding their own place, somewhere that wasn't in the center of Billund, and Kjeld remembered the
gorgeous landscape near Randbøldal.

Kjeld: *I thought we might go and live out there, so I drove out and spoke
to the owner of Korshøjgård. He might possibly have been thinking of
selling. It turned out to be an elderly horse dealer, Anton Mortensen, and
his farm was absolutely not for sale, I was informed. We gave up the plan
and moved to Skovparken.*

Over the next ten years, Kjeld made a success of LEGO, and he and
Camila had two girls and one boy. One summer's day in 1988, when
Kjeld wasn't off traveling, for once, he went to a horse show with Sofie,
who'd just started riding. Father and daughter were enjoying the atmosphere and the sights and smells of the beautiful, shining animals when
suddenly Kjeld bumped into his old friend from the riding school and
the summer camps. They were very pleased to see each other again, and
Poul Erik, who knew what Kjeld did for a living, said that he owned a
business selling riding gear in Vejle. He was also on the board of Dansk
Varmblod (Danish Warmblood), an organization for enthusiasts and
breeders of saddle horses. Kjeld invited him to Schelenborg, and when
Poul Erik Fugmann saw the empty sheds on the estate, he exclaimed,
"You've got to have horses here, Kjeld!"

No sooner said than done. The stables were renovated and fitted
with stalls. With Poul Erik as an expert adviser, Kjeld began to buy
horses, setting up a stud farm for show jumpers, which was named
Stutteri Ask (Ask Stud Farm). Working together, the two former riding
companions decided they wanted a project that involved both breeding and sports. They looked for somewhere in central Jutland where
they could build a dressage center and stallion station with room for
fifty horses, and once again, Kjeld thought of the beautifully situated
farm in Randbøldal.

Kjeld: *I picked up the phone and called Anton at Korshøjgård.*

"Hi, Anton, it's Kjeld from Billund. You still have the farm, and I'm wondering if you might be thinking of selling it?"

"You know what?" he replied. "It's funny you called, because I've just turned eighty, and I'm not walking so well anymore, and my daughter says I need to go to a nursing home, so actually I'd be happy to sell!"

He named the price he wanted for the farm, and I said, "Well, that sounds very reasonable, Anton, you've got a deal!" He was a bit disappointed by that, the old horse dealer. He'd been looking forward to haggling over the price, in proper Jutish, you know.

The new dressage center at Korshøjgård, which featured stables and a riding ground as well as other facilities, was named Blue Hors, and Poul Erik oversaw day-to-day operations.

"What will Kjeld do, then?" asked the *Hippologisk Tidsskrift*, an equestrian magazine, when they visited in the autumn of 1992.

Kjeld answered that his job as managing director of LEGO took up the vast majority of his time, and for that reason they'd need to employ people to fill the various positions at Stutteri Ask and Blue Hors.

The magazine depicted Kjeld as someone who'd thrown himself headlong into riding and dressage, primarily out of an old love of horses. He now wanted to turn his investments into a reasonably profitable business. Just like LEGO, Stutteri Ask and Blue Hors wouldn't necessarily have to be the biggest in the area, but, ideally, they'd be the best. Hence, this was why Kjeld sat at home late into the night, he explained, poring over spreadsheets that taught him more about his new hobby and business venture. He enjoyed getting deeply involved in a company that, unlike LEGO, was small enough to grasp clearly at a glance, whether that was on a walk to the stables or the training ground, or through updating the database of breeding horses with their pedigrees, descriptions, offspring, results in the sport, race dates, scans, projected foaling dates, and so on.

Kjeld: *The business has never done very well, I can tell you, but it has given me so much pleasure over the years. To have the horses and the breeding* *as close by as we do at Schelenborg, it's just wonderful. I really like going out to see them, especially when they're in the pasture and with their foals, which will often cautiously come over and give you a little nip. For me, there has always been something very healthy and therapeutic about having a close relationship between humans and animals. I think one of the most exciting things is how you get to the core of a horse's psyche. With horses, too, a lot of learning happens through play, and I can't help comparing it a bit with the faith in games and learning we have always had at LEGO.*

Kjeld and Poul Erik parted ways at a time when horses became a passion that Kjeld also shared with his wife and children, although he no longer rode. Sofie still did, however, and in the early years of the new millennium, she focused her energies on riding in Klelund Dyrehave, a deer park between Billund and Esbjerg. Thomas had been a competitive rider for a number of years, and, for a while, he ran a stud farm for Arabian horses near Schelenborg. And Agnete, the youngest of the three, would eventually become one of the country's most talented dressage riders, representing Denmark at the 2016 Olympics in Rio, on a horse called JoJo.

Kjeld's current contribution to Danish equestrian sports had lasted nearly three decades and focused on the two complexes he set up, Stutteri Ask in Funen and Blue Hors near Billund, which housed every horse- and riding-related facility conceivable and were constructed around big, modern riding grounds with space for nearly a thousand spectators. For Kjeld, it was not just about competitive sports but also about creating a family experience, and he put on festivals that were almost reminiscent of the classic LEGOLAND concept.

The same basic idea, creating an experience for the whole family, was apparent in Kjeld's grand plan for the 2010s: he wanted to build a LEGO Brand House in the middle of Billund. The idea popped into his head when they moved the company's in-house museum into his grandfather's house, just off Hovedgaden. While the move was taking place, there was a lot of talk about whether they should open the Idea House to the public. This became a particularly pressing issue since AFOLs from around the world started making pilgrimages to Billund, where it all began. But Ole Kirk's house and the long factory building from 1942 weren't suitable exhibition spaces because they didn't have the facilities or space required for a public museum.

In 2007, Billund and Grindsted were merged into one large district. The two mayors came to an arrangement by which the new district would be called "Billund," but the town hall, complete with staff, offices, and archives, would be moved to Grindsted. The move left a large, unsightly, empty building in the main square in Billund, less than a hundred yards from the Lion House, and the local government had not yet made a decision about what to do with it.

The plot was in the middle of town, once home to the dairy, and close to Billund Stream. It was too tempting to pass up. By this time, Kjeld was convinced that the new LEGO museum shouldn't be the traditional type of museum. Instead, he planned to build a large, vibrant, modern "Brand House" that paid tribute to the brand through architecture. Inside, there'd be an experience center where children, parents, and grandparents from across the world could play with bricks, have lots of hands-on building experiences, and get a fun, educational insight into LEGO's values and history.

LEGO's visionary owner already had some ideas about who'd design the museum. Danish architect Bjarke Ingels would be his choice to realize his dream of a building that reflected the ideas behind the LEGO brick and the LEGO System, and created a space for people to play.

In April 2010, when the LEGO Prize was awarded to Nicholas Negroponte, the founder of "One Laptop Per Child," which aimed to enable millions of children in the developing world to break the isolation of poverty through education and communication, Kjeld invited Bjarke Ingels to give a keynote speech. When the ceremony was over, he took the star architect sightseeing in Billund.

Kjeld: *After presenting the award, I drove Bjarke around the town, including past the old town hall, and I casually said, "You know, we could put a fantastic LEGO building there."*

Then we chatted back and forth about the idea, and it ended up with Bjarke saying that it sounded exciting, and that it was definitely something he might be interested in.

We then announced an architectural competition, where we invited three different architects, including Bjarke's design studio, BIG. He had come with all this equipment, pulled out all the stops, and presented a modular building with outdoor terraces and so on. There was no question that he was getting the job.

Kjeld's early interest in Bjarke Ingels partly had to do with the fact that Denmark educates more architects per capita than almost any other country. Danish architecture has risen to international prominence over the years, resulting in a number of high-profile projects. Like many other Danish architects, Bjarke Ingels played with LEGO bricks during his childhood, and as he said when it became clear that BIG would be given the commission in Billund:

It's a huge dream for us at BIG to be allowed to design a building for and with the LEGO Group. The LEGO brick has been tremendously significant for me personally, and I can see from looking at my nephews that the bricks' role in helping children become creative thinkers and makers has only grown stronger in a world where creativity and innovation have become a key feature of nearly all aspects of society.

Despite significant hurdles during construction, the project advanced more or less according to plan over the next few years, and on October 8, 2015, a ceremony was finally held to celebrate the groundbreaking and provide a peek at the ongoing construction. It turned into a festival, with the whole town flying flags from morning until night, and the shops staying open past six o'clock. All three thousand tickets were swiftly snapped up by Billund townspeople and LEGO employees.

For twenty kroner, you got not only a tour of the construction site itself, but also two sausages with bread as well as a soft drink, and access to a series of speeches by Bjarke Ingels, Jørgen Vig Knudstorp, and

Construction was once again underway in Billund, where the cranes were always working above an expansion to LEGO or a KIRKBI investment. Where there had once been a co-operative dairy and later a town hall, there would now be a LEGO House. Left: the System House, Ole Kirk's house from 1924 and the factory building from 1942. At the top is Godtfred and Edith's house from 1959 and the Billund Center.

Kjeld Kirk Kristiansen. Kjeld, who had recently crashed his Segway and broken his leg, had to content himself with giving his speech from a wheelchair in his conservatory at home. He said that the building that was now called the LEGO House had long been a personal dream of his, that he wanted to create a dynamic place where children and adults—both together and as individuals—could build with LEGO in all sorts of ways, hopefully in ways they had never thought of before:

> *The family and I feel that there's a bigger purpose we're working on, children's play and learning, and so it's important that we explain to parents even more about how valuable play is. LEGO House is unique because it is, and always will be, the only one of its kind in the world. That's important to me.*

Construction started making real headway throughout 2017, and with the building's white exterior surfaces, it soon began to resemble a tall, glowing iceberg smack-dab in the center of Billund where, apart from the church tower, there wasn't another building more than thirty feet high. The structure was finished in September, having been constructed from twenty-one oversized LEGO bricks, a detail that was most obvious from a drone. DUPLO Maximus, one might say.

Immediately inside the building, visitors found themselves in an enormous enclosed space in the center of the building, devoid of columns or other load-bearing structures. At almost twenty-two hundred square feet, it included a restaurant, café, and, of course, a large, well-stocked LEGO Store, in addition to the entryway. From this central plaza, children and adults could go exploring, either heading down to the basement, which featured a theater, to learn about LEGO's history, or investigating plenty of opportunities for the adults in the family to take a trip down memory lane and rediscover the LEGO sets and building experiences of their childhood.

Children were inevitably drawn toward the upper floors, which featured four experience zones named Red, Blue, Green, and Yellow, where learning through play was the underlying pedagogical basis. The Red (creative) Zone was for free play, while in the Blue (cognitive) Zone there were problems and challenges to solve. The Green (social) Zone was a world devoted to characters and storytelling, and in the Yellow (emotional) Zone, the LEGO bricks had to be used to express feelings. Young staff members were everywhere, ready to challenge and inspire children and adults to play with LEGO.

At the very top of the building was the "Gallery of Masterpieces," featuring select sculptural works of LEGO art built by AFOLs from all over the world. And in the middle of all four experience zones, from floor to ceiling, rose a forty-five-foot-tall tree built out of six million bricks, called the "Tree of Creativity." During the initial phase, the tree had been the only source of the disagreement between architect and commissioner. Ingels proposed a gigantic mobile of floating LEGO elements, but Kjeld preferred something more rooted, and he got his way;

LEGO House was officially opened in 2017 by the Danish Crown Prince, his wife, and their four children, who had a wonderful day. On the top floor, among the more abstract LEGO models built by fans from across the world, Crown Princess Mary was guided around by Kjeld (left), Bjarke Ingels, and LEGO House manager Jesper Vilstrup. *Photo: Jens Honoré/LEGO House.*

the tree of life, like Yggdrasil from Norse mythology, stretched its evergreen branches toward the sky yet kept its roots planted in the Scandinavian soil and culture from which LEGO sprang.

After the opening, architects and art critics from all over the globe made the pilgrimage to Billund to see the new collaboration between BIG and LEGO, and few could find much fault. There was near-total enthusiasm about how they had managed to transform a company's product and philosophy into such a sensational building. One or two commentators couldn't help noting the surrealistic contrast between the new, streamlined building, radiating international modernism, and the provincial town surrounding LEGO House.

The reviewer in *Arkitekten* magazine wrote that arriving in Billund and approaching the white spaceship of the LEGO empire almost felt like entering a parallel universe: "If the building strikes you as a mirage, it's because it rises out of—apologies, Billund—nothing. LEGO House puts one in mind of a ravishingly beautiful bride who has ended up at an old-timey pub or a German office-furniture fair."

LEGO House was built during a period in LEGO's history that was as adventurous as the 1980s. LEGO's 2015 results showed a profit of over nine billion kroner, due not least to the success of LEGO Ninjago in 2011 and the latest series for girls, LEGO Friends, which launched in 2012. Both were "big bangs," meaning that they were LEGO's own inventions. They had been in development for several years and were the subjects of an exhaustive worldwide marketing campaign.

The two product lines continued the gender segmentation encouraged by the management team during the crisis in the first decade of the new century. In addition to the Ninjago warriors and the Friends, the distinction between boys' and girls' toys was further emphasized in 2012 with the DUPLO Princess, which featured Disney-like princesses in DUPLO sets: Sleeping Beauty's room, Snow White's hut, and Cinderella's coach and castle. It seemed to represent a break with the notion that DUPLO products should be the same for boys and girls, a notion that had prevailed for forty years.

"Give the girls what they want," said Louise Swift, head of DUPLO Marketing, explaining that 70 percent of DUPLO sales were to boys, and that mothers around the world were looking for girls' products. The DUPLO Princesses and LEGO Friends offered them that, meeting with great enthusiasm among girls and many mothers, but also delighting Kjeld, who was himself a grandfather. As he noted in his speech at LEGO's eightieth anniversary party in 2012:

I have six grandchildren, all girls, so LEGO Friends is my favorite product at the moment. The two oldest, five and six, go absolutely nuts for it. They know the names of the Friends girls and can identify with the story, and they like to build. Although girls also play with other LEGO products, it's nice that we can now offer them something so great.

Another equally significant factor responsible for LEGO's relentless growth during the first half of the 2010s was the LEGO Ninjago product line. It was launched alongside several different digital initiatives, into the slipstream of hit films like *Kung Fu Panda* and the classic *Teenage Mutant Ninja Turtles,* which was about four mutated turtles in the sewers of New York who occasionally emerge to fight crime.

The director of LEGO Product Group Two marketing, Michael Stenderup, had high expectations in the run-up to the launch in January 2011, and felt certain that the series would sell twice as well as the previous big initiative, LEGO Power Miners. "Boys are virtually all the same worldwide. They want something that's cool, that involves going on a mission, with a conflict, and with strong, iconic characters. Ninjago has that."

To bolster the element of conflict in the Ninjago universe, LEGO constructed a spinner, which is a sort of spinning top with a LEGO figure on the top. The idea was that a group of boys would each pit their spinner against the others until one participant was left as the winner. Playing cards were included alongside the spinner and LEGO bricks, which gave the spinners different attributes.

"But wasn't LEGO, as it had in the late 1990s, moving away from its DNA and its core business?" the employee magazine asked. The marketing director didn't think so.

"Boys want conflict, and we're in no way trying to shift the focus from the classic LEGO products, but we can see that if we want to sell more, we need to invest hard on other types of play as well."

In other words, LEGO was going with the zeitgeist, responding to what appeared to be a widespread notion among parents in the Western world in the 2010s: that boys and girls were fundamentally different, and that it was impossible, and maybe downright wrong, to try to even out or alter their biological differences.

Opposed to this widespread view of child-rearing were a number of researchers, including the American sociologist and professor Elizabeth Sweet, who researched how play and toys affect gender. She believed, like LEGO, that play was vitally necessary for children because it helped them to learn, grow up, adjust to the world, and become fully fledged human beings. Unlike LEGO, however, Sweet observed that it was difficult to form one's own identity as a child when modern-day toys were so gender-stereotyped.

"Research shows that different kinds of toys help children to develop different kinds of skills. . . . All of those skills are essential for a fully functioning human."

Kjeld: *We took an enormous amount of flack as early as the 1990s, when we started making pink bricks, and especially when we launched LEGO Friends in 2012. But why? It was perfectly natural, I think, for us to adapt our products to consumers and to the era. We provided even more wonderful opportunities for children to build and play, and, fortunately,*

LEGO Friends was the sixth product targeted at girls in a thirty-year period. The series was designed for girls between five and eight, and the five diverse teenage girls from Heartlake City took consumers by storm. Olivia's house was the bestselling LEGO product of 2012, relegating LEGO Ninjago, LEGO Star Wars X-wing Fighter, and LEGO City Police Station to runners-up.

there are actually differences between boys and girls, especially once they reach a certain age.

At that point, girls prefer something that appeals to their desire to role-play. They want to build a framework for their games and identify with the various characters and settings they create. For boys, it's much more about the action and designing and building something big. That's why I think we've chosen the right, natural path. Today, we've reached the point that more than 25 percent of our users among children are girls, and it's rising all the time.

LEGO Star Wars, LEGO Creator, LEGO Technic, LEGO City, LEGO Ninjago, and LEGO Friends were the most popular lines in the first half of the 2010s, followed by steady sellers like Harry Potter, Mindstorms, and DUPLO. However, not everything LEGO touched turned to gold; their large-scale investment in the online game LEGO Universe, for example, was a flop. In 2012, it was discontinued after only a year on the market. Nevertheless, there was still good reason for Jørgen Vig Knudstorp to gather the international press together when the annual results were announced in Billund on February 25, 2015.

On top of the news that 2014 had yielded a seven billion kroner profit, which was the best-ever result for the LEGO Group, Knudstorp, who had now been CEO for ten years, delivered a highly entertaining performance at the press conference. Wearing a razor-sharp gray suit and matching tie, he gave a fluent American-English welcome to the European, Asian, and American press. He immediately made a reference to the recent Oscars ceremony in Hollywood, when the animated *The LEGO Movie* was nominated in the category of Best Original Song and the theme song "Everything Is Awesome" was performed onstage at the Dolby Theatre in Hollywood.

The idea and staging were arranged by LEGO's licensing partner, Warner Bros., and they spared no expense. Minifigure cowboys suddenly ran down from the stage and among the rows of chairs to hand out LEGO-brick Oscar statuettes to actors and celebrities like Bradley Cooper, Meryl Streep, Clint Eastwood, and Oprah Winfrey. And after the award ceremony, the recipients all allowed themselves to be immortalized with their LEGO Oscars in press photos, snapshots, and selfies, which were diligently shared on social media. Awesome!

The over-the-top number was the highlight of the evening for many people, serving as an invaluable worldwide advertisement for the animated film, as well as the LEGO brand. By comparison, a Danish newspaper wrote, a traditional thirty-second ad in the middle of the Oscars would have cost more than ten million kroner.

On a slightly smaller stage at Billund three days later, Knudstorp began by saying that they were looking at a new record year. LEGO had outdone itself again. Then, in an elegant reference to the Oscars ceremony, he broke into song, dancing jerkily to the catchy chorus: "Everything is awesome / Everything is cool when you're part of the team."

Knudstorp then switched gears and transformed the expected, sys-

The LEGO Movie had its American premiere in February 2014. It tells the story of Emmet, an ordinary Minifigure who lives his life according to the safety of the LEGO instruction manual. Then one day he is confused with a LEGO master builder who has to save the world from an evil tyrant. . . . Photo: Warner Bros.

tematic review of the annual results into a mini popular science lecture on the importance of play. He got all the journalists and photographers involved as test subjects, giving each of them a little bag of six LEGO bricks and asking them to build a duck in forty seconds, then show it to the person next to them. It was an exercise in play and learning, and learning by doing, with some of the sharpest pens in the international business press as test subjects.

Knudstorp's media stunt was a hit, and the reverberations had barely settled before the successful CEO set out new goals and objectives in the LEGO employee magazine. With the aid of *The LEGO Movie*, the company had reached new consumers across the globe. And there were even more potential consumers out there, as Knudstorp pointed out:

> *The world is becoming increasingly well-off, and although there is great uncertainty in the world, I believe that low inflation and low oil prices will bolster positive development in the markets we are in. Our brand has huge potential and is still unknown in large parts of the world. A good example of opportunities for growth is Malaysia, where we opened an office in 2014, and where our consumer sales grew more than 100 percent. There are many such countries in the world where we aren't active.*

LEGO successfully pursued this strategy for a number of years. In the second half of the 2010s, the total globalization Godtfred and his team had pictured during those euphoric moments in 1960 realized was virtually an established fact. Over the entire decade, the size and wealth of LEGO swelled, primarily due to growth in markets they had found difficult to penetrate for decades, including in Europe, North America, Russia, China, and the rest of Asia.

After 2015, LEGO began to gain even more momentum in East Asian markets. The major initial steps were taken during the five previous years, with hubs established in Shanghai, Singapore, London, and Enfield, Connecticut, where there were regional head offices with units and management divisions separate from the headquarters in Billund.

Kjeld: *There were many exciting activities going on in our hubs, and it wasn't just about sales and marketing in the market in question. It could also be issues around product development and licensing deals. These hubs were usually led by one of our senior managers, who was also part of the management team here in Billund. This has been a way of ensuring that we're global in our thinking, in every way. And it also meant that, in London, for instance, it was easier to find specialists in all sorts of fields. It hasn't always been easy attracting people to Billund. In fact, over the years, it's often been easier to get foreigners, someone from New York, for example, to settle in Billund than to get a Copenhagener to do it.*

A sign of the rapidly growing Asian market was the emergence of Chinese AFOLs. Jared Chan, based at the Shanghai hub, was tasked in 2017 with developing LEGO's relationship with these new hard-core fans and ambassadors for the LEGO idea. He recalled that AFOLs in China were quite young compared to the rest of the world but were certainly no less dedicated ambassadors of LEGO's brand. Everything they built and exhibited showed Chinese children and parents the scope of what the LEGO bricks could be used for. One striking example was from a group of AFOLs based in the major city of Nanjing in the eastern part of the country, who built Da Guan Yuan, a very famous garden described in the eighteenth-century novel *Dream of the Red Chamber*. The model rapidly became iconic, contributing to China's cultural exports, explained Chan, since the model was exhibited not only around China itself but also at international fan conventions such as Brickworld in Chicago. It was a form of cultural exchange between two countries that had occasionally had political differences. LEGO, it seemed, could bring them together.

When the LEGO Group presented its annual results for 2015 on March 1, 2016, they revealed that the company had grown for the twelfth year in a row. Their profits were now approaching 10 billion kroner, and the number of employees had grown from 14,800 to 17,300 in a single year. At the beginning of his presentation, Knudstorp promised the justifiably excited press corps that he wasn't going to sing or dance that year, although he did allow himself to briefly skip for joy over their continued progress. The numbers were almost unbelievably good, not just in terms of profit but also the equally astonishing fact that LEGO was now reaching a hundred million children across the world. Awesome, indeed!

Yet while the CEO was giddy with happiness over the fact that LEGO had doubled in size over the past five years, its owner had long since begun to air his concerns over the, as he put it, fierce, almost preternatural, growth. "Can we keep up? Can we recruit the staff we need, and will we have time to give all these new employees a good introduction to the company and our core values?"

Kjeld's anxieties were fueled in 2016, when LEGO saw both turnover and earnings fall. By the time these worrying, although hardly catastrophic, results were made public, Jørgen Vig Knudstorp was no longer the one to share the news. There was a new man at the helm, sixty-year-old Indian-born Briton Bali Padda, who had been part of the senior management team for nearly fifteen years. He was now the first non-Danish CEO in LEGO's history, and he had the dubious honor of having to announce this less than stellar set of results. As Padda concluded, "For the past many years we have seen supernatural growth. . . . What we are seeing now is a return to more sustainable growth rates and that is also what we expect in future."

Knudstorp's departure had nothing to do with the sudden, poor annual results; instead, it was related to the new key role in store for him at the family-owned company, which was already looking forward to its hundredth anniversary in 2032. Part of his task now was to help ensure a smooth generational handover at LEGO, a handover that had been in the making for more than ten years. Speaking about the announcement of his departure, Knudstorp remarked, "My new role, in partnership with Thomas [Kirk Kristiansen], is to facilitate everything to do with the owner, and to develop and protect the LEGO brand and the idea behind LEGO, as well as to further develop the LEGO brand from a business perspective."

Knudstorp's new position at the LEGO Brand Group in KIRKBI was

In 2016, LEGO achieved record gross revenue numbers for the second year in a row, and once again, Knudstorp went briefly airborne. The assembled press had been waiting for this historic moment, and photographer Mads Hansen was ready to capture it. *Photo: Mads Hansen.*

about future-proofing the company on various levels, centered on a set of questions. What did the Kirk Kristiansen family want to do with LEGO over the coming decades? What was their vision? Their objectives? Knudstorp explained in his own words how close he would now be to the family owning the company at a press conference in December 2016, when he announced the management restructure. "In my new role I am not a co-owner, but I will be taking on an active ownership role on behalf of the family, and helping it to exercise owner governance externally, so, for instance, a partner like Disney would see me as an extension of the family."

In other words, he was taking on a consigliere-like role in the family.

Kjeld was even asked at the press conference whether Knudstorp was going to start spending Christmas with the Kirk Kristiansen family.

Kjeld laughed out loud and replied, "Ha, ha, ha, ha! No, we haven't got to that point yet, but I've been toying with the thought of adopting him!"

Kjeld's actual son, thirty-seven-year-old Thomas, had been on the board of LEGO for nearly ten years by that point and was considered by his father and two sisters to be the most active owner in the fourth generation. At the press conference, he spoke publicly for the first time, explaining the thinking behind the decision to involve Knudstorp more deeply in the generational shift and the LEGO brand:

> *The reason we are doing this is that we want to avoid getting into a situation where things suddenly run away from us and we try to push growth for growth's sake, at the expense of the quality of the experience of play, or in a way that isn't coherent with the LEGO idea anymore. In that case, we will have failed. We've got to safeguard against that for the future.*

Thomas was born in Billund in 1979, the same year his father took over the position of managing director at LEGO. As a child, he'd never had the same veneration for the company that Kjeld had. At one point they'd set up a table and chair opposite the model builders so that Thomas could go and build there after school, the way his father had once done, but he never got into the habit.

> **Kjeld:** *I loved building with our designers, so when Thomas was about twelve or thirteen, I asked him one day whether it might be an idea to ask the Development Department if he could have his own corner in there. He did, but he didn't go there much. I think it was too soon. He wasn't motivated at all. Thomas could have had some good chats with people like Jens Nygaard, the man who invented LEGO Minifigures, or some of the others, who could tell him something about how they came up with the idea for their models or designs. But it never really caught on with Thomas. Maybe I actually ended up scaring him off.*

For most of his childhood and youth, Thomas mainly knew his father to be working constantly or away traveling. When Dad finally did come

An emotional moment at Vejle Fjord in June 2016. From left: Jørgen Vig Knudstorp, Thomas, Kjeld, and Søren Thorup Sørensen from KIRKBI A/S. They had decided that Knudstorp would switch roles, from CEO of LEGO A/S to working chairman of the LEGO Brand Group, whose activities worked in partnership with Thomas under KIRKBI. Kjeld asked for a picture of the four of them. He felt that the generational shift had finally taken place and Jørgen's future role had also been assured. They shook hands, agreeing that he would help the owning family to realize its visions toward the year 2032. *Private collection.*

home and the family ate together, he would later go into his office and keep working. That's how Thomas remembered it.

Neither he nor his sisters had a particularly positive relationship with the company while they were growing up. For them, LEGO was the reason they couldn't be like the other kids in their class and the reason why their father and grandfather ended up quarreling at family get-togethers. It didn't help matters that none of the three children really learned much about the factory: what people actually did there, and how the whole thing hung together. They simply saw LEGO sets streaming in through door, and they were allowed to build all the sets they wanted, but they had to remember to speak up if they found mistakes in the instructions. As Agnete recalled, "I wish sometimes that Mom and Dad had spoken about it more and opened up to us more about what was going on. Instead, it turned into this weird thing with bricks that stole all Dad's time and made him argue with Granddad, and we were teased at school."

It took all three of them the rest of their childhood and part of their young adulthood to understand that the reason they weren't more actively involved in LEGO was that their parents wanted to shield them, to keep them at arm's length from the decisions they would eventually have to make about their inheritance, and all the big, weighty questions about their potential involvement in the family-owned firm. In Agnete's words:

> Dad made a big thing of telling us kids that there were no expectations when it came to LEGO, and that we shouldn't feel like that. Maybe it was because he had once felt pressured into it, and he just didn't want to put us through the same thing. But it actually had the opposite effect, and almost ended up shutting us out. It was, and is, a really difficult balance for parents. Now that we're grown-up with children of our own who will one day inherit LEGO, we feel the same thing ourselves.

In the late 1990s, as things started going badly for LEGO, Thomas was turning twenty, and he had no idea what he wanted to do with his life. He and his sisters had been told by their father not to think about an active career in the company but to first find their own path in life. But Thomas just couldn't. He didn't have a clue what to do, and he'd searched in various different directions at once. Business? Agriculture? Or should he be a schoolteacher? Thomas ended up doing a two-year course in marketing management at the business college in Aarhus, and at some point he also started agricultural training.

Then something decisive happened. In 2003, it became clear to everybody in the family that LEGO's poor performance was weighing heavily on Kjeld's mind, and that he wasn't quite sure what was going to happen to the company. In this moment of adversity, his son suddenly noticed something in his father that he hadn't seen before and which he felt he understood:

I was in my early twenties, and I'd reached the age where you get curious about what's driving changes in your parents. What fascinated me most about Dad at that point was that even though things were looking pretty bleak and everyone was basically saying, "You know what, Kjeld, forget all that stuff about the bricks and just get LEGO sold ASAP," there was still this drive and passion in him that just kept going.

There was a voice deep down that said, "Nonsense, there's something in this!"

Of course, the willpower I saw in him could well have been purely about the legacy that previous generations had built up, which he felt obliged to continue. But there was more to it. It was the LEGO idea itself,

In 2017, thirty-seven-year-old Thomas Kirk Kristiansen's apprenticeship was over. He had been on a ten-year journey to define his role in the global business. At last, he was ready to take charge. *Photo: KIRKBI A/S.*

the belief that he could help make a positive impact on children's development. That was the passion I suddenly saw in my father. And it piqued my interest.

For the first time, Thomas thought he understood what Kjeld meant when he said LEGO was more than a toy company. If that were really true, thought Thomas, then there was still enormous potential, not just in the bricks, but also in the idea that by engaging children in play, a framework could be created for their development.

It was probably more of the teacher than the farmer in Thomas that saw the big picture, and he was now wondering whether there was a future for him at the company that had been a source of so many problems in the past. The farmer in him may have liked watching things grow and thrive, but the schoolteacher also enjoyed watching things develop, especially children.

Kjeld: *I remember we were driving home from a skiing holiday in 2003, and, at one point, Thomas said, "Dad, I was actually hoping we could sit down when we get home and you could tell me a bit about what's going on, so I can follow along a bit more. And if there's anything I can help with, I'd like to."*

It was very positive, and a clear sign for me that Thomas was beginning to think about whether he could play a role in LEGO. I had never advised the children against joining the company, or encouraged them, but even then, when we were going through our major crisis, I thought the most important thing was that they each had a good life. And not one necessarily connected to LEGO. There can be many wonderful things about inheriting a business, but there are also a lot of issues to live with. So for me, it has always been about them finding their own feet, finding out precisely what they want to do with their lives. That was my advice to them.

In 2004, Thomas announced to the entire family that he had figured out what he wanted. He didn't yet know where at LEGO he would focus his efforts, but he felt sure that this was the path he wanted to pursue:

When major crises crop up, it sets things in motion, and you can't always
control the timing. Looking back from this point in time, it was a coinci-
dence that it was me. It could just as easily have been one of my sisters who
caught the bug first, but Agnete wasn't at that point in her life yet, and Sofie
had decided to try a few other avenues first. I was exactly at that point in
my life where the whole thing was coming together, and it lit a fire in me.

At the age of twenty-six, Thomas joined the board of LEGO A/S, initially in the role of observer. Two years later, he swapped that role for a
permanent seat, and that same year, he also joined the board of KIRKBI
A/S. Additionally, he took on a role with the newly established LEGO
Brand & Innovation Board, where he, his father, and Knudstorp, among
others, did their best to define and put into words LEGO's future.

Sitting at the meeting table alongside seasoned businesspeople who
knew the rituals and the rhetoric was something of a mental mouthful
for a young man with no experience of management, who had never
been involved in the day-to-day running of a commercial or industrial
firm. It began a ten-year period that Thomas describes today as a long
journey, full of education and personal development:

Listening to meetings in the boardroom when I was super young and
totally inexperienced with it all was incredibly overwhelming. In the be-
ginning, I barely understood half of what was being said and done. It was
a big leap, going from sitting in meeting after meeting, year after year,
just mentally beginning to understand what was going on, to being a full-
fledged member of several boards. I thought I had to know everything
about everything and be as smart as everyone else put together. And it
was hard to come to terms with the fact that I couldn't; Thomas, you can
forget all about that!

It wasn't until I reached that point that I could relax my shoulders
and say to myself, "Okay, there must be something to do with family
ownership and that function and role that only we can play." You can
bring in people from the outside will all sorts of skills, but the thing we
can do as a family that no one else can . . . that's what I started focusing

on. It was about sticking to our core values, trying to push the culture in the right direction and constantly sticking to the LEGO idea, so our employees could follow and understand that LEGO could, and would, make a difference to children all across the world. That's what drives me today, and what I hope to be able to pass on to the next generation.

The next generation, the fifth since Ole Kirk Kristiansen, consisted solely of girls between the ages of nine and fifteen. Most of them had been involved in the company since 2012, in a very special capacity. Sofie, Agnete, and Thomas had learned from their experiences as children—that they wanted more knowledge and insight into LEGO—and created a special development platform within the family, which they called LEGO School. They even hired a trained teacher to lead the so-called preparation program.

At the press conference in December 2016, when Jørgen Vig Knudstorp announced his new role as special adviser to the family, Thomas told the newspapers that it was the value of family ownership that had made LEGO the company it was today, and if in a generation or two the owners no longer played an active part, it would be the end of LEGO as they knew it. "That's my biggest worst-case scenario, so we want to do everything we can so that the next generation also knows what they're getting into, but also how to be engaged owners."

This is where the LEGO School comes in, as a bridge to the future, giving Ole Kirk's great-great-grandchildren the opportunity, as part of a group, to think about the family's ownership of the company and eventually to consider their own role. As Thomas explains, "The important thing for me is basically that there's a light at the end of the tunnel for them. That they get excited, that they get that feeling: 'Yes, this is what I want, because this is where I can help make a difference for children all across the world!' That's what the next twenty years will be about."

In practice, the LEGO School was open once a month for a whole day, adding up to eight or ten schooldays, plus a summer camp, over the course of a year. The girls met for themed classes, which were always based on an active involvement in the company. They wouldn't

The three heirs in the fourth generation of the family have each developed their own special interests and life's work that have nothing directly to do with owning LEGO. Sofie (top left) runs Klelund Dyrehave, south of Billund. Thomas has built a golf resort, Great Northern, in Kerteminde. Agnete (right) is a dressage rider and participated in the Olympics in 2016 on Jojo Az. *Bottom left:* Summer 2018. Kjeld enjoys the evening sun by the horse paddock at Schelenborg with his grandchildren. *Photos: Chresten Bergh/Jysk Fynske Medier, private collection.*

simply sit, playing with LEGO; they would see up close how the bricks were molded, sorted, packed, and marketed. They would also visit the Product Development Division together, where they could learn about design and innovation. Once in a while, Grandpa Kjeld would come by and tell tall tales about when he was a boy in Billund, wandering the factory floor. The girls would also go on joint excursions to LEGO House, which they called "Grandpa's playroom." They even visited the factory in Kladno, in the Czech Republic, or went on trips in a smaller group, or individually, for example, with LEGO Foundation in South Africa, to gain more insight and broaden their perspective.

LEGO School also introduced the girls to big, difficult concepts such as philanthropy and the work of the foundation, sustainability, and environmental responsibility, and taught them a little about how a company functioned and was managed. Although it was all done in a playful way, it prepared them for when they would later have to deal with the board, the finances, and the accounts. As Agnete, mother to three of the girls, noted, "I think it's incredibly important that we develop a generation that really wants to get involved with this and wants to take it further. That's basically the whole point of it: we have something really crazy and huge here, something that is only on loan, and it needs to be passed on."

And what did Kjeld say to a "family school" that made greater demands of his and Camilla's grandchildren than he had wanted to make of his own kids? He was not only proud of his children's initiative but also enthusiastic about the concept, and, of course, he was pleased that the LEGO School's colorful, creatively decorated premises were on the same floor as his own office in the KIRKBI building on Koldingvej. As Kjeld put it in the *Jyllands-Posten* in December 2016: "It's wonderful that the fifth generation is taking pleasure and pride in being part of the family, and it's also a way of making it easier for them to handle the situation when it comes to their classmates and overall surroundings."

What the shift between the fourth and fifth generation will look like, and how many of the cousins will want to be actively involved as adults, is anybody's guess. It's unlikely to be as smooth as the handover between Kjeld and Sofie, Thomas, and Agnete, since by that point there will be twice the number of owners to take into account. The handover from Kjeld to his three children, which marked a historic change at LEGO from sole to multiple ownership, was also an attempt to create a model that could benefit and inspire the fifth generation. At its core, Kjeld's notion of a "smooth generational shift" was based on respect for individual freedom and the desire to allow the heirs to live their own lives, without necessarily having to feel an obligation to LEGO. As Agnete put it:

As a family, we have had lots of discussions and chats about how to struc-
ture it and agree on what way we want to be involved, and what opportu-
nities we have. And we three siblings have landed on a model in which one
of us is more active than the other two, and that there's more than one
way to be an owner. For example, you can choose a more passive role, as
Sofie has done. That should be okay too, we think. It's not like we chose to
be born into this. That's the reality in many families, and you've got to try
to figure out a way of being part of it. I think, quietly and patiently, we've
come to a good, common understanding of that. We've all got to have a
place; it's about family life.

Sofie's decision to be a passive owner was grounded in her desire to
fully explore her long-cherished love of nature, which partly stemmed
from all the trips to Schelenborg while she was young. She could simply
be herself in the woods with the animals, without any additional expectations. Today, she runs Klelund Dyrehave, a deer park south of Billund.
It is one of Denmark's largest parks, home to red deer, roe deer, wild
boar, and many other native species. Having owned the park since 2005,
Sofie, with the help of other talented people, has given an area of more
than five square miles back to nature, creating a better environment for
animals and plants:

The place I feel most at home has always been in the woods with animals.
It's where I can feel who I am. That's why Klelund Dyrehave isn't just a
"nature project" or "work" or an "interest"; it's essential for me to put
my love of nature into practice. I think I always knew that being part of
nature was as important to me as breathing. So I'm very grateful that my
family has supported me in my desire for freedom, allowing me to devote
myself a 100 percent to my life with the woods and animals. Their loving
support and understanding brings us even closer together, and it means
a great deal to me. Even though I've made a different choice, I'm very
proud of my family history, so it feels good to maintain a smaller, passive
share as an owner.

Thomas adds that the many conversations within the family and between the three siblings in recent years have made certain things clear, and, in fact, have strengthened the family's bond:

> *That's what's so difficult, of course, when you're a family that also has a business together. There are so many things that can go wrong on a family level, because you have to agree on some difficult things or, at least, on a common direction. That's why we have to constantly make sure that the family is thriving and doing well, and we can only do so if people don't feel locked in. It's situations when people feel trapped that are explosive.*

The generational shift, which has been ongoing for more than a decade, also gave Kjeld and his children the opportunity to agree on how to use the wealth the company creates, which is administered by the family's private holding and investment company, KIRKBI A/S. On *Forbes* magazine's list of the world's richest people in 2021, spot 274 was taken by four Danes with the middle name Kirk. According to *Forbes*, Kjeld, Sofie, Thomas, and Agnete are worth 54.4 billion kroner each. Their private assets are managed by KIRKBI A/S, which the media often describes as "LEGO's bank" and "the Kirk family reserves."

It was Godtfred Kirk Christiansen's family that formed KIRKBI Invest A/S in 1984 in an attempt, as one newspaper bluntly put it, "to separate LEGO's almost virtuous profile from the company's hard-boiled financial and investment businesses." KIRKBI was an amalgamation of the names Kirk and Billund, and the company got off to a turbulent start when Godtfred, as head of the board, decided to invest thirty million kroner in the Copenhagen-based bank C&G Banken, which, after several "creative" deals, went bankrupt in 1988, uncovering a long trail of illegal activities. The case was a sensation in the media, and took a toll on LEGO's reputation.

From the early 1980s, KIRKBI's stated aim was to achieve a better return on LEGO's money than any ordinary bank could attain. They invested in other companies and securities, buying property domestically

The freeform, abstract use of LEGO, always part of the brick's DNA, has today been developed into an art form. In 1968, Dagny Holm set the tone with her animals, houses, and scenes at LEGOLAND, and today there are "brick artists" all over the world.

Nathan Sawaya, for example, who gave up a career as a lawyer in New York in 2004 to become a full-time artist, using LEGO as his medium. His iconic *Yellow: The Leap* explores Sawaya's identity as an artist.

and abroad. Their strategy was conservative and took a very long-term view; in other words, they bought to own, not to sell.

Originally an investment company only, KIRKBI today is a multipronged organization that deals with three fundamental tasks: to protect, develop, and strengthen the LEGO brand across the LEGO branded entities; to pursue an investment strategy that ensures a sound financial basis for the activities of the owner family and contributes to sustainable development in the world; and to support the owner family and their activities, companies, and philanthropic work and help prepare for future generations' active and engaged ownership.

Søren Thorup Sørensen, KIRKBI's CEO since 2010, had worked with many family-owned companies in his former career as an auditor and was naturally interested in the question of what leads to success with that type of ownership. The key, he believed, was to keep the family together, which, in LEGO's case, was what the modern KIRKBI helped to do, as he explained:

When I joined in 2010, Kjeld made it clear that the KIRKBI of the future should be built in harmony with what was most important for the family and its members. His ambition had always been that LEGO should be owned and controlled by the Kirk Kristiansen family, and that there would be an active owner in each generation. That's why much of what KIRKBI does today centers around building and reinforcing the infrastructure that helps the Kirk Kristiansen family, and Thomas as the most active owner, to succeed.

Back in 2010, Kjeld said to me, "There's ten billion kroner in KIRKBI that we want to invest in a sustainable way, and I would also like you to build a family office, so that our family has somewhere to go, and where they can get different things done. KIRKBI will be the glue in the family, even extending beyond the bonds of blood. I want you to imagine that when my grandchildren grow up and need help with something, their first thought will be to go to KIRKBI."

When Kjeld described his vision to Søren Thorup, there were 30 people employed at KIRKBI, which managed 10 billion kroner. Today there are 180 staff members in the head office in Billund, as well as in offices in Copenhagen and Baar, Switzerland. It not only manages an investment fund of 85 billion kroner and takes care of the family members' private reserves, but still functions as a "family office," helping individual members to concentrate on their passions beside LEGO. As Søren explained:

> *Thomas, for example, has built a golf course near Kerteminde. Sofie runs Klelund Dyrehave, Agnete the estate at Julianelyst. And then there are Stutteri Ask and Blue Hors, which are Kjeld's passions. Many of the administrative tasks related to these extensive businesses (accounts, payroll, legal matters, travel, and so on) are performed by KIRKBI for members of the family. This function was an important part of Kjeld's vision in 2010, when he remarked, "We are a family of entrepreneurs, and we need to spend as much time as possible on what we're passionate about, thus maintaining our commitment to LEGO and KIRKBI." Over the past ten years, that vision has become a template for KIRKBI's development.*

KIRKBI owns 75 percent of LEGO, with the remaining 25 percent owned by the LEGO Foundation. Everything is therefore controlled by the family, with Kjeld having the final say. For now. In spring 2023, when Kjeld turns seventy-five, he will resign as chairperson of the board of KIRKBI A/S and turn over all responsibility to Thomas and the next generation.

> **Kjeld:** *As for the future, I've taken the initiative of setting up a little foundation, dubbed "Kjeld's Foundation," and there will be three impartial people on the board. The idea is that if, at some future date, the active owners of LEGO can't agree about something fundamental to do with the ownership, Kjeld's Foundation will go live. It will then have to figure things out and decide who to go with, basing their decision on the overall LEGO idea and the values the companies have always stood for, which are written down in the LEGO Idea Paper.*

Kjeld still wants to shape LEGO, but he doesn't want to restrict the strategic decisions or actions that future generations may take. Nor does he want to rule out a partial sale, acquisition, or launch on the stock exchange, although those scenarios aren't ones he likes to think about. But he knows that it's impossible to say what might be for the best in the future, so that in fifty years' time they can continue to develop the LEGO idea, which, as mentioned above, was given expression and written form in the LEGO Idea Paper. The paper outlined the conceptual basis behind the LEGO brand; it is tantamount almost to a kind of "family constitution," but it's just as familiar to all LEGO employees.

Broadly speaking, the LEGO Idea Paper distills Kjeld's ideas about visions and strategies dating from the 1980s and 1990s, an effort that was carried out by Jørgen Vig Knudstorp at the instigation of, and in collaboration with, Thomas. Using the word "we," it describes the human values the LEGO company is based on and what the LEGO brand represents. The paper begins with "Our Fundamental Belief" and the words "As a family and owners of the LEGO brand and the LEGO branded entities we fundamentally believe that 'Children are our role models.'"

If there is ever any need for Kjeld's Foundation to weigh in, its job will be to navigate its decision based on the LEGO Idea Paper and the foundation's articles of association, which emphasize that no conflict within the family can be allowed to damage the companies' operations or prevent them from being successful.

A generational handover is bound to be a complicated matter in any family-owned business, and it's rare to see most of them reach a fourth generation, let alone in LEGO's case, with the fifth.

That fifth generation is already getting a helping hand in the classroom. This prospect has enabled Kjeld and his children to agree on some guidelines as to how to spend all the money streaming into KIRKBI from LEGO. As Thomas puts it, LEGO has historically been about being a business that earns money in order to grow, in order to earn more money, in order to grow even more, in order to earn even more money, and so on:

Until recently, it has very much been the case that we have primarily had to optimize to improve the bottom line and show that we are in control of things and can run a decent business . . . of course, always with the main objective being to make a difference to the children in whom we have so much faith. Today, the company has become so large, just from a purely commercial perspective, that, as owners, it enables us to think differently about the profits we're making.

These uses include making sustainable investments through KIRKBI A/S, as well as training programs and other forms of philanthropic aid aimed at the world's most vulnerable children and families. That aid is through the LEGO Foundation and Ole Kirk's Foundation.

The LEGO Foundation is one of Denmark's biggest industrial foundations, with reserves of fifteen billion kroner, and is very generous in its distribution of funds. The foundation has grown significantly over the past ten years. Back in 2012, it employed just thirteen staff members and distributed eighty million kroner. Today, there are a hundred employees, and in 2020, the foundation gave out one and a half billion kroner, a sum that will only increase over the coming years.

The theme running through the LEGO Foundation's aid work is that children have a right to play and to learn through play, no matter where they live on the planet or what their circumstances may be. As Thomas, the chair of the board, has remarked on behalf of his family, "Our ambition, and it probably won't be fulfilled in my lifetime, is to reach all children around the world to provide a meaningful experience of play and learning."

The LEGO Foundation focuses on the importance of play for children's development and on rethinking the context of learning, and it has partnerships in more than thirty countries, concentrating its efforts particularly in South Africa, Ukraine, Mexico, and Denmark. The foundation also offers humanitarian aid in areas of the world where children are deprived of good-quality kindergartens and schools, whether those are refugee camps in East Africa, the Middle East, or places such as Bangladesh.

Everywhere, the LEGO Foundation works with leading experts, educators, parents, influential bodies such as UNICEF, governments, and ministries whose stated aim is to equip, inspire, and activate advocates for learning through play. Speaking of this kind of philanthropy, Thomas says:

> *For me, it really doesn't matter whether LEGO gets credit for the aid work or not. If I feel that what we're doing is helping to move the world in a better direction, then I'm just proud that we can inspire others to also follow that path and create partnerships that enable us to reach as many children as possible, offering learning through play.*

Ole Kirk's Foundation is somewhat smaller. Kjeld is the chairperson there, while Camilla sits on the board. The foundation supports projects that help promote quality of life for children and their families. This kind of social engagement is the foundation's primary focus, but it also considers cultural, religious, and humanitarian issues.

In 2016, for instance, Ole Kirk's Foundation gave six hundred million kroner toward constructing the children's wing of the Rigshospital in Copenhagen, the BørneRiget. It is a separate children's hospital that has set entirely new standards for the treatment of children, young people, mothers, and their families, and is scheduled to be finished by 2025. Play will be an integral part of everyday life at the children's hospital and the various courses of treatment, because as the foundation itself has commented about the project, which is the first of its kind in the world: "Children intuitively acquire new knowledge through play and understand and experience the world through play, even when they are ill."

The family's efforts to make a personal, charitable impact in the world have occasionally come under criticism, such as in *Berlingske Business* in March 2016. After profits in the billions were yet again announced in Billund, with yet more billions subsequently going into KIRKBI, the newspaper called for a greater and more outward-looking philanthropic commitment from Denmark's richest family in an era when American philanthropists in particular, such as Warren Buffett and Bill Gates, devoted large parts of their personal fortunes to various charity projects.

"Why don't we see Kjeld Kirk Kristiansen, for instance, actively get-

The new headquarters in Billund, home to more than two thousand employees, is called LEGO CAMPUS. Kjeld said of the building, "The architects from C. F. Møller came up with a fantastically exciting project, and everyone was very happy. It was a lovely office building, but so neutral it could have been used by a pension fund. There just wasn't enough of a sense of LEGO. So I took the architects into my office and showed them pictures of the boy proudly showing off his LEGO creation. That picture made them understand what it would take to build a proper head office for LEGO." *Photo: Niels Aage Skovbo.*

ting involved in projects and leaving deep, important footprints that will last for generations to come and really make a difference?"

Part of the answer is probably that the Kirk Kristiansen family is from Jutland. Unlike for American philanthropists, there isn't a cultural history of parting with the kinds of million- and billion-kroner sums that have been increasingly spent on philanthropic and sustainable causes in recent years. The family believes this is already happening through the LEGO Foundation and Ole Kirk's Foundation, and also via KIRKBI's and the family's "passion investments."

> **Kjeld:** *I like to think that we're giving something back, because we have made so much money for so many years, and it can only be a positive thing that we do good things for other people through KIRKBI. We have professional investment people and a strategy in which we say that our core capital is one thing where we need to do as well as we possibly can. And then we have additional capital besides that, which, to begin with, we called "passion capital," but we now call "thematic investments." This is where the family can get help from our investment people to invest with their hearts, get involved with sustainability-related projects and tree-planting, and inject money into companies that are exciting and innovative in terms of climate change mitigation. Projects that don't necessarily have a particularly high return, but perhaps offer some development opportunities, in terms of improving the environment and climate for the future. And, finally, I have had the chance to get involved and invested in the development of Billund; in partnership with the local government, we would like to make it a "Capital of Children," and, in time, hopefully, a powerhouse driving the development and understanding of children's play and learning. Somewhere where you can see the world through children's eyes, on several fronts.*

In March 2021, for the third year in a row, Niels B. Christiansen, LEGO'S CEO, presented more record-breaking annual results that have been a key part of the history of the world's largest toy manufacturer. Building for more than ninety years, from initially small, modest profits, the story is one of incremental improvement, of constant investment, expansion, and transformation, and of continued growth interrupted by occasional setbacks. LEGO has had to take a few serious financial hits along the way, but every time, they have managed to claw their way back up to renewed success and progress.

These ninety years of revenue have had crucial, invaluable significance for Billund and the surrounding area, creating a sense of loyalty and mutual responsibility between LEGO and the local government. For more than fifty years, the first person the CEO calls when LEGO's annual financial statements are published has been the mayor of Billund, because he knows it will always have an impact on the local administration's coffers, and to a certain extent also on its political decisions, not to mention on the residents' tax rates.

Niels B. Christiansen had previously experienced a similar kind of mutual trust in his previous job at Danfoss, which is also a family-owned business and has as symbiotic a relationship with the town of Als as LEGO has with Billund.

It's a colossal strength, having these fundamental values and culture when you're a large family-owned company that's also a part of a small community. It's nice to be in an environment where a promise is a promise, where you trust one another, and where you're not thinking the other person is out to cheat you or pull a fast one on you. You simply treat one another properly, and I really appreciate that.

The accounts presented in March 2021, when LEGO outperformed everyone else in the toy industry yet again, despite the COVID-19 pandemic, revealed that sales to consumers had grown by 21 percent and that turnover in 2020 was 43.7 billion kroner. In 1932, when Ole Kirk printed his very first price list for his wooden toys, sales amounted to 3,000 kroner.

According to Niels B. Christiansen, who has been at LEGO since 2017, the explanation for the company's success over so many years is mainly an emotional one. Not just the emotions that consumers around the world associate with LEGO's products and the LEGO brand, but also the emotions that have been gathered and condensed, over time, into the company culture and the special LEGO spirit, which has gradually spread to generations of employees. It's this spirit, in Christiansen's opinion, that is still palpable today, even though LEGO has more than twenty thousand employees spanning the entire planet.

> *Many companies can talk about the good values they have. But I don't think their employees feel those values in the same way and to the same degree as we do every day. At LEGO, values aren't something written on a piece of paper that the managing director reads out loud. Here, values are what we do, and values are part of our decisions at every level.*
>
> *Of course, the LEGO spirit is constantly in flux, staying relevant to the era, but at the same time it still has the original Kirk Kristiansen, Billund-style imprint. Many important processes in the company can take place in different parts of the world, but there are some things that form the heart of the company, and those just have to happen in Billund, where it all began. For example, the design of our products. We have between 250 and 300 designers of more than 50 different nationalities in Billund, and we're sticking to that. So if there's a gifted designer we want to get our hands on, but who doesn't want to work in Billund, well, then it's not going to happen. I also believe that the CEO of the LEGO Group at any point in time should be based in our global headquarters in Billund, managing the company from here. And I believe—and this may seem controversial—that it is rather important to have a CEO who is Danish. And if not Danish, a person with a profound understanding of the importance of the company history, values, and spirit, if you want to be certain to retain the core of the LEGO spirit.*

Niels B. Christiansen, who in his press conference on March 10, 2021, attributed the strong annual results to the employees, believes the great challenge of the future will be digitalization, with LEGO continuing to invest massively in this area in order to stay at the forefront of trends and keep pace with the many digital temptations in a child's bedroom.

Today, LEGO elements for the European market are still primarily molded in Denmark. The elements are packed into LEGO boxes in the Czech Republic, which is also where the European distribution warehouse is located. LEGO boxes for North and South America are produced in Mexico, while the Chinese and Australian markets are covered by production in China. The development of molding technology, as well as research and the creation of sustainable elements based on materials such as recycled plastic or sugarcane, takes place in Billund.

Examples of their new digital ventures are LEGO Super Mario and LEGO Hidden Side, where, with the aid of "augmented reality," you can use an app on your smartphone to become a ghost hunter. This technology expands on our physical world by adding a layer of digital objects to reality, objects that can be seen through glasses, headsets, smartphones, and tablets. As the CEO commented to a newspaper in March 2020: "Children today don't distinguish between digital and physical play. They switch imperceptibly between them and enjoy a fluid kind of play in which the physical and digital boost each other."

LEGO's investments in digitization also include expanding the capacity and facilities on the company's website, LEGO.com, which had a quarter of a billion visitors in 2020, as well as more generally ensuring that LEGO remains relevant in a future where everyone in the industry agrees on one point: things are only getting more digital!

And if you're one of those people who is sick of doing increasingly more shopping on the faceless internet, if you want to buy your LEGO bricks at a LEGO Store and have a physical experience of the brand, then there's been good news from Billund on that score as well. In 2021, 120 brand-new shops, 80 of them in China, have opened, meaning there are now a total of more than 800 LEGO-branded shops worldwide.

Over the past decade, LEGO has grown faster than anyone would have thought possible in the years immediately after 2004. This rapid growth begs many of the same questions that people asked Godtfred in 1960, or Kjeld in the 1980s: are there any limits to how big LEGO can become, and what the LEGO brand can sustain?

> **Kjeld:** *In my opinion, there aren't. What are we supposed to compare ourselves to? We're not a toy brand; we're more of a lifestyle brand, and you can see how all this technological development, and especially the spread of the internet, has created a fantastic group of adult LEGO fans who build the most wonderful things, which also inspire children, and the whole development around play and learning. No, I don't think there's any end in sight just yet.*

In the spring of 2021, looking back over the past fifteen years, a highly satisfied Kjeld remarked that they were the best of his life, in terms of family life, as well as work. Many things had fallen into place, he felt, such as the generational handover and LEGO House and the influence they had regained over the LEGOLAND parks through various acquisitions and ownership of a 47.5 percent share in Merlin Entertainments, which owns the eight parks worldwide. His family has given him even more grandchildren, and in 2017, he received a very special seventieth

birthday present from Camilla, which turned out to be an adventure vacation to be taken anywhere on Earth.

Kjeld chose Africa. It was a continent that has remained largely unexplored by LEGO, and which Kjeld had always considered "an incredibly exciting, different, and difficult continent." In his own plane, helicopter, and hot air balloon, guided by his good friend B. S. Christiansen, a former soldier in Denmark's elite Jæger Corps, he traveled from Polokwane in South Africa, close to the border with Zimbabwe and the murky gray-green Limpopo River "all set about with fever trees, to find out what the crocodile has for dinner," as Kipling wrote in *The Jungle Book*. The seventy-year-old and the former soldier continued through Botswana to Victoria Falls in Zambia, and, along the way, animal-loving Kjeld saw giraffes, elephants, lions, and zebras roaming free on the savannah. He took more than two thousand pictures and videos, split a watermelon at a 160 feet distance with a single rifle shot, and felt, at times, like the boy he'd once been, in the wilds of Billund in the late 1950s.

Now, he's having to navigate life as a retiree, something his father always struggled with. But Kjeld looks forward to it. He feels almost like he wants a little table in the corner among the designers again, where he can sit and tinker with LEGO, picking up a trick or two from those masters of the imagination.

Kjeld: *I've spoken to Thomas about it, and I'm allowed to wander around the company if I get the itch. I haven't actually done much of that. But I do often get the urge to go over and pat a designer on the shoulder if he or she has made something fabulous, something that was just so well thought-out. And then I still have my horses, which have given me so much. I also want to keep having meetings with Niels and Jørgen, and I will keep up with what's going on in the company overall. But going in and interfering, in that sense—that I don't want to do. Last but not least, there's my work with the foundation and the all-new investment strategy at KIRKBI. I see a lot of opportunities there for someone like me. And I'd almost forgotten about my work with the Billund town council and my pet project, "the Capital of Children." Because I think that's what I'd most like to be remembered for: having thought a lot about children, about their development, games, and learning, and the importance of play in general.*

Onward and upward. Or, as one of his daughters said of her father, "All those ideas! There must be a lot going on inside him. And over the past ten years he has had his resources freed up to think even more crazily, quirkily, and creatively. Anything could happen!"

This is how we take our leave of him: in a state of wonder, thinking about his family's dreams, ideals, and ambitions, strategies, plans, and visions, surrounded by stacks of annual reports from times past, market analyses and budgets, folders of patent applications, newspaper clippings, price lists, and photo albums featuring four generations of fathers, mothers, and children. Presiding over all of it is a smiling, elderly man with his shoes off, on his way around the world. He is the emissary of play, bringing an important message from "the Capital of Children" in Denmark: "It's our mission to make the term 'play' into something that doesn't just belong to childhood. It's still the case, sadly, that when you grow up a bit, you're supposed to stop playing. Nonsense. Let's stand up for fun and play—for our entire lives!"

ACKNOWLEDGMENTS

Thanks due to . . .

. . . the members of staff at the LEGO Idea House, the Local History Archive for Grene Parish, the Grindsted Local History Archive, the Fredericia Local History Archive and Vejle City Archive. Thanks also to Anders Aistrup, Tom Alsing, Karin Berg, Camilla Boesen, Hans Erik Christensen, Ning de Coninck-Smith, Jette Glargaard, Kathrine Glargaard Andersen, Mathias Glargaard Andersen, Niels B. Christiansen, Jens Christian Hansen, Helle Hegelund, Thomas Hegelund, Birgit Hornsleth, Kim Hundevadt, Peter Jessen, Gunhild Kirk Johansen, Christian Klauber, Jørgen Vig Knudstorp, Camilla Kirk Kristiansen, Kjeld Kirk Kristiansen, Sofie Kirk Kristiansen, Thomas Kirk Kristiansen, Jes Larsen, Ulla Lundhus, Lisbeth Aagaard Lykke, Linda Nielsen, Jette Orduna, Rebecca Schollert Mervild, Ulla Mervild, Tine Froberg Mortensen, Ole Magnus Pedersen, Mogens Rüdiger, Erik Skov, Ulla Skov, Pernille Schou, Kenneth Schultz, Peter Svendsen, Agnete Kirk Thinggaard, Søren Thorup Sørensen, Kenn Tarbensen, and Lasse Zäll.

BIBLIOGRAPHY

Andersen, Jens. *Astrid Lindgren: The Woman Behind Pippi Longstocking* (2018).

Andersen, Marc Malmdorf. *Leg* (2019).

Baichtal, John & Meno, Joe. *The Cult of LEGO* (2011).

Brown, Kenneth D. *The British Toy Business. A History since 1700* (1996).

Byskov, Søren. *Tro, håb og legetøj. Landsbyfolk og industrieventyr i Billund 1920–1980* (1997).

Carroll, Lewis. *Alice's Adventures in Wonderland* (1865).

Collins, Jim. *How the Mighty Fall—And Why Some Companies Never Give In* (2009).

Coninck-Smith, Rasmusen and Vyff. *Da skolen blev alles. Dansk Skolehistorie bd.5, Tiden efter 1970* (2015).

Cortzen, Jan. *LEGO manden. Historien om Godtfred Kirk Christiansen* (1996).

Coupland, Douglas. *Microserfs* (1995).

Dael, Helmer-Petersen & Juncker (red.). *Børnekultur i Danmark 1945-2020* (2021).

Den jyske Historiker. *Virksomhedshistorie* (2005).

Doyle, Mike. *Beautiful LEGO* (2013).

Evermann, Carlsen Winther & Jørgensen (red.). *Leg gør os til menne- sker. En antologi om legens betydning* (2013).

Fredlund, Jane. *Så lekte vi* (1973).

Gad, Holger. *Bondefrigørelse. Dansk landbrug i fortid, nutid og fremtid* (1989).

Hansen, Ole Steen. *LEGO og Godtfred Kirk Christiansen* (1997).

Hansen, Willy Horn (red.). *50 år i leg* (1982).

Henningsen, Peter. *Hedens hemmeligheder. Livsvilkår i Vestjylland 1750–1900* (1995).

Henningsen, Poul. *Om leg* (2019).

Hildebrandt, Steen & Rørth, Charlotte. *Hildebrandt møder . . .* (2003).

Huizinga, Johan. *Homo Ludens: A Study of the Play-Element in Culture* (1949).

Hundevadt, Kim. *Stifinderen* (2001).

Jarl, Anette Bruun (red.). *På sporet af en ny kommune* (2006).

Jensen, Carl Peter. *Modstandskamp i Vestjylland* (1985).

Jensen, John V. *Tyskere på flugt* (2020).

Jensen, Thea Bank. *Småt legetøj, stort legetøj, godt legetøj* (1967).

Jessen, Peter. *En by og dens brugs. Billund Brugsforening 1894–1994* (1994).

Karoff & Jessen (red.). *Tekster om leg* (2014).

Kirk, Hans. *Fiskerne* (1928).

Knudsen, Holger. *De hellige. Erindringer om de gudelige forsamlinger og Indre Mission socialhistorisk set* (1985).

Kristensen, Evald Tang. *Danske sagn som de har lydt i folkemunde* (1980).

Larsen, Kurt Ettrup. *En bevægelse i bevægelse. Indre Mission i Danmark 1861-2011* (2011).

LEGO House. *Building a Dream* (2017).

Lindholm, Mikael & Stokholm, Frank. *LEGO. Globaliseringen af den gode idé* (2011).

Lipkowitz, Daniel. *LEGO Bogen* (2009), *Great LEGO Sets: A Visual History* (2015).

Linn, Sudan. *Forbrugerbørn: Varernes erobring af barndommen* (2006).

Lunde, Niels. *Miraklet i LEGO* (2012).

Mailer, Norman. *Cannibals and Christians* (1966).

Milne, A.A. *Winnie-the-Pooh* (1926).

Muhr, Sara Louise. *Ledelse af køn. Hvordan kønsstereotyper former kvin- ders og mænds karrierer* (2019).

Ogata, Amy F. *Designing the Creative Child. Playthings and Places in Midcentury America* (2013).

Olsen, Lars Hedebo. *Kay Bojesen. Linjen skal smile* (2014).

Page, Hilary. *Playtime in the First Five Years* (1953).

Papert, Seymour. *Mindstorms: Children, Computers, and Powerful Ideas* (1980).

Pée, Liselotte (red.). *Gutes Spielzeug von A-Z. Kleines Handbuch für die richtige Wahl* (1976).

Pilegaard, Ulrik and Doyle, Mike. *Forbidden LEGO. Build the models your parents warned you against!* (2007).

Rasmussen, Hanne and Rüdiger, Mogens. *Danmarks historie 7. Tiden efter 1945* (1990).

Resnick, Mitchel. *Lifelong Kindergarten. Cultivating Creativity through Projects, Passion, Peers, and Play* (2017).

Robertson, David. *Brick by Brick: How LEGO Rewrote the Rules of Innovation and Conquered the Global Toy Industry* (2013).

Sawaya, Nathan. *The Art of the Brick. A Life in LEGO* (2015).

Schmidt, Ingrid & Kaj (red.). *BILLUND. Der var engang* (2003).

Sigsgaard, Jens. *Barnets verden. Træk af barnets sjælelige udvikling* (1946), *Det legede vi med. Gammelt legetøj i Danmark* (1982).

Sommer, Otto. *Erindringer om Grindsted-Grene Sogne* (1980).

Spies, Margrethe. *Fra hytte og slot. Danske hjem i tyverne og trediverne* (1977).

Sørensen, Niels Arne (red.). *Det amerikanske forbillede? Dansk erhvervsliv og USA ca. 1920-1970* (2010).

Tapscott, Don. *Wikinomics: How Mass Collaboration Changes Everything* (2006).

Trap Danmark. *Billund Kommune* (2021).

Thygesen Poulsen, Per. *LEGO. En virksomhed og dens sjæl* (1993).

Torpe, Helge & Kobayashi, Shiguro. *Den tredje vej. En kreativ ledelsesform* (1977).

www.brickfetish.com

www.brightontoymuseum.co.uk

www.brothers-brick.com

www.hilarypagetoys.com

www.inverso.pt

INDEX OF NAMES

Note: Page numbers in *italics* indicate/include captions.

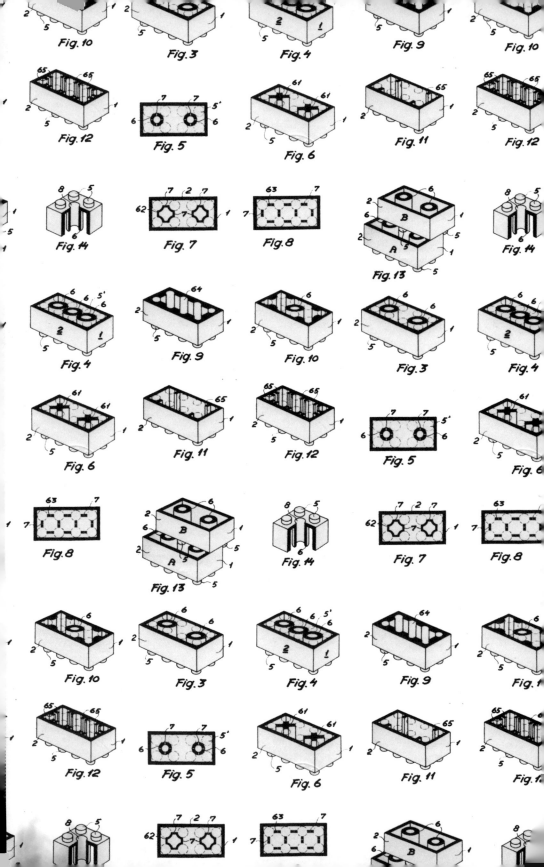

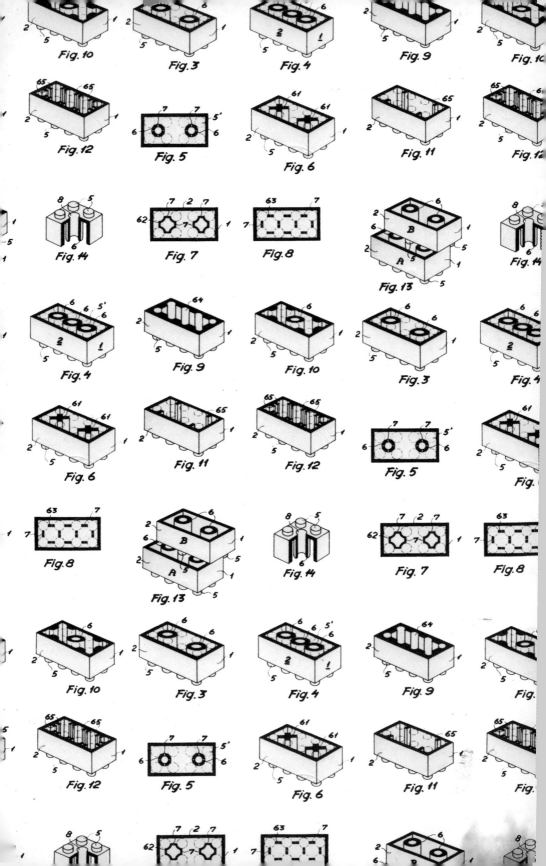

Fig. 10   Fig. 3   Fig. 4   Fig. 9   Fig. 10

Fig. 12   Fig. 5   Fig. 6   Fig. 11   Fig. 12

Fig. 14   Fig. 7   Fig. 8   Fig. 13   Fig. 14

Fig. 4   Fig. 9   Fig. 10   Fig. 3   Fig. 4

Fig. 6   Fig. 11   Fig. 12   Fig. 5   Fig. 5

Fig. 8   Fig. 13   Fig. 14   Fig. 7   Fig. 8

Fig. 10   Fig. 3   Fig. 4   Fig. 9   Fig. 10

Fig. 12   Fig. 5   Fig. 6   Fig. 11   Fig. 12